Ageing Masculinities, Alzheimer's and Dementia Narratives

Bloomsbury Studies in the Humanities, Ageing and Later Life

Series Editor
Kate de Medeiros

Bloomsbury Studies in the Humanities, Ageing and Later Life responds to the growing need for scholarship focused on age, identity and meaning in late life in a time of unprecedented longevity. For the first time in human history, there are more people in the world aged sixty years and over than under age five. In response, empirical gerontological research on how and why we age has seen exponential growth. An unintended consequence of this growth, however, has been an increasing chasm between the need to study age through generalizable data – the 'objective' – and the importance of understanding the human experience of growing old.

Bloomsbury Studies in the Humanities, Ageing and Later Life bridges this gap. The series creates a more intellectually diversified gerontology through the perspective of the humanities as well as other interpretive, non-empirical approaches that draw from humanities scholarship. Publishing monographs and edited collections, the series represents the most cutting-edge research in the areas of humanistic gerontology and ageing.

Series editorial board:

Andrew Achenbaum, University of Houston, USA
Thomas Cole, University of Texas Health Science Center, USA
Chris Gilleard, University College London, UK
Ros Jennings, University of Gloucestershire, UK
Ulla Kriebernegg, University of Graz, Austria
Roberta Maierhofer, University of Graz, Austria
Wendy Martin, Brunel University, London, UK

Forthcoming titles

A Poetic Language of Ageing, edited by Oddgeir Synnes and Olga Lehmann
Age and Ageing in Contemporary Speculative and Science Fiction,
edited by Sarah Falcus and Maricel Oró-Piqueras
Ageing and Embodied Time in Modern Literature and Thought,
by Elizabeth Barry

Ageing Masculinities, Alzheimer's and Dementia Narratives

Edited by Heike Hartung, Rüdiger Kunow
and Matthew Sweney

BLOOMSBURY ACADEMIC
LONDON · NEW YORK · OXFORD · NEW DELHI · SYDNEY

BLOOMSBURY ACADEMIC
Bloomsbury Publishing Plc
50 Bedford Square, London, WC1B 3DP, UK
1385 Broadway, New York, NY 10018, USA
29 Earlsfort Terrace, Dublin 2, Ireland

BLOOMSBURY, BLOOMSBURY ACADEMIC and the Diana logo are trademarks of Bloomsbury Publishing Plc

First published in Great Britain 2022
This paperback edition published 2023

Copyright © Heike Hartung, Rüdiger Kunow, Matthew Sweney and contributors, 2022

Heike Hartung, Rüdiger Kunow, Matthew Sweney and contributors have asserted their right under the Copyright, Designs and Patents Act, 1988, to be identified as Authors of this work.

For legal purposes the Acknowledgements on p. xiii constitute an extension of this copyright page.

Series design by Rebecca Heselton
Cover image: Samovar by Kazimir Severinovich Malevich, 1913, oil on canvas, 88.5 × 62.2 cms © Bridgeman Images

This work is published open access subject to a Creative Commons Attribution-NonCommercial-NoDerivatives 3.0 licence (CC BY-NC-ND 3.0, https://creativecommons.org/licenses/by-nc-nd/3.0/). You may re-use, distribute, and reproduce this work in any medium for non-commercial purposes, provided you give attribution to the copyright holder and the publisher and provide a link to the Creative Commons licence.

This book is available as open access through the Bloomsbury Open Access programme and is available on www.bloomsburycollections.com. It is funded by the University of Graz and Department of Health, Care, and Science of the Office of the Regional Government of Styria, Austria.

Bloomsbury Publishing Plc does not have any control over, or responsibility for, any third-party websites referred to or in this book. All internet addresses given in this book were correct at the time of going to press. The author and publisher regret any inconvenience caused if addresses have changed or sites have ceased to exist, but can accept no responsibility for any such changes.

A catalogue record for this book is available from the British Library.

A catalog record for this book is available from the Library of Congress.

ISBN: HB: 978-1-3502-3061-3
PB: 978-1-3502-3748-3
ePDF: 978-1-3502-3060-6
eBook: 978-1-3502-3062-0

Series: Bloomsbury Studies in the Humanities, Ageing and Later Life

Typeset by RefineCatch Limited, Bungay, Suffolk

To find out more about our authors and books visit www.bloomsbury.com and sign up for our newsletters.

Contents

Notes on contributors   vii
Acknowledgements   xiii

Introduction: Alzheimer's disease as a gendered affliction – masculinities between dementia ventriloquism and symptomatic readings   *Heike Hartung and Rüdiger Kunow*   1

Part One   Conceptualizing masculinities, dementia care and embodiment

1   From a 'care-free' distance? Adult sons about their parents with dementia: A cross-cultural enquiry   *Martina Zimmermann*   19

2   Masculinities in Brazil: Identity tinkering and dementia care   *Annette Leibing and Cíntia Engel*   37

3   Becoming one of the *Others*: Embodying and eliminating fabricated natures   *Melinda Niehus-Kettler*   53

Part Two   The poetics of dementia and masculinity: Between eulogy and negation

4   Living oblivion: Poetic narratives of dementia and fatherhood in Pia Tafdrup's *Tarkovsky's Horses*   *Katharina Fürholzer*   73

5   Anne Carson, dementia and the negative self   *João Paulo Guimarães and Daae Jung*   91

Part Three   Masculinity and dementia in film: Between laughter and violence

6   Of bees, boobies and Frank Sinatra: Masculinity and Alzheimer's in contemporary European film comedies   *Stefan Horlacher and Franziska Röber*   105

7   Writing the past to fight Alzheimer's disease: Masculinity,
    temporality, and agency in *Memoir of a Murderer*
    Raquel Medina   125

Part Four Perspectives on masculinity and dementia in memoirs
           and fictional narratives

8   Stories of exile and home: Dementia and masculinity in
    Arno Geiger's *Der alte König in seinem Exil* and Ian Maleney's
    Minor Monuments   Michaela Schrage-Früh   145

9   Narratives of Parkinson's dementia and masculinities:
    Jonathan Franzen's *The Corrections*   Teresa Requena-Pelegrí   163

10 Illness memoirs, ageing masculinities and care: The 'son's
    book of the father'   Heike Hartung   179

Index   197

Contributors

Cíntia Engel is a Brazilian researcher with a PhD in Social Anthropology and an MA in Sociology, both from the University of Brasília (UnB). She is now an assistant professor at the Federal University of Bahia (UFBA). Her PhD thesis is entitled 'Sharing and caring for dementias: between drug interactions and routines'. She is currently working on topics related to dementia, geriatric and home care, and the complexity of pharmaceutical care.

Katharina Fürholzer initially trained as a state certified translator (Spanish), then studied Scandinavian Studies, Literary Theory and Comparative Literature, and American Literary History in Munich and London. In 2017, she received a Joint PhD from the Universities of Münster and Ghent. From 2017 to 2019, she worked as a postdoctoral research fellow at the Institute of History, Theory and Ethics of Medicine at Ulm University with a research focus on Literature and Medicine. Since November 2019, Katharina has been a visiting scholar at the Comparative Literature & Literary Theory Program at the University of Pennsylvania where she pursues a research project on poetry and aphasia. Recent publications include *Lyrik und Medizin* [Poetry and Medicine], Ed. Florian Steger, Katharina Fürholzer (2019) and *Das Ethos des Pathographen. Literatur- und medizinethische Dimensionen von Krankenbiographien* [Ethics of pathography. Ethical dimensions of illness biographies from the viewpoint of medical humanities] (2019).

João Paulo Guimarães's research generally concentrates on contemporary American poetry and science studies. He received a PhD in English from SUNY Buffalo in 2017, with a dissertation on the relation between poetic language and the so-called 'languages of nature' (the divine word, the genetic code, cybernetic information, biosemiotics, etc). He was Irish Research Council postdoctoral fellow at University College Dublin (UCD) from 2018 to 2020. At UCD, his project, 'The Old Garde', investigated how older experimental American poets challenge the notion that vanguardism is a caprice of youth and the idea that old age is a time of recapitulation, reconciliation and resignation. He is currently a junior researcher at the University of Porto.

Heike Hartung is an independent scholar in English Studies who teaches at the University of Potsdam and the University of Rostock, Germany. She is currently a member of the European research project 'Gendering Age: Representations of Masculinities and Ageing in Contemporary European Literatures and Cinemas' (MASCAGE) at the Center for Inter-American Studies, University of Graz, Austria. She has earned her PhD in English Studies at the Freie Universität Berlin and her PhD habil. in English Literature and Cultural Studies at the University of Potsdam. In her publications she applies the methods of literary theory and cultural studies to the interdisciplinary fields of ageing, disability and gender studies. She is the author of the monograph *Ageing, Gender and Illness in Anglophone Literature: Narrating Age in the Bildungsroman* (2016) and the edited collection *Embodied Narration: Illness, Death and Dying in Modern Culture* (2018). She is a founding member of ENAS, the European Network in Aging Studies, and a co-editor of the Transcript Aging Studies publication series.

Stefan Horlacher is Chair of English Literature at Dresden University of Technology. His monograph, *Conceptions of Masculinity in the Works of Thomas Hardy and D. H. Lawrence* (2006, in German) won the Postdoctoral Award of the German Association of Professors of English. His latest publications comprise *Configuring Masculinity in Theory and Literary Practice* (2015), *Männlichkeit. Ein interdisziplinäres Handbuch* (2016); *Transgender and Intersex: Theoretical, Practical, and Artistic Perspectives* (2016); *Contemporary Masculinities in the UK and the US: Between Bodies and Systems* (2017), and *Comparative Masculinity Studies and the Question of Narrative* (special issue): *Internationales Archiv für Sozialgeschichte der deutschen Literatur (IASL)* 43/2 (2018).

Daae Jung is a PhD candidate in the Department of English at SUNY Buffalo. An active member of the Center for the Study of Psychoanalysis and Culture, she was on the editorial committee for *Umbr(a): A Journal of the Unconscious*. She is currently writing her dissertation titled 'The Remnant: Agamben and the Problem of Universality in Contemporary American Literature.'

Rüdiger Kunow is a retired Full Professor and Chair of the American Studies programme at Potsdam University. He is a founding member of ENAS, the

European Network in Aging Studies, and currently involved in the European research project 'Gendering Age: Representations of Masculinities and Ageing in Contemporary European Literatures and Cinemas' (MASCAGE). He served as speaker of the international research project 'Transnational American Studies', of the European Union research and teaching project 'Putting a Human Face on Diversity: The U.S. In/Of Europe', and was Director of the interdisciplinary research project 'Cultures in/of Mobility' at the School of Humanities of Potsdam University. Until 2008 he held the position of the President of the German Association for American Studies. His major research interests and publications focus on cultural constructions of illness and ageing, and the relations of human biology and culture. His most recent publication is *Material Bodies* (2018), a book-length study of how human life and particularly the human body, as sites of questioning, even of limitation, mark the involuntary dimension of human existence as they impose inexorable limits on individual or collective hopes and projects.

Annette Leibing is a medical anthropologist (PhD University of Hamburg, Germany), who had her first academic position at the Institute of Psychiatry at the Federal University of Rio de Janeiro. There she founded and directed, during five years, the CDA – a multidisciplinary centre for mental health and ageing, with a special focus on dementia. After a postdoctoral fellowship at McGill University (Dept. Social Studies of Medicine), funded by a Guggenheim scholarship, she is now full professor at the Nursing faculty at the Université de Montréal, and member of several research groups. Her research focuses on issues related to ageing, by studying – as an anthropologist – Alzheimer's and Parkinson's disease, ageing and psychiatry, pharmaceuticals, elder care and, stem cells for the body in decline, among others.

Raquel Medina has previously worked at the University of Massachusetts-Amherst (USA) and Aston University (UK), and is currently Visiting Research Fellow at Aston University. She is the author of *Cinematic Representations of Alzheimer's Disease* (2018), *Surrealismo en la poesía española de posguerra* (1997) and co-editor of *Sexualidad y escritura* (2002). She has published numerous articles and book chapters on contemporary Spanish poetry, women writers, and cultural studies. Her current research focuses on cross-cultural representations of ageing and dementia in film, fiction and non-fiction narrative, and poetry. She is the Director of the International Research Network CinemAGEnder, co-director of the Dementia and Culture Network, and Executive Director of the European Network in Aging Studies (ENAS).

Melinda Niehus-Kettler lived in the Republic of Ireland and worked as a freelance EFL teacher in Germany for more than ten years. She then studied for a BA in English & American Studies and Jewish Studies (2016), as well as an MA in Anglophone Modernities in Literature and Culture (2019). She obtained both degrees *mit Auszeichnung* ['with distinction']. In 2020, her Master's thesis 'Naturalising Perceived Otherness' was nominated for the Graduation Award at the University of Potsdam. As the publication of the thesis was also 'strongly recommended' in its official evaluation, Melinda decided to continue working on this research project that aims to re-/conceptualize embodied power structures and to challenge cycles of violence. She is currently a PhD candidate with a focus on British Cultural Studies at the University of Potsdam.

Teresa Requena-Pelegrí is Associate Professor in US literature and culture at the University of Barcelona. Her teaching focuses on US literature of the nineteenth and twentieth centuries and cultural studies. Her research interests are centred on the representation of masculinities in US literature. She has participated in different international research projects on gender and masculinities and she is currently a member of the European research project 'Gendering Age: Representations of Masculinities and Ageing in Contemporary European Literatures and Cinemas' (MASCAGE). Her recent publications explore diverse aspects of masculinities in contemporary US fiction: 'Fathers Who Care: Alternative Father Figures in Annie E. Proulx's *The Shipping News* and Jonathan Franzen's *The Corrections*' (2014), 'Green Intersections: Caring Masculinities and the Environmental Crisis' (2017), and 'The Interrelated Materiality of Masculinities and the More-Than-Human-World in Jane Smiley's *A Thousand Acres*' (2019).

Franziska Röber is a PhD student and research assistant at Dresden University of Technology and received her Master of Education in English studies, colours and interior design in 2017. She is currently working on her PhD project titled 'Still Creating A Fuss: Negotiating Age and Sexuality in British Sitcoms (1990–present)'.

Michaela Schrage-Früh is Lecturer in German at the National University of Ireland, Galway, where she is also currently part of the research team of the European research project. Gendering Age: Representations of Masculinities and Ageing in Contemporary European Literatures and Cinemas' (MASCAGE). She has published widely on Irish, British and German poetry and fiction, and is the author of two monographs, *Emerging Identities: Myth, Nation and Gender in the Poetry of Eavan Boland, Nuala Ní Dhomhnaill and Medbh McGuckian* (2004) and *Philosophy, Dreaming and the Literary Imagination* (2016). She has co-edited *Ageing Women in Literature and Visual Culture: Reflections, Refractions, Reimaginings* (2017) as well as a special issue of *Nordic Irish Studies*, titled *Women and Ageing in Irish Writing, Drama and Film* (November 2018), and a special issue of *Life Writing*, titled *Women and Ageing: Private Meaning, Social Lives* (January 2019) She is co-founder of the Women and Ageing Research Network (https://womenandageing.network/).

Matthew Sweney is an editor and translator, lecturer at Palacký University Olomouc, Czech Republic and researcher in the European research project 'Gendering Age: Representations of Masculinities and Ageing in Contemporary European Literatures and Cinemas' (MASCAGE) at the Center for Inter-American Studies, University of Graz, Austria. He earned his PhD in English and American Studies at Palacký University Olomouc. In addition to ageing and masculinity, he writes on the overlaps of literature, film and cultural studies, and translates contemporary poetry from Czech to English.

Martina Zimmermann is a UK Research and Innovation Future Leaders Fellow and Lecturer in Health Humanities and Health Sciences in the Department of English at King's College London. She trained as a pharmaceutical scientist in Erlangen, Germany, specialized in neuropharmacology in Milan, Oxford and Frankfurt, and obtained her Habilitation in Pharmacology from Goethe University Frankfurt in 2013. Over time, her research interests increasingly shifted towards literary study, and she holds a second PhD in the Health Humanities. She has published two Wellcome-Trust-funded open-access monographs on scientific and cultural dementia narratives, *The Poetics and Politics of Alzheimer's Disease Life-Writing* (2017) and *The Diseased Brain and the Failing Mind: Dementia in Science, Medicine and Literature of the Long Twentieth Century* (2020).

Acknowledgements

The contributions to this volume have been written as part of the European research project 'Gendering Age: Representations of Masculinities and Ageing in Contemporary European Literatures and Cinemas' (MASCAGE), funded by Gender-Net Plus ERA-Net. We acknowledge with gratitude the financial support of the University of Graz and the Department of Health, Care and Science of the Office of Regional Government of Styria, Austria for open access funding of this book collection. The realization of this book was made possible by the support of Ben Doyle, editor at Bloomsbury, and Laura Cope, who helped with the details of the production process.

The scope of this volume reflects the possibilities for scholarly exchange within the MASCAGE project with research teams in Spain (Universidad de Castilla-La Mancha), Ireland (University of Galway), Austria (University of Graz), Sweden (Södertörn University), Estonia (Tallinn University) and Israel (Bar-Ilan University). The interdisciplinary exchanges within this group have moved from occasional personal workshops in the contributing countries to virtual exchanges in response to the coronavirus pandemic. Although much has been lost with the foreclosure of personal interaction, some things have also been gained in the more frequent virtual interfaces. Contributors related to the European and North American Networks in Aging Studies (ENAS & NANAS) have further broadened the range of this volume, which brings together experts within the fields of Masculinity and Age Studies with early career researchers.

Introduction: Alzheimer's disease as a gendered affliction – masculinities between dementia ventriloquism and symptomatic readings

Heike Hartung and Rüdiger Kunow

1. Alzheimer's disease and critical sociocultural constructions of old age

Dementia, and more particularly 'senile dementia of the Alzheimer's type' (American Psychiatric Association 2013), is not only a grim presence haunting senior residences and geriatric care wards, it has in many countries all over the world become part of the public conversation about diseases, care, and the prospects and challenges of late life. Since the 1990s, and thus incidentally the same time as HIV-AIDS, dementia has even become a pervasive cultural idiom and more specifically, dementia and its most visible variant, Alzheimer's, a.k.a. 'AD', has established itself as a descriptive shorthand for the condition of being 'old'.

Cognitive impairments can have many different causes and take on many different forms. *The Diagnostic and Statistical Manual* (DSM) of the American Psychiatric Association offers an evidence-based overview and a detailed description of the various neurocognitive disorders known to the medical profession. Since the present volume is interested less in the medical etiology of these disorders than in their cultural resonances, a certain generalization in terminology is possible, even called for. Hence, we will reiterate in our arguments the prevalence given to Alzheimer's disease as a suitable umbrella term while recognizing that other related disorders exist.

AD is a serious condition of the body, more especially of the mind, but at the same time it is a site of resistance. The etiology of Alzheimer's disease, like that of other forms of dementia, mounts serious challenges to normative concepts of the self which are crucial elements of the cultural history of the West. The losses of speech, memory, mobility, of control over bodily functions run counter to, in fact openly challenge, Enlightenment concepts of the self and its celebration of independent self-fashioning. At the same time, these neurocognitive disorders present multiple forms of resistance to our communicative, everyday routines in social interaction. AD patients behave in ways that other people may find erratic, because they run counter to what may be expected of 'normal' people and this seeming intransigence then adds to or reinforces the social and cultural marginalization of these patients.

While the social and cultural spaces of Alzheimer's are thus often tenuous, even troubled, the temporal coordinates of the disease seem stable, even obvious. AD is a disease of ageing. Old age, however understood specifically, has never been the most popular period of the life course, and the various forms of cognitive impairment occurring later on in life clearly feed into this dark vision. In other words, existing general fears of ageing have been superseded by fears of getting or being 'demented' in old age. Researchers are even speaking of an '"Alzheimerization" of ageing' as an expectation of inevitable latest-life decline (Gilleard and Higgs 2000, 40). AD has in this sense become a widely shared historically new dystopia of the life course. In this 'Alzheimer's-obsessed era' (Gullette 2011, 169), the public conversation about AD is of course vast and varied. Aagje Swinnen and Mark Schweda are even speaking of a 'Dementia Boom' (2015, 10): the exponential growth of public and private representations. A Google search for 'dementia' yields 97 million hits, while 'dementia stories' produces a whopping 176 million. Representations of AD are a motley crew: that can occur in formal, expert contexts as well as in informal, mundane ones. They can take oral or written form, in traditional media as well as in the new digital ones. The proliferation of AD in a variety of media such as memoirs and blogs, expert papers, personal accounts, film and literary genres has nevertheless exhibited a remarkable concurrence in themes, images and stories told about the disease. This frequently takes the form of a *Bildungsroman* in reverse, recording the progressive un-learning of abilities and knowledge as the illness unfolds. These losses and the ways in which they present challenges to patients and caregivers, together with the question of how these losses and challenges approach the limits of representation and question traditional views of selfhood and human development have been explored from the various perspectives in different cultural contexts and practices. They focus on: literature (Maginess 2018; Falcus and Sako 2019; Hartung 2016), film (Medina 2018), life writing (Zimmermann 2017; Kunow 2015, 2019) and a combination of these cultural representations and discourses (Swinnen and Schweda 2015; Bitenc 2020; Leibing and Schicktanz 2020).

Drawing on this wealth of cultural critiques of dementia, we focus in this volume on Alzheimer's disease as a deeply gendered affliction. Whereas older women have been more in the focus of Age Studies because of the even more punitive cultural constructions of female old age, in general, male patients and male caregiving in the context of AD still has to be explored in its cultural repercussions. To address this blank spot in previous research, the focus chosen in this volume on the specifics of dementia as a disease of ageing masculinities aims at an analysis of the gendered difference in relation to the syndrome. Furthermore, specific aspects of male identity construction in the context of mental illness will be explored. From the perspective of cultural critique (to which we will return at the end of this introduction), dementia, like other biomedical pathologies, can perhaps best be understood as a figure of interruption: resisting normative constructions of the human self and its wonted range of behaviour. AD intrudes into the most 'normal' everyday routines and makes life in its wonted ways impossible; it intrudes into the fabric of relations between self and others, 'virtual' and physical reality, and in communication it interrupts the flow between linguistic signs and their signified.

Clinical data suggest that, as the disease progresses, dementia patients increasingly encounter considerable difficulties in matching the ideas in their mind with the conventional means of expression (Meteyard and Patterson 2009). The progressive loss of communication and comprehension skills manifests itself in a shrinking of vocabulary (dyslexia), losing one's place while reading, and poor comprehension of what is being read. Oftentimes, patients still know words but cannot connect them in ways to form comprehensible sentences, as in this recorded exchange:

Elinor How are you, Mother?

Lil Oh, in a fast muff, getting out of the wet ditches.

Elinor Wet ditches, well, that's interesting.

Lil Oh, I'm in a dedeford, they're, they're having a beurz. I mean, they're having a cressit. And would be considered hijardi. Would be picking dependent stuff. I mean they're showing up prepays and other things.

Elinor That's good.

Fuchs 2005, n.p.

This passage from Elinor Fuchs's memoir of her mother's dementia, *Making an Exit* (2005), also foregrounds the performative function of language in AD discourses: as a successful business woman, Fuchs's mother Lilian Kessler was used to giving speeches in public. At a stage when most of her former capabilities are no longer available, she still goes through the routines of a speech in a small circle of relatives who encourage her emotional success in such a performance. In a kind of dramatic monologue, she gives a nonsensical speech reminiscent of Samuel Beckett's modernist minimalism, as Fuchs points out: 'Meanwhile, as Beckett would say, that wasn't "such a bad little canter"' (Fuchs 2005, 109).

As this example shows, literary criticism provides possibilities for making sense of what is usually perceived as the losses of AD in the medical framework. However, the position of cultural critique vis-à-vis dementia is complex and sometimes marred by generalizations and silences. Certainly, it is not circumscribed by the primary and pressing material problems of appropriate care or therapy options. Important as these are, cultural critique has little to offer here. Instead, and from a perspective concerned less with healing the cognitive pathologies associated with dementia than with its cultural pathologies, this critique can turn to the cultural archives and interrogate the resources they offer for the representation of determinate otherness.

The cultural presence of the disease is occasionally framed by various forms of organized creativity – creative engagement projects would be the technical term here – among them theatrical performances, sculpting and painting, life writing, also poetry. These performances are designed to open 'avenues for meaning-making between people who cannot communicate through traditional, rational language [and] can help put meaning back into what we fear are meaningless lives' (Basting 2009, 164). These representations, and side by side with them professional portrayals, are of course extremely varied in content and form, ranging from award-winning movies such as *Still Alice* (2014) via self-help manuals to semi-private blog spots.

The entry of dementia into popular discourses, facilitated to no small degree by the new social media, may have popularized the disease; whether it has also popularized its victims remains an open question, and a crucial one for cultural critique. From this perspective, dementia is an example of what Aihwa Ong, in a different context, has called 'the cultural logics of subject making' (1999, 6) and all the distortions and omissions implied in these logics.

'Popular' seems an awkward term anyway in the context of a terrible disease which offers little hope for improvement and for which no cure is available. Nonetheless, the term is useful here because it points to a continuing process during which dementia has travelled from the clinical domain into the public sphere, while gerontological or geriatric experts have lost some, if not much of their former interpretive authority. As a consequence, the overall understanding of dementia is being modified 'from the bottom up', by the voices of the people directly involved – or so it might seem. So we should not forget here that the cultural embrace of dementia and here again, especially AD, can at times be smothering so that the disenfranchisement of patients in their everyday routines is reiterated and reinforced by well-meaning popular representations.

Such a note of caution is even more important since the demotic character of dementia and especially of AD anchors the disease firmly in the popular culture of the Global North[1] at the same time that it also opens it to the analytic competence of cultural critique. The conjunction of mental impairment and cultural practices can be expected to offer useful information about both the status of such an impairment in contemporary culture, especially that of the United States, and also about the chances and limits of culturally available means of expression. This is especially true of what has sometimes been called a cultural 'master narrative' of dementia, a form of dementia storytelling which de- and prescribes how the entry of mental impairments into a person's life is

---

[1] It is important to make this distinction because, as Lawrence Cohen and others have shown, the reactions to cognitive impairments, especially in older people, are largely determined by social and cultural traditions and assumptions about later life, not all of which follow the patterns of the Global North.

to be scripted, what the intermediary steps are, how that person fights the disease, etc.[2] Taken together, these analytical steps would then point to the favourite and by now familiar diagnosis that dementia is – like so much else – culturally constructed.

Important as such work is, it is not enough. What is also necessary is a shift of terrain, not, as some might expect, from the medical-therapeutic domain to visions of empowerment offered by cultural practices such as painting, poetry, or performances. What we in this volume regard as the new terrain opened by cultural critique is one in which dementia is no longer seen as principally located in the individual patient, being 'her' or 'his' impairment, and by extension her or his problem. Instead, the purpose of this book project is to demonstrate how dementia is circulating incessantly in the public sphere, in formal and informal contexts, in conversations, written and filmic texts, etc. This change of terrain opens critical inquiry to a complex of analytical questions, among them how dementia is being (re)presented here in terms of gender, what the stories are that are being told about it, what types of narratives are used, who is speaking for whom and, perhaps most importantly, what the silences and lacunae are in the public conversation.

It is certainly tempting to understand such cultural critique as a form of 'cultural therapy', a critical praxis directed at alleviating some of dementia's cultural burdens by exposing 'the figures of power that operate in dominant discourses or ideologies' (Hardt 2011, 19; Grossberg 2010, 93–6). Such a reading might well be called reparative because it is not held in thrall by hegemonic epistemologies of power (in this case, those of the geriatric or the medical profession in general) but instead looks for those cultural resources that may allow us to imagine alternative, better and empowering ways of life for dementia patients. Showing how social and cultural norms 'reside in and find a concrete manifestation' (Armour and St. Ville 2006, 6) in the human mind in its impaired stages can open up a space for reflection (and action) concerning not only cultural meaning but just as importantly also the civic meaning of human life in its frail, dependent and limited condition.

---

[2] For this discussion and the possibilities of a counter-narrative cf. Bitenc (2020, 16–17, 99–121), and with a more literary-critical focus England (2017).

The cultural readings of dementia proposed in the essays collected here are gesturing in this direction but at the same time are also seeking to move beyond this framework, and they do so especially in two directions: they give sustained attention to the gendered nature of the various forms of dementia and they also explore a phenomenon that we are calling here 'dementia ventriloquism'.

2. Dementia ventriloquism: Speaker positions in AD

It is frequently assumed that since dementia patients can no longer speak for and of themselves – at least not in the ways ordained by our culture – others must take over the job[3] – and there has to this day been no lack of such others as thousands of dementia stories and blogs show.

A good example of this kind of ventriloquism is a post from an Alzheimer's caregiver about a Christmas situation with an Alzheimer patient:

> 'The Greatest Gifts of All' By Amy Goyer, 23 December 2015, 11:18 AM
> The way Alzheimer's disease has ravaged my dad's capabilities is especially hard to bear during holidays. ... Linda [the blogger's sister] and I looked at each other and teared up. My heart broke for him. But then he squeezed my hand and said, 'But I like this one, too' [that year's Christmas tree] and gave me a little smile. ... [dad has glaucoma which has affected his visual processing and verbal communication is getting more difficult for him.] ... I helped him touch the tree and he looked up at the lights, and said, 'I see it!' ... My heart overflowed. ... We must always remember that deeply familiar things, such as holiday rituals and music, may bring up memories and very rich connections. We must never stop including loved ones; always reach out. Never give up. Even if we can't see or hear it, something may be getting through. And we must never, ever get so caught up in sadness or self-pity that we miss the truly important moments of great joy and meaning.
> https://blog.aarp.org/author/amy-goyer

Reading this report, one cannot miss the sense of control which the blogger exercises over both, 'Dad', the Alzheimer's patient, and her own reactions. The

---

[3] There is an echo of Marx's *The Eighteenth Brumaire of Louis Napoléon* where he speaks of subaltern peasants. The reduced mode of being registers here also in an economy of representation: 'They cannot represent themselves, so they must be represented' (Marx 1963, 51).

memory evoked here is meant to bring home the lesson for which 'Dad's Christmas' is providing the example and occasion, namely the moral imperatives involved in caring for Alzheimer's patients. In this way, what is meant to pass as an AD memoir is less 'about' the ravages of the disease than about the ascendancy of the caregiver over the recipient of her care.

Many attempts have been made to counter or at least curtail some of the disenfranchising power of such ventriloquism. One of these is the 'Meet Me at MoMA', part of Francesca Rosenberg's MoMA Alzheimer's Project. In December 2011, people suffering from various degrees of AD were invited to look at van Gogh's painting *Starry Night* (1889) while their responses were recorded. Afterwards, these responses were assembled into a text by the project organizers acting as facilitators.

Ventriloquizing, 'a projected or simulated Other signification' (Banerjee 2008, 78), is a key factor shaping the cultural presence of dementia. Speaking of and for the afflicted, ventriloquism seems to secure a continued social and cultural presence for 'them', even if such a presence might exist only in memory. Oftentimes, informal stories about dementia patients are declared as memorials. Also, Jonathan Franzen's by now 'classic' dementia narrative, 'My Father's Brain: What Alzheimer's Takes Away' opens with the declaration: 'Here's a memory' (2001, 81). As the text chronicles Earl Franzen's gradual subjugation to the 'subtractive progress of Alzheimer's' (90), the memories recorded are getting invested with a double entendre. This is quite typical of the genre of the dementia memorial: there are events that happen in the life of the patient but these events also happen in the parallel universe of textualized memory so that the text gets to be speaking about two lives at one and the same time (or textual moment). And, even while Franzen avoids the openly ventriloquizing posture adopted in many other dementia memoirs written by next-of-kin, his text is curiously ambivalent about whose story this really is: 'My memories of my father's initial decline are vividly about things other than him. Indeed, I'm somewhat appalled by how large I loom in my own memories, how peripheral my parents are' (82).

Postcolonial critique has taught us that the cultural/textual praxis of 'speaking for' is never really innocent. Rather, it is one that involves us in a complex politics of representation: 'All speaking, even seemingly the most immediate, entails a distanced decipherment by another, which is, at best, an interception', an interruption in the direct flow of communication between speaker and the persons or groups he/she is speaking for (Spivak 1999, 309). Dementia ventriloquism thus gives presence to and at the same time withholds the presence of those it speaks about while leaving them curiously 'ungendered'.

Although Samuel Beckett has never spoken either for or about persons with dementia, his work has implications for representations of the illness. His later plays have been described as dramatizing the quandaries of the human mind (Takahashi 1982, 72). *Ohio Impromptu* (1981) is interesting for the question of dementia ventriloquism. The very short play displays a situation in which a generic listener (L) and a generic reader (R) are positioned at a table opposite each other. They are 'as alike in appearance as possible' (1984, 285), and thus suggest in their symmetrical poses two parts of a single, split consciousness. It is only the reader who speaks, reading out a third-person narrative from the book in front of him/her. The contents of this narrative concern the story of a man who has suffered a separation from his beloved. Unable to sleep, he encounters a stranger who has been sent to him by his lover, 'the dear name', to 'comfort' him (1984, 287). This minimal story is repeated and ritualized, while the narrative trajectory moves from 'Little is left to tell' (1984, 285) at the beginning to 'Nothing is left to tell' (1984, 288) at the end of the play. In this way, the play illustrates a problematic aspect of representing dementia in narrative, since the experience of dementia also disrupts the 'sense of an ending' or the illusion of wholeness, which a story with a beginning, middle and ending perpetuates.

The last variation in this short play's reflection on storytelling can be read as an approximation of dementia, or as dementia ventriloquism:

> What thoughts who knows. Thoughts, no, not thoughts. Profounds of mind. Of mindlessness. Whither no light can reach. No sound. So sat on as though turned to stone. The sad tale a last time told.
>
> 1984, 288

The movement in the play's embedded narrative is from a position of closeness to the first character's – the lover's – thoughts to one of externalized speculation, so that in addition to the mistrust in narrative there is also a progressive denial of interiority. Nevertheless, this analytic of regression is balanced by the play's focus on relationship: the love relationship, the linguistic repetitions evoking familiarity, the 'comfort' of the reading voice. In bringing both these perspectives of familiarity and distance together, Beckett's play illustrates important aspects of the representation of dementia.

3. AD, gendered care and ageing masculinities

We return to the question of how representations of AD relate to ageing masculinities. Like all diseases, dementia is deeply gendered. Clinical data from various countries tell us that the incidence of dementia is higher in women: 'Two-thirds of clinically diagnosed cases of dementia and AD are women, according to U.S. and most European reports. The primary reason offered for this gender difference is women's greater longevity' (Beam et al. 2018, 1017).

This is also the reason why women have been more in the focus of dementia studies, also in their role as the primary caregivers to dementia patients. And while women have been, and continue to be, in that role, male caregiving for spouses or parents with Alzheimer's disease still has to be explored in its cultural repercussions. Therefore, the focus chosen in this volume on the specifics of dementia as a disease of ageing masculinities aims at an analysis of the gender difference in care as well as specific aspects of male identity construction in the context of mental illness from the perspective of cultural critique. Bringing together insights from Masculinities Studies and Age Studies for the first time, this volume focuses on the gendered perspectives in cultural representations of AD. Such a focus is meant to initiate a new and more complex approach which looks at dementia as a disease affecting more than one person, invoking and challenging traditional as well as unconventional views of ageing masculinities.

Care has historically been associated with women and femininity, a focus that remained strong even in Carol Gilligan's feminist ethic of care, in which she argued for the necessity of a 'mode of thinking that is contextual and narrative rather than formal and abstract', and conceived the activity of care as centred around 'the understanding of responsibility and relationships' (1982/2003, 19). Arguing against a different morality for men and women in

Gilligan's gender-based psychological theory, Joan Tronto has situated care in a contextual metaethical political theory that retains the relational aspect of care but foregrounds questions of inclusion and boundaries as well as aspects such as relativism, utopianism and (individual) rights (1987, 660, 663). Nevertheless, she has shown that traditional modes of male care have been associated with the public realm and with hegemonic masculinities. In this framework, male care encompasses protecting society and engaging in economic activity and men are thus 'granted a pass from caring' in the domestic sphere (2013, 92). However, as Tronto also points out, both gender conceptions and those of care are shifting in contemporary societies. The 'Care Collective', for instance, has formulated a vision of 'universal care' that is related to a 'politics of interdependence' and embraces more inclusive models of kinship than those of the traditional nuclear family. As the authors of *The Care Manifesto* point out, dependence and care continue to be 'devalued and even pathologised' because 'autonomy and independence have historically been lionised in the Global North and gendered "male"'. Indeed, notions of unfettered male autonomy and independence remain symbolic of 'manhood', defined primarily in opposition to the 'soft', caring and dependent world of 'domesticity' (2020, 23).

How do these gendered concepts affect the situation of people with dementia? The position of the feminist philosopher Eva Feder Kittay seems most adequate to this situation, who argues that dependency is a fundamental human relationship, both for men and women, and should, therefore, be the foundation for theorizing the subject. Reflecting her own position as a moral philosopher and as mother of a cognitively disabled child, she promotes an inclusive sense of subjectivity and care: 'We human beings are the sorts of beings we are because we are cared for by other human beings, and the human beings' ontological status and corresponding moral status need to be acknowledged by the larger society that makes possible the work of those who do the caring required to sustain us' (2010, 412). To bridge the gap between concepts of gender, masculinity and the person with dementia, her way of depicting the human in its broadest sense, brings us back to the function of art and literature in representing dementia: '[T]here is so much to being human. There's the touch, there's the feel, there's the hug, there's the smile ... there are so many ways of interacting. I don't think you need philosophy for this. You need a very good writer...' (2010, 408; emphasis in text). An example for such a very good writer who has embraced the 'limitations' of both old age and mental illness, is Samuel Beckett. At the age of seventy-five, he famously summarized his poetic practice of diminishment:

> It's a paradox, but with old age, the more the possibilities diminish, the better chance you have. With diminished concentration, loss of memory, obscured intelligence – what you, for example, might call 'brain damage' – the more chance there is for saying something closest to what one really is.
> qtd. Shainberg 1987, n.p.

In spite of one monograph on the topic (Jeffers 2009), the relation in Beckett's work to notions of masculinity still needs to be further explored. By contrast, its engagement with old age and (mental) illness has been widely acknowledged and researched. Beckett is an extremely useful reference in the present context, because his work addresses in fundamental and undaunted ways the central issue that lies at the heart also of a cultural critique of Alzheimer's disease, namely the question of the relation between the human subject in its most frail condition and the cultural inventory of representations.

4. Conclusion as departure: AD and cultural critique

In the beginning, we characterized Alzheimer's as a site of resistance, of intransigent refusal of conforming to the normativities vested in the Enlightenment self. In these concluding remarks we want to offer brief reflections also on AD as a site of resistance to the routines of cultural critique.

In this perspective, we would do well to acknowledge that there is no inside of AD that would be fully accessible to outsiders, and this includes critics. This is not to say that no such inside exists – this would be a demeaning view of people suffering from the disease. Instead, what we want to solicit attention to is the idea that the oftentimes broken pieces of communication – linguistic, gestural, or otherwise – from the patients themselves cannot and perhaps should not be read mimetically, as being somehow expressive of intersubjectively shared meanings.

Such an acknowledgement would seem to suggest a different approach to these expressions, one that might be called symptomatic.[4] This would involve a focus on and commitment to what the text is unable to say. A symptomatic reading does not stop at recognizing surface features of a given text, nor does it seek to 'normalize' it, making it conform to established protocols of expression, such as genre or use of symbols and metaphors. Instead, it concentrates on the gaps, contradictions and non-sequiturs and reads them as traces or symptoms of a larger unresolved problem. The text as symptom also places readers and critics at a distance from expressions which they acknowledge they cannot fully comprehend.

Such a symptomatic reading of people with Alzheimer's and their expressions has energized reparative cultural activities such as 'Meet Me at MoMA' or the Alzheimer's Poetry Project. They seek to give a voice to those who are silenced by the standards of everyday communication without ventriloquizing them, speaking for them. Examples of similar such readings can be found throughout this collection.

Symptomatic readings of texts associated with Alzheimer's disease open up a space for reflection (and action) concerning not only their linguistic or communicative meaning but just as much the status in public conversation of human life, especially in contexts where the normative assumptions about what makes life human are up for debate.

With this in mind, the question of how much mental malfunction a society and a culture will accept in old people (and not only there) without regarding them as irretrievably Other is fast becoming an increasingly important ethical issue which the present collection is committed to exploring further.

Bibliography

Althusser, Louis, and Etienne Balibar. *Reading Capital*. Translated by Ben Brewster. London: New Left Books, 1970.

---

[4] There is no space here to enter into a full elaboration of the concept and its ramifications. The term itself has entered critique through the work of Louis Althusser where it is meant to designate a reading that focuses on what the text in question represses or fails to express fully. Cf. Althusser and Balibar's *Reading Capital* (1970). Althusser's ideology-critical commitments do not guide our use of the term. Cf. also Eve Kosofsky Sedgwick's *Epistemology of the Closet* (1991).

American Psychiatric Association. *Diagnostic and Statistical Manual of Mental Disorders*. 5th ed. Washington, DC: American Psychiatric Publishing, 2013. http://www.psychiatry.org/practice/dsm

Armour, Ellen T., and Susan M. St. Ville. 'Judith Butler—In Theory.' *Bodily Citations: Religion and Judith Butler*. Eds. Ellen T. Armour and Susan M. St. Ville. New York: Columbia UP, 2006. 1–12.

Banerjee, Mita. *Ethnic Ventriloquism: Literary Minstrelsy in Nineteenth-Century American Literature*. Heidelberg: Winter, 2008.

Basting, Anne Davis. *Forget Memory: Creating Better Lives for People with Dementia*. Baltimore: The Johns Hopkins UP, 2009.

Beam, Christopher R., Cody Kaneshiro, Jung Yun Jang, Chandra A. Reynolds, Nancy L. Pedersen, and Margaret Gatza. 'Differences Between Women and Men in Incidence Rates of Dementia and Alzheimer's Disease.' *Journal of Alzheimer's Disease* 64.4 (2018): 1077–83.

Beckett, Samuel. 'Ohio Impromptu.' *Collected Shorter Plays*. New York: Grove Press, 1984. 283–8.

Bitenc, Rebecca A. *Reconsidering Dementia: Narratives Empathy, Identity and Care*. New York: Routledge, 2020.

Care Collective, the (Andreas Chatzidakis, Jamie Hakim, Jo Littler, Catherine Rottenberg, and Lynne Segal). *The Care Manifesto: The Politics of Interdependence*. London: Verso, 2020.

Cohen, Lawrence. *No Aging in India: Alzheimer's, the Bad Family, and Other Modern Things*. Berkeley: U of California P, 1998.

England, Suzanne E. 'Private Troubles, Master Narratives: Dilemmas of Dementia Care in a Short Story.' *The Gerontologist* 57.5 (October 2017): 963–8. https://doi.org/10.1093/geront/gnw086.

Falcus, Sarah, and Katsuro Sako. *Contemporary Narratives of Dementia: Ethics, Ageing, Politics.* New York, London: Routledge, 2019.

Franzen, Jonathan. 'My Father's Brain: What Alzheimer's Takes Away.' *The New Yorker* (10 September 2001): 80–91.

Fuchs, Elinor. *Making an Exit: A Mother-Daughter Drama with Machine Tools, Alzheimer's, and Laughter*. New York: Metropolitan Books, 2005.

Gilleard, Christopher, and Paul Higgs. *Cultures of Ageing: Self, Citizen and the Body*. Harlow, UK: Pearson, 2000.

Gilligan, Carol. *In a Different Voice: Philosophical Theory and Women's Development*. Cambridge, MA: Harvard UP, 2003.

Grossberg, Lawrence. *Cultural Studies in the Future Tense*. Durham, NC: Duke UP, 2010.

Gullette, Margaret M. *Agewise: Fighting the New Ageism in America*. Chicago: U of Chicago P, 2011.

Hardt, Michael. 'The Militancy of Theory.' *South Atlantic Quarterly* 110.1 (2011): 19–35.

Hartung, Heike. 'The Limits of Development? Old Age and the Dementia Narrative.' *Ageing, Gender and Illness in Anglophone Literature: Narrating Age in the Bildungsroman*. London, New York: Routledge, 2016. 170–220.

Jeffers, Jennifer M. *Beckett's Masculinity*. New York: Palgrave Macmillan, 2009.

Kittay, Eva Feder. 'The Personal is Philosophical is Political: A Philosopher and Mother of a Cognitively Disabled Person Sends Notes from the Battlefield.' *Cognitive Disability and its Challenge to Moral Philosophy*. Eds. Eva Feder Kittay and Licia Carlson. Malden, MA and Oxford: Wiley-Blackwell, 2010. 393–413.

Kunow, Rüdiger. 'Forgetting Memory: Poetry and Alzheimer's Disease.' *Recovery and Transgression: Memory in American Poetry*. Ed. Kornelia Freitag. Newcastle: Cambridge Scholars Publishing, 2015. 281–96.

Kunow, Rüdiger. 'Lives without Memory: Alzheimer's Narratives.' *Developing Transnational American Studies*. Eds. Nadja Gernalzick and Heike C. Spickermann. Heidelberg: Winter, 2019. 103–12.

Leibing, Annette, and Silke Schicktanz, eds. *Preventing Dementia? Critical Perspectives on a New Paradigm of Preparing for Old Age*. Oxford: Berghahn Books, 2020.

Maginess, Tess, ed. *Dementia and Literature. Interdisciplinary Perspectives*. London, New York: Routledge, 2018.

Marx, Karl. *The Eighteenth Brumaire of Louis Bonaparte*. New York: International Publishers, 1963.

Medina, Raquel. *Cinematic Representations of Alzheimer's Disease*. London: Palgrave Macmillan, 2018.

Meteyard, Lotte, and Karalyn Patterson. 'The Relation between Content and Structure in Language Production: An Analysis of Speech Errors in Semantic Dementia.' *Brain and Language* 110.3 (2009): 121–34.

Ong, Aihwa. *Flexible Citizenship: The Cultural Logics of Transnationality*. Durham, NC: Duke UP. 1999.

Sedgwick, Eve Kosofsky. *Epistemology of the Closet*. Berkeley: U of California P, 1990.

Shainberg, Lawrence. 'Exorcising Beckett.' *The Paris Review* 104 (1985). https://www.theparisreview.org/letters-essays/2632/exorcizing-beckett-lawrence-shainberg [17 December 2020].

Spivak, Gayatri Chakraworty. *A Critique of Postcolonial Reason: Toward the History of the Vanishing Present*. Cambridge: Harvard UP, 1999.

Swinnen, Aagje, and Mark Schweda. 'Popularizing Dementia: Public Expressions and Representations of Forgetfulness.' *Popularizing Dementia: Public Expressions and*

Representations of Forgetfulness. Eds. Aagje Swinnen and Mark Schweda. Bielefeld: Transcript Verlag, 2015. 9–20.

Takahashi, Yasunari. 'The Theatre of the Mind: Samuel Beckett and Noh.' *Encounter* (April 1982): 66–73.

Tronto, Joan C. 'Beyond Gender Difference to a Theory of Care.' *Signs: Journal of Women in Culture and Society* 12.4 (1987): 644–63.

Tronto, Joan C. *Caring Democracy: Markets, Equality, and Justice*. New York, London: New York UP, 2013.

Zimmermann, Martina. *The Poetics and Politics of Alzheimer's Disease Life-Writing*. Basingstoke: Palgrave Macmillan, 2017.

Part One

Conceptualizing masculinities, dementia care and embodiment

Part One

Conceptualizing preschoolers'
development and education

From a 'care-free' distance? Adult sons about their parents with dementia: A cross-cultural enquiry

Martina Zimmermann

1. Introduction

How do adult sons perceive of themselves as they confront their parent's older age and memory loss? In an earlier work I introduced the concept of care-free distance in the context of adult sons writing about their parent with dementia (Zimmermann 2017, 49–73). By this concept I meant that adult sons would be able to write from a position less affected by the burdens and pressures of the actual caring experience, which would influence how they represent their mother or father.[1] This chapter wants to interrogate this care-free notion with a view to unpicking how dealing with an ageing parent impinges on the son's identity and self. I will not directly focus on responsibilities of care here, given that gender does not necessarily determine how caring is perceived differently (Sharma, Chakrabarti and Grover 2016). Rather, I take the caring role of the adult son as their connector to ageing – confronting them with their own ageing and potential memory loss as they navigate, in their own midlife, care for their parents.

Ageing has long been considered 'antithetical' to hegemonic masculinity – a concept that includes the following themes: (1) concealing emotions, (2) being

---

[1] I had made this claim in the awareness that, in comparison to adult daughters, adult sons often continue to be less involved in the active care of their parent. But already at the time I cautioned that, according to a series of sociological studies, since the 1990s men have increasingly become involved in caring, approaching female levels (Zimmermann 2017, 26).

the breadwinner and being admired and respected, and (3) projecting an air of toughness, confidence and self-reliance (Springer and Mouzon 2019, 200, 186). I will use these themes to think through how adult sons cope with an ageing parent and their memory troubles. How do they deal with emotions; what role does their professional status play in how they write and, linked to this, how is their self-reliance projected? Taking into account that identity perception also depends on the cultural context and the carer's demographics, including age, education and ethnicity (Sharma, Chakrabarti and Grover 2016; Springer and Mouzon 2019), I will take a cross-cultural approach, looking at the accounts of three adult sons in Italy, Britain, and the United States.[2]

Michele Farina's *Quando andiamo a casa? Mia madre e il mio viaggio per comprendere l'Alzheimer. Un ricordo alla volta* ('When are we going home? My mother and my journey to understand Alzheimer's. One memory at a time' 2015) offers a journalistic account of experiences with dementia in Italy. In writing a documentary, Farina can adopt a distanced reporting style; concurrently, his narrative reveals itself as a gradual rapprochement with his own fears of succumbing to dementia after his mother's death. *Take Me Home: Parkinson's, My Father, Myself* (2007) by English writer Jonathan Taylor explores relational aspects of identity further. Taylor's search for his father's past becomes equivalent to the search for his own identity, given that Taylor is no longer recognized by his father with dementia. How much does the choice of narrative form in these accounts depend on the parent's memory loss or on the son's profession? And how does cultural tradition direct concepts of health in old age? I address these questions by reading the above two texts against *A Necessary End* (1994) by American writer and journalist Nick Taylor, who traces the ageing and dying of his mother (from vascular dementia) and father (from heart disease) against their continued desire for self-determination.

While Farina's text appears to emphasize the public debate of dementia in Italy, the accounts by Jonathan Taylor and Nick Taylor seem to be much more private engagements with their parents' illness. I look at them here together to acknowledge that illness narratives come in many forms and genres (Bolaki 2016). More so, the distinct genre chosen by Farina particularly speaks to the

---

[2] References from all three narratives are incorporated in brackets in the running text; translations from the Italian original are my own.

challenge of negotiating one's own mortality as an ageing man. Considering a range of conditions typical in older age, including Alzheimer's, Parkinson's, stroke and heart disease, this chapter explores concepts of independence, autonomy and health as central to identity and self within and beyond the framework of hegemonic masculinity.

2. Michele Farina: Borrowing the pain of others

Michele Farina, whose mother had shown first symptoms of dementia in 1994, publishes a documentary about his 'journey to understand Alzheimer's'; a journey through the 'Italy of the dementias' (25) that takes him through his mother's illness experience again. In over two years of travelling, beginning eight years after the mother's death, he 'collected stories, anger, tears, surprises, laughter' (24). In recounting these, *Quando andiamo a casa?* tackles 'stigma, enigma, taboo, social rejection, isolation: zero laughter' (61). It lays into a country 'in which doctors do not speak with the patients' (299). It is also a life-affirming manifesto for dementia as a multi-factorial condition that requires, to be understood and addressed properly, the perspective of many different parties: 'patients, families, healthcare workers, organisational structure, institutions, researchers, those with other conditions' (25). Farina encounters them all, writing the story of an entire nation.[3] He explores the manifestations and consequences of the 'collapse of families and society to meet the growing need for care' that has long been coming for Italy, other Mediterranean countries and the Global North as a whole (Comas-d'Argemir and Soronellas 2019, 317). The impact of population changes in Italy has been of serious concern since the 1980s, when the demographics already made 'old-age politics a pressing issue' (Cavigioli 2005, 50). *Quando andiamo a casa?* traces, one decade into the twenty-first century, the impact of the inadequate political and societal response to these issues as much as the effect of what neuro-psycho-pharmacologist Marco Trabucchi chastises as 'bureaucracy and indifference' (348).

---

[3] Italy's sharp North-South divide is less obvious in Farina's account, but possibly perceivable in the Milanese journalist's choice of scientist interlocutors, most of whom work in northern universities; but this choice might also be explained by the close research links among these medical scientists and clinicians.

The importance of Farina's work cannot be overstated, as it sharply resonates with healthcare policy and its insufficient implementation in other European nations. For example, Farina dismantles politicians across the spectrum for their ignorance as regards a 'national plan for the dementias' (252–4). Concurrently, he highlights the diagnosis-therapy-assistance trajectory successful at a local level, where 'patients and their families are accompanied every step of the way' (387). Compare this to the situation in England.[4] The Department of Health and Social Care published plans like 'After a Diagnosis of Dementia: What to Expect from Health and Care Services' in May 2018, but local activists continue to struggle for a dementia strategy that would implement such guidance and, among other things, allocate to each individual diagnosed with dementia an empowered and trained support who has continuity of involvement throughout the course of the disease (Zimmermann and Britton 2018).

Farina's book is a prime example of life-writing whose author-narrator seeks to stay in control. Writing about a condition that apparently impacts on one's autonomy or potency comes with the necessity to find some 'compensatory power and freedom' (Couser 1997, 185; Zimmermann 2017, 101–3; 2019). *Quando andiamo a casa?* brings Farina the reward of a journalistic success that turns him into 'a good messenger' (394) and the book's reception into a platform for national activism to overcome Alzheimer's disease 'as something vague and far away, something unlikely, something exotic' (21); it is the beginning of what is meanwhile established as a national 'Alzheimer Fest' – 'a great Festival of Alzheimer's open to all related conditions' (424).[5]

At the same time, the narrative form of a documentary ensures that Farina's personal experiences and admission of fears and inadequacies can authoritatively become part of and mix with the stories of others. His scrutiny of homecare help in Italy deserves particular mention in this context, not only because it answers concerns by scholar of ageing Kathleen Woodward (2012) who laments the narrative absence from illness life-writing of the professional carer. It also is a key moment in the text where Farina's scrutiny first turns to

---

[4] Healthcare politics is devolved in the United Kingdom; this means that the document discussed in this paragraph is valid for England, but not Northern Ireland, Scotland or Wales.

[5] 'Alzheimer Fest', accessed 16 September 2020, http://www.alzheimerfest.it/. The festival was launched in 2017 and takes place once a year.

care for his mother. Homecare is largely left to the illegal immigrant, often of Northern African, Latin American, or Asian origin. A chapter entitled 'saintly carers' explores the 'intercontinental alliance' between carers and patients, offering the vignette of a woman from the Ivory Coast and her baby son taking care of a patient who no longer walks or talks (108). Following this emotional portrait of an elective affinity, 'a family rendered multi-ethnic by dementia' (109), Farina lets the reader glimpse into the 'cross-cultural challenge' (119) of having had the Peruvian carer Ines in their own home, including social responsibilities coming with wanting to help immigrants obtain citizenship after they had spent years as part of the nuclear family (119). Or take the following example where the form of the documentary helps Farina to distance himself from his own experience. He delivers pungent criticism against the 'infantilisation of old people [...] typical for certain care systems and their capacity to make profit, to take care of the highest possible number of old people with the minimum possible number of carers' (91). With this reference to Atul Gawande's *Being Mortal* (2014), he chastises the use of tranquillizers in institutions. But in doing so, he admits that, in the care for his mother, his family had administered '"some little drops"' considering it 'a form of protection, relief, not like an instrument of coercion' (92–3). Such critical reflection, Farina acknowledges, is only possible from a position of authority and closure, attained after the mother's death: 'Why am I feeling more free now? Because [my mother] is no longer there and because regrets have taken the place of fear?' (93).

Reminiscent of patient activists, Farina relies on narrative strategies that help him emotionally to distance himself from a condition that concerns the brain (Zimmermann 2017, 101; 2019). He frequently refers to the dementia brain as a furnace being turned off and taking a long time to cool down (e.g. 15–16, 45, 102), writes of his brain as a 'kilo and 300 grams of entrails and neurons, smelling of senescence' (277) and describes himself as part of the 'generation Nutella' to avoid mention of the baby boomer generation (104). These narrative tactics all have the effect of creating analytical space between the author-narrator and his outlook, emphasizing Farina's 'attempted flight' from the reality of the disease (21) during the mother's lifetime. The emotional rapprochement with his mother's condition is perhaps best documented in how Farina had not been able to deal with his mother's incontinence. Explaining this by way of referencing Philip Roth's monumental *Patrimony* (1991) expresses Farina's speechlessness masterfully (355–7):

> Patrimony, the origin of the world. I don't know whether I was able to live 'the changes' of my mother in this spirit. I don't remember. I hope so, but it is easier to think this now: faced with it, as she was alive, day after day, for years, it must have been hard. Nappies taint us, this is the truth. Or they become everyday, which is even worse.
>
> 357

Patrimony is one of the most widely known and referenced illness memoirs (see also Heike Hartung's chapter in this collection). As such, it can serve Farina as a surrogate for writing about his own experience.

It becomes ever clearer that *Quando andiamo a casa?* is also Farina's attempt at coming to terms with his fears and loss. Only 'after the hard mourning', Farina admits, he felt the need 'to rediscover [...] things that I had never tried to know (maybe because there was no cure in sight)?' (23). In his encounters with geneticists, medical scientists and practising clinicians, Farina now works through his own risk of having inherited the condition (104), and the question of how he would deal with a positive genetic test (152). Eventually, Farina acknowledges an 'inevitable reflex: to borrow the pain of others to put our own pain in perspective (ridimensionare). Even though, in this way, sometimes we end up reliving it, in real proportions; or we weld one to the other' (392). Put differently, *Quando andiamo a casa?* comes down to Farina's rapprochement with his own potential future by way of exploring his mother's dementia in the experiences of others:

> Touring Italy I travelled in time: I returned to the past, I relived things I had forgotten. I had seen my mother again a thousand times, in a thousand faces. After all these years I, who during the disease had constructed a fortress and closed down loopholes to protect her and to protect myself, have been travelling putting her story onto the windscreen like a travel permit.
>
> 394

The result of his journey is not only a journalistic masterpiece that unconditionally centres around individual patients and carers. It comes with the important insight that: 'I set out on this journey with nostalgia for my mother, with the feeling and the fear of having to find her again, maybe follow her [...] I don't know how it will be, when I might be the primitive son of my son. But now I am less afraid' (422). Identity for Farina is a question of working through his past behaviour and attitudes to his mother's condition – and to do this in a form that is consistent with his profession and enables him emotionally to stay in control. For Jonathan Taylor, whose narrative I now turn to, identity is equally a question of negotiating with his behaviour in the past, but it is also a question of unpicking the relationship with his father – of discovering his father.

3. Jonathan Taylor: Rationalizing aggression

Take Me Home creates an identity as it documents its search. The book's dedication frames this undertaking as risky and inconclusive: 'to my father, John Taylor (1928?–2001), who would probably have hated it'. John Taylor's memory problems begin when Jonathan Taylor is still a teenager and, as such, they challenge him especially during his formative years with long-term impact on his identity. The challenge is twofold: his father no longer recognizes him; and, at a time when his parent can no longer offer 'his own version of events' (225), Jonathan Taylor discovers that his father might have committed '"identity fraud"' (45). *Take Me Home* is Taylor's version of events, pieced together in the need to figure out 'what our relationship would have been like if [my father] hadn't been ill' (193).

Taylor's father has Parkinson's disease with Capgras syndrome. In this condition, John Taylor takes his son for an impostor who claims to be his son. Aggravating the situation, he takes the impostor's 'real' identity to be that of a former colleague, who (so Taylor finds out after his father's death) caused his father great grief, eventually leading to his early retirement and subsequent depression (12–13). Changes in relationships are perceived of as one of the most difficult transitions families go through when a parent has been diagnosed with dementia (Roach, Drummond and Keady 2016); and dementia is seen as a 'threat to love relationships' (Krüger-Fürhoff 2015, 95). John Taylor's condition determines how the son has to live with several versions of himself (I am adapting Douwe Draaisma's ideas here): how he was as a child when his father was still well, how he is in the daily presence of his father's condition, how he is in the mind of his father's Capgras syndrome, and all these are perhaps 'too much to be integrated in a single self' (Draaisma 2009, 438). How does Taylor cope with such a challenge to his identity?

Illness life-writing has often been described as supporting and reflecting the author-narrator's search for continuity in a life disrupted by illness. Taylor writes continuity into the relationship between patient and carer, father and son, parents and children more generally. He identifies parallels between his parents' love story and his own falling in love with his future wife (56–7); the rejection experienced at the hand of his future father-in-law for him resonates with his own father's upset, as he refers to 'pidgin Greek or Parkinsonian English, the languages [that] fail to express the love and rage of fatherhood' (63); and, perhaps most importantly, the experience of care creates continuity (19). Its all-consuming role is broached early on, in the second chapter. Entitled 'help help help', it attends to the daily minutiae of caring, listed in intervals as short as five minutes. The exclamation refers to what the father yells when he does not recognize his son and wishes to 'get *that person* away from me' (15, emphasis original). This lack of recognition dominates much of Taylor's illness experience; at least, if we can take the book cover as an extension of Taylor's impressions: printed in glossy relief, 'help help help' runs from line to line across the entire dust jacket.

But the continuity expressed in 'help help help' goes much deeper. It points to Taylor's key coping strategy, which in turn reveals much about the severity of the father's condition (Gelman and Greer 2011; Steck et al. 2007). In Capgras syndrome, particular hostility is projected onto the double, and all familiarity and warmth are removed from the relationship (Draaisma 2009, 432). Taylor is confronted with anger and aggression, including having 'the front door slammed in my face [. . .] meals thrown at me [. . .] and slaps aimed haphazardly in my direction' (213). In this way, 'help help help' is also Taylor's own plea. It is what he screams in a drunken state, beaten up by some youths (101), but not wanting 'to go home where I'm mistaken for a "him" who could be any-him' (100). With the help of alcohol and drugs, Taylor adopts a strategy of *'willed dementia'* as a teenager, actively seeking to escape his upset (161, emphasis original). This coping mechanism now challenges his search for identity.

Identity means two things at once and in dynamic exchange: 'modelling oneself *on* the other, and the establishment of the self as distinct, individual, different *from* the other' (King 2000, 31, emphases original; see also Burke 2014). In reliance on Nicola King's definition, identity is doubly at stake in *Take Me Home*: Taylor has no clear idea of his father's past nor does he have rich positive memories of the lived relationship with him before his illness. All that remains is for Taylor to 'trace [in retrospect] the story of my father's gradual decline [...] and shape it into something meaningful' (226) – a neat summary of Taylor's book-long activities, as the memoir's near symmetric organization reflects the core business and intention of *Take Me Home*. Its two central parts cover Taylor's search for the father's own past as well as the son's happy memories of him.

In the closing part's epigraph Taylor refers to Blake Morrison's bestselling *And When Did You Last See Your Father?*, the account of a son trying to come to terms with a difficult father, a 'bullying, shaming undemocratic cheat', who also wanted 'the best for [Morrison]' (1993, 11, 132). Morrison's narrative choices bring home Taylor's emotional emergency. Morrison systematically alternates chapters of past memories with those detailing the lived experience of his father's short illness and dying in the present. Chapters exploring childhood memories are told in the present tense, in order to draw the reader into the author-narrator's remembered formative years. Taylor, by comparison, writes about the past in the past tense, admitting, in response to Morrison's question, that 'I don't know when I last saw my father "unmistakably there, in the fullness of his being, him", because I'm not sure who my father was' (261).

Taylor's efforts to answer this question go in two directions: searching out the father's past and appreciating the physicality of his condition. But the effort to tell 'a long-term, linear narrative, moving from the disease's origins to its end' (226) is fraught with challenges. A common element in illness life-writing, Taylor's account begins with a chapter entitled 'a diagnosis'. Yet, confrontation with diagnosis does not come as a key moment of change that would suddenly alter his perspective on life (Couser 1997, 82, 64; Jutel and Jutel 2017). For Taylor, there does not seem to be a time before diagnosis, as he 'was only ten years old when [his father] had his nervous breakdown, only fifteen when his disease was diagnosed, only eighteen when he started misidentifying me' (243). That said, understanding Parkinson's disease as a neurological condition helps Taylor rationalize the parent's inability to recognize or remember him (222). 'Parkinson's is a disease of neurotransmitters, of the chemicals which facilitate communication *between* cells. So I like to believe – whether or not it was neurologically correct – that the brain cells themselves, and the memories they embodied, were still intact. They were just isolated, unable to communicate with one another' (165, emphasis original). But in the end, he cannot separate the illness from the father as person. His father is '*a person* [...] a *whole* person – not just bits and pieces of tremoring hands, distended abdomens, choreiform movements, Lewy bodies' (253, emphases original; on the impossibility to separate illness from fatherhood, see also Katharina Fürholzer's essay in this collection).

In a similar way, Taylor's efforts to learn more about his father's past remain inconclusive. But, as a contemporary reviewer opined, 'it is to Taylor's credit that he fails to pin down his father' (Laing 2007). To comprehend the father and the relationship with him is much more than learning about his past or defining his pathology. Rather, Taylor comes to the conclusion that the double, which has critically determined his own identity, has been a structuring principle in his father's life and identity:

> My father's life was so full of these repeated patterns and doubles, I wonder if Capgras syndrome just mixed them up a bit. The pattern of doubles was already there, structuring his life and mind; all Capgras had to do was collapse a few of the pairings into each other [...] Capgras: it's the end-point of finding patterns and establishing connections: everything collapses into everything else.
>
> 206

Take Me Home reveals itself as testimony to the importance of relational identity that holds within and beyond a parent's memory loss and challenging behaviour.

4. Nick Taylor: Conserving family dynamics

A Necessary End (1994) addresses the question of continued self-determination in the face of ageing and illness on account of both parents and children. Nick Taylor faces the fact that 'anywhere children in the bloom of their lives must confront their parents' withering. What do our parents need? What must we do for them? What becomes of us in the process, of our minds and lives and dreams?' (28). Writing after Clare and Jack Taylor's death, Nick Taylor thinks through what really mattered – to him as well as his parents – during the final seven years of their lives. In essence, he traces his parents' shift from third to fourth age (Higgs and Gilleard 2015), from 1984 to 1991. At the same time, *A Necessary End* lets the reader glimpse into a son's coping mechanisms as he seeks to balance feelings of responsibility and the wish for freedom (and relief from responsibility), as he beholds his parents' increasing vulnerability, when they 'grasped the life I would have denied them in the interest of my own convenience' (14). Put differently, *A Necessary End* thinks through the consequences of what Michele Farina advocates in the voice of Atul Gawande: older people living their 'waning days' in a self-determined way (Gawande 2015, 9). And read against Jonathan Taylor's search for his own identity in confrontation with an ill father, Nick Taylor's 'helplessness and confusion' (31) suggest that a son may well experience a challenge to his identity in the face of his parents' ageing, even though he can take comfort from many happy memories of their lived past.

What matters most to Clare and Jack Taylor is their continued autonomy and independence, powerfully conveyed in their decision to move, in their mid-seventies, from Waynesville, North Carolina, to Chapala near Guadalajara in Mexico where they wish to spend their final years. As his parents leave their sheltered housing, under the 'unforgiving eyes of prisoners watching an escape' (8), Nick Taylor admits that it 'would have been much easier on me if, like the others, they had chosen to simply sit and wait for death' (9). But he also knows that the 'ingredients of dignity were all [his father] asked', that all he 'wanted was to meet his basic needs, health among them, and to have some money in his pocket' (76). As the son 'feared for the integrity of [his] own life' (30), what are his coping mechanisms?

Nick Taylor clearly recognizes that his parents continue to be in better health when comparing to some of their friends. Reference to these friends is scattered throughout the memoir as if the author-narrator had to keep reminding himself of his parents' successful ageing. There is the wife of a good friend of his parents, 'in a nursing home with Alzheimer's disease, [who] had forgotten who [her husband] was' (15); there are the parents of one of Taylor's friends, the mother suffering from Alzheimer's, the father, after 'a paralyzing stroke [...] in a nursing home' (32) for eight years, the last three '"unresponsive", a gray and neutral word for living death' (186). Dementia, more than any other degenerative condition, significantly increases dependency and the need for institutional care (Higgs and Gilleard 2015, 50). In linking mental decline to lack of success in ageing (Zimmermann 2020, 98), these cursory observations have a twofold effect. They bring out the momentarily still better health of Clare and Jack Taylor, and they painfully offset what Nick Taylor has been afraid of all along: the loss of his parents' self-sufficiency.

A Necessary End is about what Nick Taylor terms 'generational switch', as '[his] concerns were [those of his parents], twenty years removed' (10).[6] The memoir's longest chapter, encompassing most of the book's second half, explores in excruciating detail 'my mother's confusion and Dad's dependence' (126) during the year 1989. Previously, in 1986, Nick Taylor could still ignore 'the quirks that started appearing in [my mother's] letters [...] the wrong month, or the wrong year, at the top of the page' (45). During 1989, he describes himself as 'more conscious of their frailty' (136). The pace of the narrative slows down to moment-in-time recordings of conversational exchange. And, reminiscent of Jonathan Taylor's need to chronicle to get a hold on his father's disease, the chapter is scattered with dates and timelines, as if it helped the author-narrator to rationalize his parents' rapid change that 'was all about sadness and memory and loss and struggle and yearning' (121). Such narrative choices signal Nick Taylor's increasing acceptance of his parents' dying, as also suggested by the illustration heading the chapter. Each chapter is introduced by one of Jack Taylor's wood-block prints. But especially the ones heading this and the final two chapters trace the parents' slowing down: 1989 opens with a closed garden gate, followed by 1990 displaying a capsized ship that anticipates Jack Taylor's looking 'like some ghost ship' (163), and the final chapter, 1991, beginning with a church engraving to mark his parents' death.

Two events in the book's narrative and textual centre stand out in 1989: Jack Taylor is in need of a pacemaker; and, after episodes of memory loss and confusion, Clare Taylor has several strokes. These events force Nick Taylor to consider long-term care options, trying to avoid 'someplace sad with stale odors' (103) where his parents would have to follow 'regimented, anonymous

---

[6] 'Nick Taylor's Books', accessed 16 September 2020, http://www.nicktayloronline.com/works.htm.

routines' that cut them off from everything that had mattered to them (Gawande 2015, 9). More telling than these physical markers is Nick Taylor's discovery of a box with his mother's memorabilia. These include photos that show her 'as an ingenue [sic], full of life and promise, then as a career girl, then as a young wife, then as a working mother' (92). The reader appreciates how strongly Nick Taylor senses his parents' imminent loss around this time when the box of memorabilia is lost – just when his mother's forgetfulness becomes increasingly pronounced.[7]

As in Jonathan Taylor's case, the parent's continued cognitive capabilities condition the son's perception of himself: 'She had no memory for the immediate past, but by reaching back she resurrected my own memories' (167). In reverse, her increasing dementia destabilizes his self-confidence (Burke 2014). Nick Taylor is keenly driven by his publishing activities, including his growing reputation as a non-fiction writer. But his successes are no longer in the parents' awareness, as especially his mother is no longer able critically to appraise his writing. Taylor's own view of himself falters in confrontation with the mother's loss: 'I wanted her to have, if only for a moment, the authority I'd seen that afternoon when I was looking through her papers' (95). That said, Clare Taylor's desire for self-determination remains unbroken until the very end. Nick Taylor observes his mother's struggles to follow physiotherapeutic interventions after her stroke when she finally exclaims: 'Why don't they just let me die!' (170). It takes her son a little longer to appreciate that he has to let go, as 'this was not my mother. This was not the woman she had been, nor the woman she would have wanted to be' (177).

A Necessary End is the story of dying as part of ageing. Death, the knowledge that death will come, dominates the account conceptually – most obviously driven by its chronology. Like the other memoirs explored in this chapter, *A Necessary End*, albeit indirectly in this case, pays tribute to Philip Roth's *Patrimony*. Roth's book about his father's dying of a brain tumour offers a 'mythic version of how to negotiate the death of a parent', while also telling the unadorned truth of the pain and physicality of dying (Hawkins 1999, 118–19). Nick Taylor's account achieves a similar split between myth and reality, perhaps

---

[7] Blake Morrison similarly hoped that regaining some of his father's medical equipment 'might restore some part of my father to me' (160).

because it is a story of living in ageing and living in dying, and of the pain that comes from letting your parents live the life they want, until the very end. 'Death itself was not the problem', explains Nick Taylor, 'It was my parents' dotage that I feared. I feared their faltering, their decline, and, finally, their dependence' (27). The way they chose to live eventually determines their difficult end – the image of the bird as a symbol of freedom tracing this shift. Nick Taylor describes them as 'bedraggled birds on their last migration' (111) when they eventually pack up to leave Guadalajara for Fort Myers in Florida to be closer to him and in a more protected environment. He soon sees 'little pieces [...] fly away' (130) and traces his mother's decline through her series of strokes, her arm 'a broken wing to wave' (144). And his father's breathing, near the end 'was weaker, a flutter of a bird's wing' (189).

Still, Nick Taylor's account is mapped on the preferred plot of the redemptive ending, as the younger generation is 'so relieved to be alive' (193). Obviously, Nick Taylor observes his parents' memory in his writing. The first edition of *A Necessary End* has the elegant finish of a precious book to be cherished; it is bound in part linen, has a colour-matching head and tail band, and artistic front cut. In addition, it gives space to the father's 'delicate wood-block prints' which Nick Taylor 'considered his true calling' (3). Above all, the son conveys the parents' immortality in his own existence: 'I have my father's prints and tools and the childhood memories I asked them both to write. I have memories. Most of all, I have myself. Me. I am what my parents made and left. I am what I have to remember them by. And I am the person that they made. I will have to do with that, but all in all, it's not so bad' (193).

5. Conclusion: Masculinity and control

There are demographic as well as political reasons for being attuned to gender when considering carer narratives (Bitenc 2020, 134). Globally, seventy per cent of workers in health and social care are women (Boniol et al. 2019), although there are more and more men who provide care (Arber and Gilbert 1989; Hirst 2001; McDonnell and Ryan 2014; Zimmermann 2017, 26). Such numerical imbalance implies that caring can be seen as challenging hegemonic masculinity. In addition, older men have a lower life-expectancy than women and are often 'constructed as pre-death' (Hearn 1995, 101). It is perhaps the desire to 'bid for immortality' (Bauman 1992, 51) that, at least partly, motivates men to write about their parents in a way that, compared to adult daughters' writing, is more removed from the caring experience as such (Zimmermann 2017, 23–47).

Michele Farina, Jonathan Taylor and Nick Taylor all write after their parent or parents have died. They are professional writers, two of them active in journalism. They negotiate with the death of those who made them who they are, especially Jonathan Taylor struggling with regret about lost opportunities, as his father 'knew everything (or so it seems to me now) and I talked to him about nothing' (88). The feeling of guilt appears to permeate all three texts (Zimmermann 2017, 129), although Nick Taylor refuses to buy into 'guilt as a condition of living' (194). Blake Morrison, whose account Jonathan Taylor negotiates with, puts this succinctly in a new afterword to his memoir: 'When young, we were impatient with our parents: now we want to atone for our callowness, and to acknowledge what they were and all they did' (231). Read in this light, these authors explore implications for the adult child's identity of the parental generation's memory loss, and, as such, none of them is care-free.

Atonement comes through researching and writing their narratives. In an attempt to explain why the number of female illness narratives is so much higher than those written by men, I had previously suggested that men might find it difficult to maintain a sense of masculinity after having published their account (Zimmermann 2017, 45–6). Where these author-narrators feel compromised by their own feelings they run to the undisputed reference in the field, Roth's *Patrimony*. But their written works are more than atonement. Each of them publishes in tune with their professional aspirations. Farina turns 'pseudo-detective of "dark Alzheimer's"' (337) to scrutinize 'oasis-like care homes and hell-like care homes' (24), Jonathan Taylor writes as the literary critic-cum-author to reflect on the powers and pitfalls of life-writing, and Nick Taylor offers a poetic account of healthy ageing.

All three narratives present the reader with a redemptive ending. Nick Taylor celebrates being alive; Jonathan Taylor is getting married; and Michele Farina pursues his vision of Alzheimer Fest. Each in their own way stays in control of how they share emotions about ageing – their own ageing as much as that of their parents (Specht, Egloff and Schmukle 2013; on the issue of control, see also the contribution by João Paulo Guimarães and Daae Jung in this collection). Farina stays in control by choosing a particular narrative form. Jonathan Taylor tries to rationalize the effects of Parkinson's with Capgras dementia by approaching it as a biomedical condition. And Nick Taylor accepts his parents' wish for autonomy by placing it alongside his own professional drive. All three make sense of their experience by advocating self-determined ageing in a supportive environment. They write about a mode of ageing that they themselves hope to approach in midlife; a mode of ageing that will ensure they maintain their identity and self.

Acknowledgements

This work was supported by a UKRI Future Leaders Fellowship [MR/T019794/1]. I am grateful for discussion with Jonathan Taylor at the launch of the 'Parkinson of the disease' exhibition, Maughan Library, King's College London, 12 October 2017, and owe thanks to Neil Vickers for pointing me to Zygmunt Bauman's work.

Bibliography

'Alzheimer Fest 2020.' http://www.alzheimerfest.it/ [16 September 2020].
Arber, Sara, and Nigel Gilbert. 'Men: The Forgotten Carers.' *Sociology* 23 (1989): 111–18.
Bauman, Zygmunt. *Mortality, Immortality and Other Life Strategies*. Cambridge: Polity Press, 1992.
Bitenc, Rebecca A. *Reconsidering Dementia Narratives: Empathy, Identity and Care*. Abingdon: Routledge, 2020.
Bolaki, Stella. *Illness as Many Narratives: Arts, Medicine and Culture*. Edinburgh: Edinburgh UP, 2016.
Boniol, Mathieu, Michelle McIsaac, Lihui Xu, Tana Wuliji, Khassoum Diallo, and Jim Campbell. *Gender Equity in the Health Workforce: Analysis of 104 Countries*. Geneva: World Health Organization, 2019.
Burke, Lucy. 'Oneself as Another: Intersubjectivity and Ethics in Alzheimer's Illness Narratives.' *Narrative Works: Issues, Investigations & Interventions* 4 (2014): 28–47.
Cavigioli, Rita C. *Women of a Certain Age: Contemporary Italian Fictions of Female Aging*. Madison: Fairleigh Dickinson UP, 2005.

Comas-d'Argemir, Dolors, and Montserrat Soronellas. 'Men as Carers in Long-Term Caring: Doing Gender and Doing Kinship'. *Journal of Family Issues* 40 (2019): 315–39.

Couser, G. Thomas. *Recovering Bodies: Illness, Disability, and Life Writing*. Madison: The U of Wisconsin P, 1997.

Department of Health and Social Care. *After a Diagnosis of Dementia: What to Expect from Health and Care Services*. London: Department of Health and Social Care, 2018.

Draaisma, Douwe. 'Echos, Doubles, and Delusions: Capgras Syndrome in Science and Literature.' *Style* 43 (2009): 429–41.

Farina, Michele. *Quando andiamo a casa? Mia madre e il mio viaggio per comprendere l'Alzheimer. Un ricordo alla volta*. Milan: BUR Varia, 2015.

Gawande, Atul. *Being Mortal: Illness, Medicine and What Matters in the End*. 2014. London: Profile Books, 2015.

Gelman, Caroline Rosenthal, and Christine Greer. 'Young Children in Early-Onset Alzheimer's Disease Families: Research Gaps and Emerging Service Needs.' *American Journal of Alzheimer's Disease and Other Dementias* 26 (2011): 29–35.

Hawkins, Anne Hunsaker. *Reconstructing Illness: Studies in Pathography*, 2nd edn. West Lafayette: Purdue UP, 1999.

Hearn, Jeff. 'Imaging the Aging of Men.' *Images of Aging: Cultural Representations of Later Life*. Eds. Mike Featherstone and Andrew Wernick. London: Routledge, 1995. 97–115.

Higgs, Paul, and Chris Gilleard. *Rethinking Old Age: Theorising the Fourth Age*. London: Palgrave, 2015.

Hirst, Michael. 'Trends in Informal Care in Great Britain during the 1990s.' *Health and Social Care in the Community* 9 (2001): 348–57.

Jutel, Thierry, and Annemarie Jutel. '"Deal with It. Name It": The Diagnostic Moment in Film.' *Medical Humanities* 43 (2017): 185–91.

King, Nicola. *Memory, Narrative, Identity: Remembering the Self*. Edinburgh: Edinburgh UP, 2000.

Krüger-Fürhoff, Irmela Marei. 'Narrating the Limits of Narration: Alzheimer's Disease in Contemporary Literary Texts.' *Popularizing Dementia: Public Expressions and Representations of Forgetfulness*. Eds. Aagje Swinnen and Mark Schweda. Bielefeld: Transcript, 2015. 93–112.

Laing, Olivia. 'Through the Looking Glass.' *Guardian*, (18 August 2007). https://www.theguardian.com/books/2007/aug/18/featuresreviews.guardianreview5.

McDonnell, Eilis, and Assumpta A. Ryan. 'The Experience of Sons Caring for a Parent with Dementia.' *Dementia* 13 (2014): 788–802.

Morrison, Blake. *And When Did You Last See Your Father?* With a New Afterword by the Author [1993]. London: Granta Books, 2006.

'Nick Taylor's Books.' http://www.nicktayloronline.com/works.htm. Accessed 16 September 2020.

Roach, Pamela, Neil Drummond and John Keady. '"Nobody Would Say That It Is Alzheimer's or Dementia at This Age": Family Adjustment Following a Diagnosis of Early-Onset Dementia.' *Journal of Aging Studies* 36 (2016): 26–32.

Sharma, Nidhi, Subho Chakrabarti and Sandeep Grover. 'Gender Differences in Caregiving among Family – Caregivers of People with Mental Illnesses.' *World Journal of Psychiatry* 6 (2016): 7–17.

Specht, Jule, Boris Egloff and Stefan C. Schmukle. 'Everything Under Control? The Effects of Age, Gender, and Education on Trajectories of Perceived Control in a Nationally Representative German Sample.' *Developmental Psychology* 49 (2013): 353–64.

Springer, Kristen W., and Dawne M. Mouzon. 'One Step Toward More Research on Aging Masculinities: Operationalizing the Hegemonic Masculinity for Older Men Scale (HMOMS).' *Journal of Men's Studies* 27 (2019): 183–203.

Steck, Barbara, A. Grether, Felix Amsler, A. Schwald Dillier, Georg, Romer, L. Kappos and Dieter K. Bürgin. 'Disease Variables and Depression Affecting the Process of Coping in Families with a Somatically Ill Parent.' *Psychopathology* 40 (2007): 394–404.

Taylor, Jonathan. *Take Me Home: Parkinson's, My Father, Myself.* London: Granta, 2007.

Taylor, Nick. *A Necessary End.* New York: Doubleday, 1994.

Woodward, Kathleen. 'A Public Secret: Assisted Living, Caregivers, Globalization.' *International Journal of Ageing and Later Life* 7 (2012): 17–51.

Zimmermann, Martina. *The Poetics and Politics of Alzheimer's Disease Life-Writing.* Basingstoke: Palgrave, 2017.

Zimmermann, Martina. 'Terry Pratchett's *Living with Alzheimer's* as a Case Study of Late-Life Creativity.' *Creativity in Later Life: Beyond Late Style.* Eds. David Amigoni and Gordon McMullan. Abingdon: Routledge, 2019. 198–207.

Zimmermann, Martina. *The Diseased Brain and the Failing Mind: Dementia in Science, Medicine and Literature of the Long Twentieth Century.* London: Bloomsbury, 2020.

Zimmermann, Martina, and Anthony Britton. 'Changing Care: How a Neuropharmacologist-*cum*-Health-Humanist and a Caregiver-turned-Activist Work Together to Achieve Improved Caregiver and Patient Support.' Paper presented at the Workshop on Working Together beyond the Academy in Research in Dementia and Culture, London, 23 November 2018.

2

Masculinities in Brazil: Identity tinkering and dementia care

Annette Leibing and Cíntia Engel

Two vignettes – one about a husband who is looking after his wife, the other one about a son caring for his mother – lie at the centre of this chapter about dementia care in urban Brazil. The first narrative especially explores family dynamics around male dementia care, while the second one focuses on interactions in the clinic. And although at first glance the genderedness, as well as the cultural context of these stories, seem to be at the forefront, we argue that both categories need to be seen as changing signifiers. Within the complexity of everyday life, gender and culture are entangled with multiple and co-existing value-systems, materialities, health economics, geriatric epistemologies, personalities, questions of class and biology, and so much more. In other words, the specific Brazilian context and the gendered aspects of care play sometimes more, sometimes less a role as the stories unfold. Our focus nevertheless will be the gendered vectors – contributing forces – within the wider context of care dynamics in the two vignettes. However, thinking about gender in a specific context means a constant repositioning and identity tinkering – even in Brazil, where often the predominant image of the '*machista*' (male chauvinist) is evoked in describing local masculinities (see below).

Vignettes are incomplete narratives – they are glimpses of lives embedded in a fragmented context, but in which, ideally, concepts emerge that capture important and revealing aspects of what is at stake. Such concepts – for instance 'family insufficiency' – are analytical and necessary short cuts to complex social phenomena. Our vignettes obviously only provide a faint image of what it means to care for someone with dementia, which is a multilayered compound of activities and dispositions, and this is especially so in Brazil: the country is often perceived as highly complex and – a metaphor used at least since Bastide's classic description of Brazil from 1964 – a land of 'contrasts'. Educator Paulo Freire, for instance, described Brazil in 1998 as, 'the dramatic coexistence of different times that overcome together in the same geographical space – backwardness, misery, poverty, hunger, traditionalism, magical conscience, authoritarianism, democracy, modernity, and postmodernity' (quoted in Steinberg 2011, xxi). The same complexity can be found when talking about gender, where different historical times and concomitant value-systems co-exist – a fact that might at least partly explain the tensions found in the vignettes we will discuss in this chapter. Heilborn and da Silva Cabral (2013), in their study of young Brazilians, gender and sexual practices, come to the conclusion that notions of gender equality, even in more educated parts of society, are less commonly accepted and put into practice by men as compared to women. The authors write that:

> highly educated men demonstrate a weak adherence to the principles of gender equality, while their female peers show a remarkable flexibility in their attitudes toward and beliefs about sexuality. This unexpected disparity provokes us to suggest that there is a reinvigorated expression of gender inequality in a social stratum, in which the real progress of egalitarianism could easily be imagined.
>
> 42

More specifically speaking about gender, old age, and self-care, Coelho, Giacomin and Firmo (2016) show that in their study, most men – just like in other national contexts – avoid the topic of medical care, and link illness, as well as the ageing body, to frailty and a loss of masculinity. Male self-care, like elsewhere, is typically enacted through practices of care outside of the health domain, although such activities – playing sports, sexual activities, or physical work in general – can get medicalized, when declining functionality is perceived as pathological (Katz and Marshall 2003; Leibing et al. 2014; Medeiros et al. 2014; Pereira 2009). This avoidance of medical care needs to be seen as partial and paradoxical, and as in co-existence with a generalized Brazilian fascination with health technologies and especially with pharmaceuticals. This major phenomenon in Brazil we have called elsewhere 'pharma-literacy' (Leibing, Engel and Carrijo 2019).

One way of 'rejuvenating' old age through a hybrid – both extra- and intra-medical-domain kind of self-care – is well described by Debert and Brigeiro (2012). Already happening before, but especially after the introduction of Viagra to the Brazilian market, a major 'eroticization of old age' took place, with a concomitant quasi-obligation – more for men than for women – of talking constantly about and ideally also having (heterosexual) sex in order to continue to inhabit the universe of younger adults. Brigeiro (2000) introduces in his study a category that was frequently employed by the middle-class urban men he studied in Rio de Janeiro, 'the pyjamas'. Different from the men Brigeiro observed and who regularly met in public spaces, a man described as a 'pyjama' is someone who is passive and who stays mostly at home (imagined as wearing pyjamas and slippers); he is pitied, and perceived as dominated by his wife.

The adherence to such masculine values suggests that adopting the role of a caregiver for a Brazilian man is not always easy, although a number of studies, as well as our own observations stemming from extended fieldwork, also portray men who apparently have accepted (and enjoyed) such roles. However, as Santos and Rifiotis (2004) argue, Brazilian men generally can rely on more help from other (mostly female) family members when compared to women as caregivers. Further, the Brazilian institution of the maid in the middle and upper classes plays an important role in the capacity of caregiving, although less so in the following two vignettes. And although the affordability of the *empregada*, the maid, has changed in recent years as a result of stricter labour laws, the still very common and poorly paid household help is an important element in Brazilian cultures of care (see Vilela 2019). These women help to keep older people in the community, while (relatively uncommon) institutional nursing homes carry an extremely negative connotation of abandonment. The role of the maid as care aid is increasingly shared with the more recent phenomenon of trained professional caregivers, *cuidadoras*. The growing need for these mostly female professionals who get hired by families, as well as mushrooming public and private training programmes all over Brazil, shows the strong reliance of the State on families to be responsible for caring (and paying) for their ageing persons in need (Debert and Oliveira 2015). In the first vignette, the family had hired a *cuidadora* who helped with some of the daily caregiving tasks, while in the second narrative, the sister who lived in the same building, sometimes sent her *empregada* to help with household chores.

The lack of a solid social net in Brazil is, of course, especially difficult for poorer families, in which, additionally, the ideal of the 'provider husband and father' is often absent (de Souza 2009). The documentary *Alzheimer na Periferia* by Brazilian filmmaker Albert Klinke (2018) describes with a lot of sensitivity how five families, living on the outskirts of São Paulo, deal with the many challenges and the lack of resources they face in caring for a family member with dementia. The moral obligation to care, based on Christian family values, is a strong motivating factor in the stories narrated in the film.

Finally, most masculinity studies nowadays show that something like an 'identity tinkering' takes place regarding male caregiving – as a result, most current work insists on the fact that there are gendered aspects, but that they are much less normative than they were in the past. As an example, Calasanti and Bowen (2006) describe in their work, which took place in rural UK, how caregivers constantly crossed gender borders – a fact that can also be observed in the following two vignettes.

1. Vignette one: Caring for his wife

In 2018, Mr João turned eighty. He was born in a rural area of the northwest region of Brazil, as was his spouse, Mrs Aparecida. They got married in their twenties. Before that, Mr João was married to another woman and had three children. With Mrs Aparecida, he had seven children, six girls and one boy. In the 1960s, they were raising their children together, with the resources of the farm where they lived. But when Mrs Aparecida got pregnant with their last child, Mr João decided to migrate to the Federal District, where the new capital Brasília was being constructed and where workers were needed.

Mr João's father went first; he sold almost all his lands for a negligible amount of money, believing in a propagandized promise of a 'better life' in the Federal District. Mr João decided to do the same. He stayed for almost three years in the Federal District and saw his father come to regret not having his land anymore and having to live and die in a landscape that he could not love. But he also saw his brothers building their houses and bringing their families to live in the Federal District, where urban life was progressively appearing to provide better opportunities to study and work.

During those years, Mrs Aparecida stayed in the north-western part of Brazil and took care of their children, with the help of her family. She also started to work as a seamstress, because the money that her husband had been sending to her was not enough. She almost lost her last child in a fire that occurred in her home. Mr João did not return home to help with this crisis. Her family discovered that he had started a new family in the Federal District. But, with some insistence on the part of Mrs Aparecida and her family, he finally returned to the north-western region. They moved to the capital of a nearby state, not far from the farm, and they stayed together for many years – a period in which Mr João was described as having been a good provider, but a very strict father.

In 2000, by which time all their children were adults, Mrs Aparecida became more and more forgetful. One day, she got lost on her way home. The daughter who was still living with them took her to a doctor and, after a lot of tests, Mrs Aparecida received the diagnosis: Alzheimer's disease. At first, Mr João became her main caregiver, with the help of his daughter and a domestic worker. Just like many other husbands of women with dementia of his generation, Mr João had to learn how to deal with caring activities, something that he had never been responsible for before (cf. Santos and Rifiotis 2004). But differently than other experiences that we and other researchers have learned of (Russell 2001; Baker et al. 2010; Robinson et al. 2014) in which the husband engages intensively and almost exclusively with caregiving, Mr João did not fully adhere to being a caregiver.

One of the reasons, his daughters observed, had to do with the fact that Mr João had never been perceived as a caring husband. The daughters described him as verbally aggressive, a '*machista*'. And there was a lot of bitterness resulting from the fact that when he went to another state to pursue a better life for his family, he started a whole second family and did not provide as he had promised. The daughters were convinced that he would be a bad caregiver for his wife. Therefore, the four daughters who were living in the Federal District decided to take care of their mother there. They separated the couple. Mr João said that he would prefer being with his wife and have the daughters moving there to help him. But realizing that this option was not economically possible, he finally agreed to the decision.

That did not work very well. Mrs Aparecida wanted to be with her husband. She started to cry repeatedly and became more and more agitated. The doctors then prescribed her an antipsychotic drug, in order to deal with this 'agitation'. The drug did not work, so the daughters decided to bring their father to stay with Mrs Aparecida. And that worked: she became calmer and happier with her 'old man' (as she used to refer to him), even when dealing with his yelling.

However, although Mr João initially agreed to move, he quickly realized that being in this new place was not what he wanted. He remembered his father's fate regretting moving, and he missed his friends. His relationship with his daughters was complicated. He was being cared for – just like his wife – but he didn't have a strong voice in decisions. This was made even more dramatic when he became blind due to complications from cataracts.

The same geriatrician was attending both he and Mrs Aparecida. Initially, the consultations were provided together. And although Mr João tried very hard to convince this geriatrician to engage with his version of daily life and of what he thought his wife needed, he was constantly ignored by the geriatrician, and his way of seeing the situation was contested by his daughters. For that reason, the geriatrician decided to stop seeing them together and separated the couple one more time. Mr João was classified as a *'machista'* – a term that doctors used when discussing his case and it was even found in his patient file. According to the doctors, he didn't have the best interests of Mrs Aparecida in mind. Mr João also started to complain about the doctors that were attending him in the Federal District. He let everyone know that he was there against his will and that he was alone and disrespected – not treated as 'the man he was'.

But although he did not stop complaining about his wife's disease, and, sometimes, was irritated with her, he learned how to communicate with her like no one else. One day, one of the daughters was trying, with no success, to convince Mrs Aparecida to take a shower. She was very irritated with the situation. Mr João approached his wife and said: 'I've just enjoyed my bath; the water is warm and delightful. Are you going, too?' She grabbed her towel and said: 'I'm going to take a shower, too'. The daughter at this point told me that her father helped a lot with daily care, so despite the fact that she considered him responsible for some daily distress, she also believed that he was an important part of caring for her mother. It's 'complicated', she said. For that reason, they were also insisting that it would be important for him to stay there and Mr João repeatedly used the argument, 'she is my wife, and now she needs me'. But sometimes he became sad and mad about his destiny: 'I'm stuck, this is no life for me, she was such a good wife before, now she is like that! I'm paying for my sins from the past'.

In the Federal District, other relationships with the wider family – the daughters' husbands and the grandsons – also became part of the intricacy of daily care. These caring activities revealed further aspects of the expectations and norms regarding masculinity, especially that of the younger men. Although there were four daughters living in the Federal District, three were more involved in managing the division of care: Marta, Julia, and Joana – all in their forties. Joana was divorced and, because of that, she was chosen as the one that would live with their mother and father. Marta and Julia used to visit constantly and, some days of the week they took Mrs Aparecida to stay in their homes. Joana told me that her sisters insisted that as she didn't have a husband, it would be easier for her to share the house with their parents. She loved her mother very much and was happy to take care of her, but she was ambivalent about her sister's argument. She observed that a husband could be a complication in caring for the elderly, but also an important partner. On several occasions, she came back to this point when comparing her sisters' husbands.

Marta's husband used to be evaluated in the family as a caring and 'good' husband. He was a strong provider but was also really engaged at home. He used to do some of the daily home care, but a major contribution of his was that he took over transportation to doctors' appointments, as well as solving the multiple bureaucratic needs of the family. He was very attentive when talking with Mrs Aparecida and she liked him, and, his best characteristic: 'he does not get in the way'.

Julia's husband, on the contrary, was known as the one that 'gets in the way'. That meant that he would limit his wife's attention given to her parents, would complain that she did not take enough care of her nuclear family, because she spent a lot of time with her parents. Mrs Aparecida clearly showed that she did not like him, and neither did Mr João. They felt he had repeatedly mistreated them. That situation would compromise the time that Julia would put into caring, as well as the trust of the other sisters regarding Julia's care work. This aspect – that it is the couple that influences how Julia, as an individual, is able to care – is rarely discussed in the literature (although there are many studies on couples in which one of them is the person with dementia). Here, Julia's relation to her husband is central in the evaluation and division of care. We found this distinction between a 'good' and a 'bad' husband in other contexts as well.

In fact, caring for older parents with dementia was a constant source of debate and reflections about masculinity itself within this family. The constant references to types of masculinity, but also possible implications for sexuality were important topics of discussion, and especially when the care of grandsons was required, but also questioned. Marta's son, who was 18 years old at the time, was very close to his grandmother. When she was at his house, he would help his mother with the care work. He showed a lot of interest in his grandma's disease, and did Internet searches about Alzheimer's that he discussed on several occasions with his aunts. His interest became an essential part of the care work, because every time someone needed information, he would be able to find an answer on the Internet. He would refer to himself as a 'dedicated son', one that would always engage with his parents.

While on one hand he was considered a 'good boy', especially for his attentive way of relating to his grandmother, on the other hand some family members doubted his straightness: care and masculinity became evaluated in connection with an ambiguous sexuality, especially in young men. Joana once told me that she never let her sons (both in their twenties) do domestic chores or activities of caring when they were children because she had been taught that this could compromise the making of a straight man. She believed that this was one of her main responsibilities as a mother. In 2018, though, she told me that she was regretting that a little bit; she was feeling that her sons were not very open to helping at home, that times had changed and she said this even though they were close to their grandma. And she also thought that they were just like their grandfather and father in one problematic aspect: they were '*machistas*'.

One of those young men once told me that he didn't know how to do some things, he didn't feel prepared, although he wanted to help. The other one explained that he, as a man, did not have the body built for care. It would be humiliating for him to try. They had different perspectives about why they didn't feel that they should or could help. One was more convinced that a lack of experience was at the core of his inability; and the other one believed that it was because of his male body not made for care. Both preferred to help their mother and grandma with money – in the context of the families' limited budgets, an aspect of care that was much appreciated.

2. Vignette two: A follow-up consultation at the geriatric clinic

It was a day at the specialized out-patient clinic in Brazil's Federal District, when mostly individuals with a dementia were seen. Following the established protocol, a second-year geriatric resident would start the detailed consultation, and a more senior geriatrician would join towards the end of the session, in order to discuss the medication regimen the resident wanted to prescribe.

The resident called out the name of Mrs Madalena, who was sitting in a wheelchair in the waiting area. We all entered one of the tiny cubicles in which the examinations take place. The small space was now packed with a desk, behind which the resident took her place, the chairs for the three sisters who accompanied their mother, and Mrs Madalena's wheelchair, while Mrs Madalena's son sat with me, the anthropologist, on the examination couch. Through the barred windows we heard birds in mango trees in the patio, and through the open door of the cubicle a cacophony of voices from the other examinations taking place, only separated by thin walls made of white varnished panels.

The son beside me looked at his hands, while the cheerful voice of the resident asked Mrs Madalena some questions about her well-being that were either not answered or were answered with grumbling noises. The young geriatrician scrolled through the thick patient's file and then turned to the sisters. In a more matter-of-fact tone, she asked the three women about what had been going on since the last consultation. What followed was a long discussion of each medication Mrs Madalena was taking and of several symptoms – from sleep to bowel movements (for more detail, see Leibing, Engel and Carillo 2019):

Dr C. How much are you giving?

Daughter As you wrote it down: at 4 pm give one [pill].

Dr C. Of 25 [mg].

Daughter Of 25; and at night one of 100, around 9 pm and . . .

Dr C. (surprised) Ah, you are giving a whole of 100 or . . . ?

Daughter Yes, a whole one. With that she sleeps all night.

Dr C. Who is giving the medications? She lives with your family?

(. . .)

Once again, I was astonished by the technical details in a conversation that sounded sometimes like doctors talking among themselves, and not like a geriatric resident speaking with a family member without medical training. Another example:

> **Dr C.** The Hidrocloro is a diuretic, before it was the Moduretic. (...) That's because the Moduretic was a combination of amiloride with hidrocloro, so I changed it, because now she is only using the Hidrocloro.

The resident then turned to me and explained that the diagnosis was 'probable Alzheimer's disease' – probable because of the many other comorbidities. It is 'the cowardly disease', commented one of the daughters, in the sense of a coward who is attacking someone who cannot defend herself. She explains: 'she [my mother] was so vain, so beautiful, always so very well dressed, nails, pedicure – even at home. And now this.' The daughter adds that she found her mother playing with her faeces on several occasions.

The son, sitting beside me, had stayed quiet for almost half an hour, in a serious and introverted mood. Then he spoke for the first time:

> **Son** She is sleeping all the time.
>
> **Dr C.** That was after we readjusted the medications?
>
> **Son** Yes. There are days she lies down, doesn't even take the meds at night, so I try ... ahm ... But when she is a little more awake, I put a little bit of perfume on her, so she feels good about herself.

The old woman: screams [and says something unintelligible.]

Up to this point two aspects of Mrs Madalena's care stand out – the central role medications play in Mrs Madalena's care, and the silence of the son – two factors that are interlinked in this narrative.

Medications

As in most consultations, medications play an important role in 'fine-tuning' Mrs Madalena's symptoms through a constant adaptation of dosages and types of pharmaceuticals, but also of circumstances: when families are perceived as having limited capacities of care, tranquillizing and the controversial antipsychotic medications are prescribed in higher doses than in families that are perceived as well-functioning in terms of caregiving. The geriatricians we interviewed were aware of the dilemma and deplored the situation, but said that sometimes they had no choice (see Engel 2017; Leibing 2009). The informal diagnosis of 'family insufficiency' was regularly used by health professionals to circumscribe this lack of care capacity, where then medications were prescribed to counterbalance symptoms that would otherwise disturb even more greatly the fragile equilibrium at home, such as being awake at night. However, Mrs Madalena was now sleeping too much. Dosage and, sometimes, type of medication needed to be adjusted. It seemed that at a previous consultation the resident at that time had augmented dosages, because of the severe tensions the family was experiencing, fuelled even more by the financial issues caused by the one brother who was distrusting the caregiving son.

Medications in this context can be seen as bio-social objects – objects (e.g. pills) that not only alter Mrs Madalena's biology (like blood pressure and synaptic connections), but that additionally alter – or are altered by – social relations. As an example, pills are prescribed for calming too agitated patients, and therefore relieving family tensions. In the case of the caregiving son, augmented dosages are based on the geriatrician's perception of a family conflict resulting in not good enough care: this can be based on the opinion that a son is not a good caregiver, lacking caring attitudes of work seen as typically female, while higher doses might also follow one brother's logic, that the son lacks care skills because his primary interest is his mother's money and not her well-being (see below). Finally, medications and medical technologies also impact on the relationship between families and the State, when, for instance, certain medications and geriatric diapers are distributed for free, sometimes linked to promises made by politicians and playing a major role in some elections, in which several politicians were elected over the last thirty years, based on their programmes targeting older people.

The silent son

A second important factor is the astonishing exclusion of the son during the consultation. From the beginning, while the very long discussion about each of the multiple medications took place, the daughter answered the resident's question about 'Who is giving the medication? She lives with your family?' with: 'No, although we live in the same building; she lives with G. [the son who is sitting beside me]. He recently went to the Public Defender, but it is so complicated . . .' The daughter then explains that the unemployed son is trying to get custody of his mother, so that he can have access to her bank account with her small pension and pay the daily expenses, but one of his brothers is trying to prevent that, arguing that G. does not want to work and is only after his mother's pension. And although now it is clear that the son is taking care of his mother in her apartment, the discussion of the care regimen continues with the daughters; the male caregiver gets ignored, until the moment when long into the consultation, he speaks up and observes that the new medications made his mother sleep too much. At this moment he still speaks softly, almost timidly, but gets increasingly agitated.

The son complains about the lack of recognition he receives for his dedicated work, because some of his siblings and, especially one brother, were accusing him of having an easy life and of merely wanting his mother's money. He describes in detail what he called 'sacrificing myself': the difficult, never-ending, and sometimes disgusting, work he has to do – traditionally female work – that goes unacknowledged by his family. His voice gets louder and he becomes more and more agitated, while other residents and one of the senior geriatricians start entering the tiny room to try to calm him down. The son starts to cry. After this episode, the son was prescribed an anti-depressant.

3. Care and recognition

The two vignettes provide a picture of different generations of men engaging with dementia care and how such care work is performed and evaluated with regard to male identities. Caring, with its female connotations, deeply unsettles the men's identities: at stake is the authority of a father, husband, and former 'head of the family' now facing the disregard of daughters and doctors and doubt about his abilities as a caring husband. An adult man, a son and full-time caregiver encounters distrust because he needs the pension money of his mother. Further, there is a son-in-law who is classified as 'good' or 'bad', depending on how much time he demands from his wife. Finally, a young man, a grandson, is being investigated about his sexual orientation – if he is too caring, he is suspected of being gay – while at the same time not caring enough means being classified as potentially '*machista*'.

In fact, there are various kinds of masculinity being disputed in these encounters that vary depending on the generation, but also on conflicting images of what it is to be a man. One could speak here about a culture war – a battle around the intertwined different value-systems and personal and national ideals of manhood, constantly nurtured by, public figures, soap opera characters, churches, celebrities, jokes, resulting in more or less embodied values. Progressive values that question rigid, traditional masculinities are part of this mix, and some values even come to be regretted, for instance in the way to raise a boy, because, as one interviewee explained, 'times have changed'. At the same time, the two narratives reveal how an extremely conservative view of gender rules and sexual orientation is interacting with more progressive perspectives. As shown in many more recent masculinity studies (e.g. Boratav, Fisek and Ziya 2014; Scheibling 2020; Santos and Rifiotis 2004), Brazilian men also adhere to multiple masculinities and negotiate maleness within care work. In our two vignettes, men and women compose narratives in which there is a tension between the desire to increase men's caring side, while trying equally to avoid creating too feminine behaviours, within a strong homophobic paradigm.

One specificity here, compared to most of the literature on masculinities with an evolutionary perspective (showing a transformation of rigid role models to more fluid ways of conceiving gender over time,) is that in some parts of the Brazilian population in the last years, values bound to ideas about masculine ideals are actually getting more conservative. In fact, after a progressive government in Brazil under presidents Luiz Inácio Lula da Silva (2003–11) and then Dilma Rousseff (2011–16), in which male identities became more attuned to greater equality in gender roles, including a greater tolerance towards the blurring of gender boundaries and LGBTQ+ identities, the present government celebrates male identity as ultra-traditional, supported by the enormous movement of fundamentalist evangelical churches with their strict heterosexual role models. In fact, one reason often heard by voters for their admiration of the current president, Bolsonaro, is that the sacred image of the family was ignored by the former government, a critique that strongly relates to sexual identities. The recent exclamation by president Bolsonaro that Brazil is a 'land of *maricas* [effeminate persons, sissies]',[1] referring to the fear of Brazilians preoccupied with uncontrolled Covid-19 numbers in the country, shows the denigration of men who care too much about health, as well as the ideal of toughness, strength and carefree attitudes towards health associated with 'real' maleness.

Our reflections on the topic are only a first step: ideally, accounts of masculinities should be longitudinal, in order to see how cultural change reflects on identity tinkering and practices of recognition. What we can affirm is that looking at how masculinities are performed in dementia care can open up complex reflections on sometimes contradictory national and generational perspectives of what it is to be a man and how people deal with these questions on a daily basis.

Bibliography

Baker, Kevin, Noelle Robertson, and David Connelly. 'Men Caring for Wives or Partners with Dementia: Masculinity, Strain and Gain'. *Aging & Mental Health* 14.3 (2010): 319–27.

Bastide, Roger. *Brasil, Terra de Contrastes*. São Paulo: Difusão Europeia do Livro, 1964.

Boratav, Hale B., Güler O. Fisek, and Hande E. Ziya. 'Unpacking Masculinities in the Context of Social Change: Internal Complexities of the Identities of Married Men in Turkey'. *Men and Masculinities* 17.3 (2014): 299–324.

Brigeiro, Mauro. *Rir ou chorar? Envelhecimento, sexualidade e sociabilidade masculina*. Rio de Janeiro, dissertação de mestrado em Saúde Coletiva, Instituto de Medicina Social, Universidade do Estado do Rio de Janeiro, 2000.

Calasanti, Toni, and Mary E. Bowen. 'Spousal Caregiving and Crossing Gender Boundaries: Maintaining Gendered Identities'. *Journal of Aging Studies* 20 (2006): 253–63.

Coelho, Juliana S., Karla C. Giacomin, and Josélia O.A. Firmo. 'O cuidado em saúde na velhice: a visão do homem'. *Saude e Sociedad,* 25.2 (2016): 408–21. https://doi.org/10.1590/S0104–12902016142920.

---

[1] Quote (our translation): 'I am sorry for the deaths, but we all have to die one day. There is no sense in fleeing from this [Coronavirus] reality, we have to stop being a country of *maricas* [sissies]'. (Folha de São Paulo, 10 November 2020; https://www1.folha.uol.com.br/poder/2020/03/veja-o-que-bolsonaro-ja-disse-sobre-coronavirus-de-certa-histeria-a-fantasia-e-nerouse.shtml)

Debert, Guita G., and Amanda M. de Oliveira. 'A profissionalização da atividade de cuidar de idosos no Brasil.' *Revista Brasileira de Ciência Política* September–December (2015): 7–41. https://dx.doi.org/10.1590/0103-335220151801

Debert, Guita G., and Mauro Brigeiro. 'Fronteiras de gênero e a sexualidade na velhice.' *Rev. Bras. Ci. Soc.* 27.80 (2012): 37–54. https://www.scielo.br/scielo.php?script=sci_arttext&pid=S0102-69092012000300003&lng=en&nrm=iso

de Souza, Márcio Ferreira. 'As análises de gênero e a formação do campo de estudos sobre a(s) masculinidade(s).' *Mediações* 14.2 (2009): 123–44.

Engel, Cíntia. 'Corpos e experiências com demências: seguindo emaranhados de subjetividades e substâncias.' *Anuário Antropológico* II (2017): 301–27.

Heilborn, Maria L., and Cristiane da Silva Cabral. 'Youth, Gender, and Sexual Practices in Brazil. *Psicologia & Sociedade* 25 (2013): 33–43.

Katz, Stephen, and Barbara Marshall. 'New Sex for Old: Lifestyle, Consumerism, and the Ethics of Aging Well.' *Journal of Aging Studies* 17.1 (2003): 3–16.

Klinke, Albert. *Alzheimer na Periferia*. Vimeo, 2018. https://vimeo.com/ondemand/alzheimernaperiferia

Leibing, Annette. 'From the Periphery to the Center: Treating Noncognitive, Especially Behavioral and Psychological, Symptoms of Dementia.' *Do We Have a Pill for That? Treating Dementia.* Eds. Jesse Ballenger, Peter Whitehouse, Constantine Lyketsos, Peter Rabins, and Jason Karlawish. Baltimore: The Johns Hopkins UP, 2009. 74–97.

Leibing, Annette, Cíntia Engel, and Elisângela Carrijo. 'Life through Medications – Dementia Care in Brazil.' *ReVista Harvard Review of Latin America*, Winter 2019 (part II). https://revista.drclas.harvard.edu/book/leibing-change-title?fbclid=IwAR2d-iYb9rThSUpk1L6AYYgkw-f8wxcF64gVGIV3cBEUjqdV4BI8JHxuL38

Leibing, Annette, Julien Simard, Virginie Tournay, and Nicolas Noiseux. 'Participating in Clinical Trials: Masculinity, Stem Cells and Heart Disease.' *PluriAges* 5.1 (2014): 17–21.

Medeiros, Paulo Adão de et al. 'Participação masculina em modalidades de atividades físicas de um Programa para idosos: um estudo longitudinal.' *Ciência & Saúde Coletiva*. 19.8 (2014): 3479–88. https://doi.org/10.1590/1413-81232014198.16252013

Pereira, Erik G.B. 'Reflexões sobre práticas corporais, identidades e masculinidades.' *Rev. Bras. Psicol. Esporte Motricidade Hum* 1 (2009): 37–43.

Robinson, Carol, et al. 'The Male Face of Caregiving: A Scoping Review of Men Caring for a Person with Dementia.' *American Journal of Men's Health* 8.5 (2014): 409–26.

Russell, Richard. 'In Sickness and in Health: A Qualitative Study of Elderly Men who Care for Wives with Dementia.' *Journal of Aging Studies* 15 (2001): 351–67.

Santos, Sílvia, and Theophilus Rifiotis. 'Masculinidade no envelhecimento: o caso dos homens idosos no papel de cuidadores familiares.' *Fazendo Gênero* 1998, (2004): 1–8.

Scheibling, Casey. "Real heroes care": How Dad Bloggers Are Constructing Fatherhood and Masculinities.' *Men and Masculinities* 23.1 (2020): 3–19.

Steinberg, Shirley R. 'Brazil: A Land of Many Contrasts.' *Counterpoints* 385 (2011): xxi–xx.

Vilela, Renata. 'Quem são as empregadas domésticas no Brasil?' *Reconta Aí* [26 December 2019], https://recontaai.com.br/quem-sao-as-empregadas-domesticas-no-brasil/

3

Becoming one of the *Others:* Embodying and eliminating fabricated natures

Melinda Niehus-Kettler

In my (lived) experience, taking care of someone does not necessarily equal caring about someone. While spending time with and around people diagnosed with (forms of) dementia, I have heard about and seen them being in-/deliberately neglected or completely ignored by (under-)paid carers, unpaid caregivers, as well as unrelated relatives. I have heard and seen them being mocked behind their backs, i.e., insulted and degraded by the use of words, laughter, and even the cuckoo gesture. Most of them have been confined in one way or another; many have dissociated themselves. Most of them are rarely listened to – even when they can and feel the need to narrate and relate. Some of them have lost the use of words. In the last years, I have witnessed self-proclaimed authorities describing people with dementia as acting shamelessly, and people diagnosed with dementia feeling deeply ashamed for their (allegedly) shameful behaviour.[1]

Since living with dementia increasingly limits personal narratives of storytelling and autobiography, it feels crucial to find ways of relating – and ways of imagining someone's identity being affected by embodied and dis-embodying eliminating processes. I regard this essay as a thought experiment inspired by my kith and kin. Its objective is to describe two distinct and, at the same time, indistinct forces affecting and eliminating our *natures*: our societal power structures and dementia.

Appreciating the affective dimension and ramifications of our experiences, I will touch upon a number of theories on the workings of our power structures

---

[1] Throughout this chapter, the expression *dementia* is used as a collective term that describes symptoms such as the impairment of memory and verbal communication irrespective of whether or not this affliction has been diagnosed as caused by Alzheimer's or Parkinson's disease, etc.

from the field of cultural, particularly gender and postcolonial studies. They include theses by Michel Foucault and Sara Ahmed. Due to the limited scope of this chapter, I will outline a selection of *Othering processes* that may be conceived of as a body of theories. In essence, however, they depict forms of violence and experiences that affect and effect the fabricated natures of the *others*, e.g. *women's, the invalid's* and *non-westerners'* perceived identities. I conceive of these processes as constituted by the most effective elements of our power structures: phenomena such as categories and binary systems, everyday and institutional discourses that dehumanize and discredit, confining practices, as well as bodily experience/s, for example shame.

From my limited perspective, I can only imagine the cognitive dimension of the experiences that alter a person living with dementia. Thus, my briefly introducing a notion that I have termed *Percept Cycles* visualizes embodying processes and, thereby, the implications and implicatures of the very personal and universal percepts that make up our bodies of percepts and knowledge. As this may help our conceptualizing how our perceptual make-up and (tacit) knowledge in terms of someone and something grow in the course of our lifetime, it may help our imagining how dementia unravels and tears holes in this very tissue of intertwined percepts. Providing food for thought, I will conclude by setting my concept of Percept Cycles briefly into dialogue with Pia C. Kontos's observations and rationales described in 'Ethnographic Reflections on Selfhood, Embodiment and Alzheimer's Disease'. This approach offers, I believe, a way of grasping how all of our diverse percepts, e.g. sensation, emotions, objects of perception, as well as (metaphorical) concepts, constitute and contribute to our embodied individuality, agency, and modes of communication. *Au fond*, my conceptualizing embodiment relies on the 'concept of a body (…) that [includes] both the corporeal and psychological, but also the political, social and cultural dimensions' (Hartung 2018, 13).[2]

---

[2] Due to my non-medical education, my personal and cultural background, I will delineate *western* constructions of Otherness. Told through the metaphorically and literally limited perspective of one of the *healthy* and *female others*, my delineations will focus on the *others'* perspectives. It is a given that I can only speak for myself, though. And whereas my loved ones' stories may be conceived of as part of my story, I feel they are *not my stories to tell*. Moreover, it is imperative to appreciate the powerful differences among and within the groups of the perceived *others* and *norms* – and the disparities among their experiences and perspectives. I do not suggest that anything such as a homogenous group of *others*, e.g. *female, invalid*, or *non-western* people exists. Still, the Othering processes they live through appear to be remarkably similar. As I am still deliberating the advantages and disadvantages of universalism and identity politics, the terms that are capitalized and/or given in italics should be regarded as social constructs – they are marked accordingly. By using these expressions I am mostly complying with the style of the authors whose works I have studied, among other things, to simplify the reading process.

1. Fabricating and eliminating natures

Othering is not just occupying a point of view but *choosing* a perspective and criteria that 'allow humanity to be divided into two groups: one that embodies the norm and whose identity is valued and another that is defined by its faults, devalued and susceptible to discrimination' (Staszak 2009, 43). To make these hierarchies appear more *natural*, they are commonly reasoned from (allegedly harmful) bodily particularities defined by questionable categories such as *sex*, *race*, and/or *state of health*. This way, dichotomies, e.g. *female/male, black/white, sick/healthy* are made to make sense. On the whole, our dominant human norms, e.g. *male*, *sane*, and/or *western* individuals, are in a position to impose their categories as they commonly constitute the authorities and the standard against which all the *others* are measured.

Drawing on Foucault's theories on disciplining discourses, we can presume that human beings are categorized for the benefit of our authorities. Perceived Otherness and identity are based on our classification and binary systems that represent forms of institutional as well as social control (Foucault 1995, 191). Our 'body', more precisely, our bodily experience/s and knowledge may be conceived of as 'carefully fabricated' by 'manifold relations of power' (Foucault 1980, 93; 1995, 217). These are 'established, consolidated' and 'implemented' through the 'production, accumulation, circulation and functioning of' *discourses and practices* (Foucault 1980, 93; 1995, 140, 170/171, 217). The invisible workings of power, or rather, our 'disciplinary [machineries]' re-/form the individual as well as the species body (Foucault 1995, 143, 155; 163, 174). Among other things, medical, anthropologic, economic, and legal discourses 'discipline the body, optimize its capabilities, extort its forces, increase its usefulness and docility' (Foucault 1995, 155). It is also through and via discourses (and practices) that we transform simple manifestations of bodily differences into phenomena such as categories and dichotomies, e.g. *men/women, the healthy/the invalids, westerners/non-westerners*. All of which can be reduced to the binary systems *the norm/the other, normal/deviant*, and/or *human/less-than-human*. In other words, we degrade and impose a *marked change* on the natures of human bodies.

A crucial part of these discourses constitutes infra- and dehumanization. In the same vein as infantilization, infra-humanization is highly instrumental as the humiliation takes on a sanitized form. Seldom do we question diminutives. Seldom do we question belittlement. Infra-humanization co-constructs the *others* as *less-than-human* and less intelligent beings. In doing so, the in-groups deny the out-groups reason, sanity, certain (secondary) human emotions, and intellectual, e.g. language skills. The *others* are, hereby, depicted as incapable of moral conduct and controlled demeanour (Viki and Calitri 2008, 1055, 1057). By contrast, dehumanization is an arguably less subtle way of eliminating others from participation and consideration. Individuals' and peoples' identities have been fabricated and implicitly conceptualized as peril and/or devoid of (legitimate) power, as *non-human* or *sub-human* particularly for two reasonings: Either they have been constructed and re-/presented as exhibiting animalistic features, uncontrollable and irrational behaviour – or they have been regarded and treated as 'having the properties of an object', i.e., as passive entities lacking subjectivity (Rudmann and Mescher 2012, 735). Thus, the allegedly deviant *others* are understood in terms of another concept, *animals* or *objects*, while they are dehumanized and degraded either way.

With their 'essence' being 'understanding and experiencing one kind of thing in terms of another', 'metaphorical concepts', i.e., 'metaphors' are central to dehumanization and these discursive manoeuvres (Lakoff and Johnson 2003, 5, 6, 7). Metaphorical concepts can be understood as begotten and nurtured by, as well as manifestations of *natural experiences* (Lakoff and Johnson 2003, 117). These are, e.g., 'products of our bodies'; they are the result of our 'perceptual and motor apparatus, mental capacities, and emotional makeup' (Lakoff and Johnson 2003, 117). Further 'natural kinds of experiences' are products of our 'interactions with our physical environment, e.g. moving, manipulating objects' and our 'interactions with other people within our culture' – among other things, 'in terms of social, political, economic, and religious institutions' (Lakoff and Johnson 2003, 117). Against the backdrop of Othering and embodying processes, it seems imperative to acknowledge that metaphorical concepts do not merely manifest in and define 'the words we use', they are also part and parcel of our tacit knowledge (Lakoff and Johnson 2003, 5, 116). And while they are grounded in (and, in turn, also affect) our experience/s, they structure our conscious thought and actions (Lakoff and Johnson 2003, 3).

Metaphorical concepts 'create realities for us, especially social realities. A metaphor may thus be a guide for future actions. Such actions will, of course, fit the metaphor. This will, in turn, reinforce the power of the metaphor to make experience coherent' (Lakoff and Johnson 2003, 156). All of the aforementioned implicit (metaphorical) concepts of the *others* as infantile, immoral, passive, as non- or less-than human beings have in common that they implicitly foster and vivify our perceptions and conceptions of the, for example, *female, sick,* and/or *non-western others* lacking control, integrity, and cognitive, e.g. language skills. The perceived contradictory concepts of the *others* as powerless, frail, and inanimate *or* as powerful entities endangering society both entail and justify (hegemonic) hierarchies and *custody*. They re-/generate our alleged need of protection from the *others'* dispositions. Contemplating the experiences of people living with dementia, we can ascertain how monitored changes in mood, regressing to childhood memories, and progressive difficulty communicating with words are easily instrumentalized as reasons to protect them – and as evidence of their lacking humanness and control. In turn, they are un-/consciously conceptualized and treated as entities undeserving of bodily autonomy, visibility, and authority. They derive parts of their perceived identity as the *others* from dehumanization and isolation.

In sum, epistemic, psychological, and emotional violence, e.g. in the form of dehumanization structured by metaphors, are positively correlated with our proclivity to use physical violence (Rudmann and Mescher 2012, 741). They are part and parcel of everyday and institutional discourses. They manifest in covert and overt discrediting and incapacitating measures that include laughing at someone, allegedly *harmless* mockery – social put-downs of any description. Political, medical, legal, and religious discourses as well as phenomena such as the concept of *deviance* re-/generate and perpetuate our conceptualizing the *others* as less valuable, non- or less-than-human entities. These frequently precede, turn into, and re-/generate re-/enforced isolation and (the threat of) physical assaults. It is safe to say that, within cycles of abuse, de- and infra-humanization also succeed and normalize confining and eliminating processes, e.g. the deprivation of liberty and/or physical abuse. Ultimately, 'houses of confinement' (Foucault 1995, 51), e.g. penal institutions, (psychiatric) clinics, hospitals, nursing homes, but also other 'sets of spatial constructs and practices' such as gender, *racial* and residential segregation are 'based on the discursive construction of [O]therness' (Staszak 2009, 46).

An element of (embodied) Othering processes that seems to have been largely neglected is what I regard as the most pivotal one: *bodily experience/s*, for example bodily experience/s of *shame*. Generally, I will understand the term bodily experience/s as encompassing and acknowledging diverse conceptions and definitions. Among other things, I appreciate the German distinction between two different notions of *experience*: In the 1930s, Walter Benjamin characterized 'lived experience' ['*Erlebnis*'] as 'being separated from *Erfahrung*' (Henning 2006, 96, 98). For one thing, the term *experience* translates into '*Erlebnis*' (plural: '*Erlebnisse*' = experiences) and denotes the immediate, the lived moment; for another thing, *experience* refers to '*Erfahrung*', which is 'accumulative, reflected upon' and, as it develops over time, 'counts as knowledge' (Henning 2006, 96). In effect, my concept of bodily experience/s is based on a combination of these experience/s. Thus, it includes what Lakoff and Johnson call 'natural experiences', e.g. experiences that come into being during our 'interactions with our physical environment', with other human beings and 'institutions' (2003, 117). However, bodily experience/s also comprise 'natural experiences' such as 'products of our bodies', e.g. sensations and emotions that we experience via our 'perceptual and motor apparatus, mental capacities', and 'emotional makeup' (Lakoff and Johnson 2003, 117). In any case, all of these forms and concepts of experience/s beget, nurture, and manifest in our identities, our perceptual make-up and knowledge. They play a vital role in our personal and trans-generational (hi)stories. In essence, they are as much sources as symptoms of what I interpret as the other *most effective elements of our power structures*. These are *discourses, practices*, and *manifestations*, e.g., manifestation of bodily particularities that are transformed into *phenomena* – within the blink of an eye, the course of a lifetime, and/or several generations.

In 'Shame Before Others', Sara Ahmed describes shame and 'the gift of the ideal' as experiences and constructs that have a largely positive impact on human beings and their relationships (2014, 106). Feeling shame is principally considered as a way to 'reconciliation' and a way of 're-integrating' those who have failed others (back) into 'social bonds' (Ahmed 2014, 106–9). By contrast, drawing on her thoughts on *failure*, I would like to highlight the ways in which bodily experience/s of shame represent crucial elements that are essential to our fabricating natures, trans-generational stigmatization, and convictions.

Thereby, they constitute and contribute to physical and psychological confinements.

Ahmed considers shame as a 'sign of' our own or someone else's 'failure' (2014, 103). By the same token, I conceive of shame as having a d-/evaluating, correcting, and self-/sanctioning dimension. Hence, these bodily experience/s have a practical, aesthetic, and symbolic function. More often than not, the perceived state of failing is based on our conceiving of ourselves as *deviating* from the established (human and abstract) *norms* and accepted epistemological and ontological standards, especially in terms of physical and psychological bodily particularities, social, sexual, and/or ethical conduct. This phenomenon and concept of *deviance* does not only define the perceived identities of the *others*, but also reinforces perceptions and conceptions of shame and Otherness. Generally, shame can be regarded as affecting our identities from an early age and the 'negation that is perceived' is commonly 'painful' and 'experienced before another' (Ahmed 2014, 103, 104). Referring to Foucault's metaphor of the 'Panopticon' and his notion of the 'imagined gaze', we may feel shame even if no-one else is physically present, though. We (desire to) regulate our(-)selves as soon as we catch our(-)selves deviating from ideals and *norms* – for *normalizing* bodily experience/s, discourses, and practices have 'trained' us to do so (Foucault 1995, 143, 163, 170, 174). Being surveilled and disciplined by our *normal* (self-proclaimed) authorities and/or surveilling and disciplining our(-)selves, i.e., seeing ourselves from their perspective and through their eyes, we experience shame as a self-/judgement as well as a self-/sanctioning measure. In this regard, (inducing) bodily experience/s of shame can be conceived of as a means to exercise control and power – to make us docile, comply and conform again. Through shame, we punish ourselves or others for failing and evoking uncomfortable feelings, e.g. making visible what is supposed to be hidden (Ahmed 2014, 104).

In our patriarchal and capitalistic societies, e.g. neoliberal, sexist, and sanist discourses and practices re-/create and perpetuate social and gender ideals. They re-/generate an error-culture that makes us feel shame for what we have constructed as less valuable and illicit attributes and conduct – as weaknesses and failings. Alleged failures include embodying one or more forms of *female*, *invalid*, *racial*, *juvenile*, and/or *differently-desiring* Otherness. Rather generally, our breaking the mould, not contributing to cycles of profit (any longer), reconsidering our own perspective/s, being vulnerable, showing emotions, and/or asking for help are regarded as shameful and worthy of punishments. The intrinsic belief, value and evaluative systems also leave a (distinctive) mark on ageing and/or invalid *men*, whose natures have been fabricated as, ideally, physically strong and emotionally controlled, independent, and authoritative.

Either passively acquiescent to authority, or actively willing and feeling entitled to shame the *others* to re-/establish their own purported superiority, some individuals evoke shame by the means of degrading discourses and practices or disregard. They effect a person's 'movement back into [themselves] [which] is simultaneously a turning away from [themselves]'; this sensory movement entails the individual having 'nowhere to turn' (Ahmed 2014, 104). Albeit to varying degrees, they experience impuissance, alienation, and a loss of legitimized mobility. Conceiving of ourselves as *deviant from the norms*, as not fulfilling *ideals* – which are, for all intents and purposes, constructed by our authorities to re-/integrate us into cycles of profit – we may literally and metaphorically dissociate ourselves. Living through shame 'involves the de-forming and re-forming of bodily and social spaces' (Ahmed 2014, 102–3).

Taking the perspective of the *others*, e.g. people living with dementia, conceptually (and perceptually), we can assume that their feeling shame and a lack of self-worth is often a consequence of their identity, cognitive state, and/or conduct being discredited through discourses and practices – and/or a lack thereof, namely neglect. Denying them bodily autonomy and their agency reinforces cycles of abuse. Our societies' sanitizing and normalizing abuse – e.g. declaring that the *others*' (actually fabricated) deficiencies and failures are *natural* parts of their identity – regenerate shame and anger (Krizan and Johar 2015). Above all else, invalidating their emotional responses and reactions to the abuse absolves our societies from questioning our ways of *taking care* of them. On balance, it may be a person's simple need for being seen, heard and, thereby, valued (again) that re-/creates 'social bonds' (*nota bene*, trauma bonds and/or shame-rage cycles as well) (Ahmed 2014, 107; Krizan and Johar 2015). We desire to be known and recognized as the person *we* feel we are – or sense we used to be before we were altered. In the end, our perceived worth and sense of self depend on how and *if* we are perceived, tended, and represented by others.

The Othering processes that I have described are constituted by interrelated and highly effective elements of our power structures – and they may be construed as forming a cyclic system. They depict what those of us who are categorized as the *others* from the very beginning of our lives might be experiencing every day, e.g. as we embody one or more forms of perceived *female, differently-abled*, and/or *non-western* Otherness. Furthermore, the very same processes transform the fabricated natures of the *norms* who only become the *others* when/if they alter and are altered. They might become the *others* as their bodies, their statuses, and/or their (self-) conceptions alter – either within the course of a lifetime, or after life-altering events such as being categorized as an *invalid*. For instance, *men* having been categorized and diagnosed with dementia are forced to change their perspective as they are un-/intentionally no longer perceived and treated as *normal* and/or authorities. At the risk of sounding cynical, as they are *becoming one of the others*, they might actually gain perspective while losing persepctive.

Othering processes could be regarded as means to re-/integrate the *others* into cycles of profit, to render them docile and unconfident. Albeit not generally maliciously chosen forms of control and protection, binary systems, dehumanizing, segregating, and isolating measures are part of divide-and-conquer tactics. They constitute forms of epistemological, psychological, physical, and emotional violence with acute and chronic effects on all of us. Above all else, they eliminate the *others'* subjectivity and self-definition, they eliminate allegedly in-alienable rights, perceived humanness, and self-worth. Still, conveniently enough, the lines between manipulation and care, between control and protection often become blurred – especially when thinly-veiled unenlightened self-interest masquerades as affection and/or altruism.

2. To cut a long (hi)story short: Embodied audio-visual hierarchies

Shame is an element of our (embodied) power structures that, just as dehumanizing discourses, neglect, separating and confining practices, eliminates the perceived *others* from (further) participation and consideration. Thereby, they become in- or less visible, but also in- or less audible. And while shame affects the *others'* already limited or illegitimized using of (social) space/s, it also co-determines how much space, which scope and position they occupy, e.g. a rather central or peripheral one, in the front or in the back. It may be regarded as implicitly co-effecting and affecting what I conceive of as *embodied audio-visual hierarchies*. These reflect and, in turn, also limit our rights to see, know, and control, as well as our rights to speak and be listened to. They illustrate and reproduce our im-/mobility within hierarchical structures, our rights to choose remaining in/visible and in-/audible and/or becoming in/visible and in-/audible. Hence, I understand these self-replicating and multidimensional organizational structures as a result and manifestation of the interrelations among our (implicit) perceptions – *and* as appealing to multiple senses. In my mind, embodied audio-visual hierarchies are part and parcel of authorship and visibility; they also rely on the effect of the disciplining, medical, and/or colonial gaze. While being manifestations of implicit power dynamics and *author*ity, for example the phenomena of the *medical* and the *disciplining* gaze interrelate with the right to speak, examine, judge, and to limit bodily, social, and global mobility. They are also interrelated with the right to command, to make others wait and (passively) receive and accept the knowledge that is being presented (Foucault 2003, 29, 48, 54; Foucault 1995, 143, 154, 170). Overall, an individual's and/or a group's subjectivity and agency are re-/defined by the authorities' gazes and discourses; they are also manifested in our very position within hierarchically structured spaces, e.g. in a church, a classroom, and/or a clinic.

On another level, our visibility, the impact of our voice and, hereby, our perceived normalcy and value are also contingent on *how much* space we occupy in public. This is, in turn, dependent on diverse forms of confinements and segregation reasoned from categories such as gender, state of health, and/or ethnic background. More precisely, we experience embodied audio-visual hierarchies within public hierarchical structures as they are manifested in the number and percentage, but also the perceived status of people who are categorized as, e.g., *male/ female, healthy/sick*, and/or *the colonizer/the colonized*. We implicitly perceive and are affected by them in a conference room, at university, in parliament, in the food service industry and health care sector, among authors of and protagonists in historical, political, religious, and/or medical discourses. Evidently, they also effect and are affected by (self-) representations in media reports, the literary canon, and film. Above all else, embodied audio-visual hierarchies are the symptoms and sources of a (hi)story of allegedly valueless Otherness. It is a story fabricated and told, rather exclusively, by the purportedly *normal* and *valuable*, in other words, by *healthy*, *male*, and/or *western* authorities.

3. Embodying our power structures

Within the theoretical framework of a larger research project, I have conceptualized the aforementioned elements of our power structures, i.e., manifestations/phenomena, bodily experience/s, discourses, and practices as diverse *percepts*. Inspired by Foucault's theories on discourses disciplining our individual and the species body, as well as Lakoff and Johnson's notion of 'Embodied/Experiential Realism', my concept of Percept Cycles originated as a visualization of embodiment and Othering processes. The interdisciplinary and non-medical approach offers, I believe, a simple and, at the same time, highly complex way of imagining and visualizing our embodying processes, but also ways of challenging trans-generational cycles of abuse that illegitimize the perceived *others*' identities and power. The point here is that, at bottom, manifestations/phenomena, bodily experience/s, discourses and practices all constitute *different forms of percepts*.

Throughout my delineations, the signifier *percept* is used for its equivocal nature and mostly as an umbrella term. If not specified, it represents several forms of percepts at once. 'Percept' can have different definitions depending on the discipline defining the term e.g. philosophy, psychology, or linguistics.[3] In the end, to allow for intrapersonal and interpersonal differences among our percepts, I need to acknowledge all the understandings and definitions of 'percept': i.e., a 'recognisable sensation or impression received by the mind through the senses' (*HarperCollins Dictionary* online, '"percept" in American English' definition 1);[4] percepts as recognition of emotions (as described in Li's *Encoding and Decoding Emotional Speech...* page 92); as an 'object or

---

[3] Some of the discrepancies among our conceptualization are explained in the *Stanford Encyclopedia of Philosophy*, e.g. in 'Epistemological Problems of Perception' (https://plato.stanford.edu/entries/perception-episprob/); and 'The Problem of Perception' (https://plato.stanford.edu/entries/perception-problem/).

[4] This definition, found at https://www.collinsdictionary.com/dictionary/english/percept, according to the website is taken from *Webster's New World College Dictionary*, 4th Edition. Copyright © 2010 by Houghton Mifflin Harcourt.

phenomenon that is perceived' (*HarperCollins Dictionary* online, British English, definition 2) as in a Rorschach test; and 'a concept that depends on recognition by the senses, such as sight, of some external object or phenomenon' (*HarperCollins Dictionary* online, British English, definition 1) – i.e., an interpretation of a perceived representation. These conceptualizations show that in different disciplines and contexts, 'percept' is actually not used to refer to an object that we perceive or a concept, but to the sensations/impressions that we experience.

This is why I would want to describe our diverse percepts as i) our 'sensations' and 'percepts of emotion'/'emotions we perceive in others'; ii) 'objects and phenomena that we perceive'; and iii) 'concepts in our minds'.

From my perspective, metaphorical concepts are both vital and fatal implicit percepts for they re-/generate, e.g., our un-/consciously conceptualizing the *others* as non- or less-than-human entities.[5]

Ultimately, all of these 'percepts' constitute crucial elements of our affective makeup and (implicit) knowledge. They ways in which they appear to interrelate and the fact that all of them have been described as 'percepts' induced me to conceive of them as forming Percept Cycles.

Indeed our diverse percepts appear to be cycling. They move in and follow a regularly repeated sequence of events. Sensations and emotions of shame or fear in terms of someone or something that we perceive may beget, nurture, and manifest in percepts in the form and in terms of everyday discourses, e.g. conversations among peers and family members. Sooner or later, most of these percepts beget, nurture, and manifest in percepts in the form and in terms of institutional discourses, everyday and institutional practices and phenomena. These might be social sanctioning measures, medical, legal, and political discourses, and/or segregating practices. All of these elements can be regarded as constituted and defined by established (metaphorical) concepts. They might beget, nurture, and manifest in new, slightly altered, and/or established

---

[5] Lakoff and Johnson explain that our 'conceptual system' is, in essence, 'metaphorical in nature' (Lakoff and Johnson 2003, 3, 115). The authors' theory of 'embodied realism' is based on 'the notion of the embodied mind for which the dimensions of tacit (or implicit) and non-propositional knowledge of the body are crucial' (2015, 16, 77; Ernst 2015, 247). They illustrate how our 'cognitive unconscious', which operates too fast to be focused on, includes all our 'automatic cognitive operations' as well as 'our implicit knowledge' (2015, 10, 13). Being a 'perceptual inference', metaphorical concepts appear to be part and parcel of, but also 'rely on [our] embodied tacit knowledge' (Ernst 2015, 247–8).

percepts – e.g. in bodily experience/s of impuissance, inferiority, and/or anger. Within a cyclic system, they form growing Percept Cycles. This way, percepts do not only accumulate, they become part of one another as well. In the end, they form and make up a multilayered tissue of compound percepts. They can be conceptualized as comprehensive *bodies of percepts and knowledge* – in more than one sense.

All in all, the elements of our power structures can be conceived of as diverse percepts that form part of and develop into numerous cycles of percepts. This way, they constitute and contribute to our *perceptual make-up* and *knowledge* in terms of someone or something. In my mind, we sense, perceive, conceptualize, and *embody* other human beings, objects, natural entities, but also abstract concepts in the form of Percept Cycles. In other words, *we embody* the elements of power structures – e.g. *manifestations/ phenomena*, *discourses*, and *practices* re-/generated by *bodily experience/s* in terms of (and as represented by) someone or something – via and in the form of percepts. By virtue of our embodying Othering processes and cycles of violence our personal and universal (hi)stories have also the power to repeat themselves. Effectively, our (trans-generational) embodied power structures implicitly form, deform, but also il-/legitimize our perceptual make-up, knowledge, and, thereby, our individuality and agency. All of which may be regarded as truly personal and, in the same way, as remarkably universal in nature. Whereas they depend on our partly shared cultural and historical frameworks, they rely on the bodily experience/s, discourses, practices and phenomena that we live through – but also on our willingness to care, listen, and question our own perspective/s.

4. Elimination from the inside?!

As time moves in cycles and life moves in cycles, our percepts move in cycles. We continuously re-/generate and experience them. As they accumulate and evolve, they take on an increasingly complex life of their own. Percepts develop into a multilayered tissue of compound percepts that are organic and, at the same time, constructed. Including percepts of resistance, this is a hybrid *materiality* of acquired and grown knowledge – which we conceptualize as a form of power. Moreover, depending on the time we have known them and the strength of the (emotional) connection to them, we embody, e.g., a person or piece of music in the form of percepts that constitute and contribute to a strongly intertwined, multilayered tissue of percepts *or* a rather holey fabric of a couple of loosely connected percepts. We conceive the identity and (hi)story of every(-)body and every(-)thing through and in the form of these growing Percept Cycles – be it our favourite person, a song, a museum object, or the abstract concept of power.

It is my conceptualizing identities as well as perceptual make-up and knowledge as an organization of percepts that enables me to grasp the concept of a person's individuality and agency. It also enables me to imagine the cognitive dimension of the experiences that a person living with dementia embodies, among other things, how dementia *dis-embodies* their wealth of knowledge and emotional relations. Contemplating these bodies of percepts and knowledge, i.e., the tissue of intertwined cycles of percepts embodied within and by a person, we can imagine these percepts starting to grow apart at some point in time. We can imagine Percept Cycles falling apart. Dementia can be conceived of as gradually eliminating our implicit compound percepts. As a consequence of dementia taking apart our percepts, we let go of others, perceivably, one at a time. As it forces us to loosen our hold on Percept Cycles that constitute, e.g., a person's identity, we might recognize emotions that we feel in this person's presence, but not their face; we might recognize their face, but not their name (e.g. Gleeson 2019).

Taking these aspects into consideration, it is crucial to acknowledge that, even though dementia alters our bodies of percepts and knowledge, it does neither eliminate our individuality, nor our agency. As delineated before, it is our societies' Othering processes that eliminate and/or illegitimize the *others*' identities, bodily autonomy, and power. For example, all of the aforementioned implicit (metaphorical) concepts of the *other*s as non- or less-than human entities have in common that they implicitly foster our conceptualizing the *others* as lacking reason, credibility, and cognitive, e.g. language skills. Particularly concepts of the (in)ability to master language are closely intertwined with concepts of (a lack of) control, the civilized *norms*, and the uncivilized *others*. Remarkably enough, it seems to be our societies' fear, actual failure (and/or unwillingness) to value and comprehend the *others'* bodily particularities, knowledge, and modes of communication that re-/generate and justify cycles of elimination. Consequently, the *others'* perspectives, forms of expression, and bodily experience/s are perceived and treated as *deviant* and *worthless*.

Nonetheless, as mentioned before, I conceive of bodily experience/s as *powerful* sources and symptoms of the other elements of our power structures, i.e., everyday language, institutional discourses, practices, and phenomena. I argue that our perceived individuality and agency are defined by and are a product of the reciprocal relations among these percepts, among the identities of the perceived *norms* and the *others*, and among their perceptual make-up and knowledge. Contemplating this, my concept of Percept Cycles and embodiment, I suggest that the other percepts that make up our humanness and power, i.e., our bodily experience/s expressed and communicated without words, but via spontaneous actions and habits still impact on the people and things around us. Even if we have lost the use of words, we still affect those around us – just as they continue to affect us. Since human communication is governed by the same conceptual system that controls thoughts and actions, language is certainly 'an important source of evidence for what that system is like' (Lakoff and Johnson 2003, 3). Still, our perceptual make-up and knowledge, including our metaphorical concepts, do not only manifest in language. They are also expressed via other modes of communication such as pictures, sounds, and gestures (Forceville and Urios-Aparisi 2009). Thus, akin to spoken words, these can be conceived of as manifestations of our personality and power.

Drawing on other, but rather similar concepts of embodiment, agency, and selfhood, I would like to incorporate Kontos's rationales described in 'Ethnographic Reflections on Selfhood, Embodiment and Alzheimer's Disease'. She uses a 'theoretical framework of embodiment, which integrates Merleau-Ponty's radical reconceptualisation of perception and Bourdieu's theory of the logic of practice' to analyse 'findings of an ethnographic study of selfhood in Alzheimer's disease' in a long-term care facility (2004, 830/831). Kontos argues that selfhood has a primordial origin as it 'emanates from the body's power of natural expression, and manifests in the body's inherent ability to apprehend and convey meaning' (2004, 837). Our bodies are regarded as 'providing the corporeal foundation of selfhood' (Kontos 2004, 837). Furthermore, she asserts the 'sociocultural dimension of the pre-reflective body' to be the 'second origin of selfhood' (837). In other words, our habitus, 'mastery of social practices' – and the way these 'mark class distinction' – are another essential part and manifestation of our 'embodiment of social structures' and selfhood (2004, 837).

Among other things, Kontos's study focuses on what I regard as the everyday and institutional practices and phenomena constituting and contributing to our Percept Cycles. This materiality of bodies of percepts and knowledge encompasses, for example, percepts constituting 'tacit' 'sociological knowledge consisting of learned and archived faculties that have become implicit through embodiment and automatised by practice' (Ernst 2015, 247). Whereas people experiencing dementia might be expected to lose this (implicit) knowledge defining their individuality, Kontos describes how some *patients* adhere to internalized beauty regimes, and how many continue to conform to social norms and rules when interacting with others (2004, 832, 833). Some people diagnosed with dementia appear to *unlearn* these embodied elements of our power structures. Others seem to hold on to discourses and phenomena such as society-imposed inhibitions, rules of etiquette, and beauty ideals re-/generated by their bodily experience/s. This way, these percepts remain part of their embodied individuality and agency.

Language is undeniably the most privileged form of communication (and the most underestimated form of violence). Kontos underlines, however, that it constitutes merely one way of expressing individuality and power. She delineates how people living with dementia '[interact] meaningfully with the world through their embodied way of "being-in-the-world"' (2004, 829). The study participants express their selfhood and agency through, among other things, 'spontaneous' actions and non-verbal communication re-/generated by bodily experience/s, e.g. through 'dancing', 'singing', 'listening', and, thereby, also paying attention to and 'caring' for other individuals (2004, 832, 834). They do not only communicate with words, but with 'gestures', 'body' and 'limb' 'movements', 'facial expressions', and 'eye behaviour'; their 'posture', 'postural shifts', 'intonation changes, the rise or fall of pitch level [...] and pauses' '[carry] implication and meaning' as well (2004, 835, 836). These descriptions can be read as depicting how our 'tacit knowledge', e.g. percepts belonging to 'the realm of cognitive-automatized faculties consisting of the basic operations of our nervous system and perceptions' (Ernst 2015, 247), is a distinctive part of our perceived identity. For example, our sensations and emotions of affection, disgust, shame, and anger are sources (and symptoms) of discourses, practices and, thereby, meaningful spontaneous wordless interactions as well (Kontos 2004, 829, 832, 833). Rarely do we appreciate the validity of these bodily experience/s, emotional responses, and modes of communication. Yet, they re-/present manifestations of individuality and agency, as well as powerful narratives in their own right – *be it narratives without words, or non-linear ones.*

Concluding, the notions of embodied Percept Cycles, identities, perceptual makeup and knowledge can, by no means, encompass the entirety of elements that constitute and contribute to our individuality and agency. Still, my concept of *bodies of percepts and knowledge* as a visualization of embodying and Othering processes might offer a perspective on embodiment and dementia that adds to Kontos's contesting that living with Alzheimer's disease entails a loss of selfhood (2004, 829, 846). My admittedly unconventional approach may allow us to discern cyclic systems that re-/generate the *others'* perceived lack of humanness, value, and power by transforming, illegitimizing and/or eliminating their *natures*, cognitive states, visibility, and forms of expression. And although dementia alters an individual's perceived identity and accumulated (tacit) knowledge, we can start from the premise that the person we know and their individuality remain with us during the progression of the disease. In accord with Kontos's reasonings, I argue that the person with dementia is neither devoid of selfhood, nor devoid of power.

Bibliography

Ahmed, Sara. *The Cultural Politics of Emotion*. 2nd ed. Edinburgh: Edinburgh UP, 2014.

'Epistemological Problems of Perception.' *Stanford Encyclopedia of Philosophy*, 5 Dec. 2016. https://plato.stanford.edu/entries/perception-episprob/ [22 May 2020].

Ernst, Christoph. 'Moving Images of Thought: Notes on the Diagrammatic Dimension of Film Metaphor.' *Revealing Tacit Knowledge: Embodiment and Explication*, Eds. Frank Adloff, Katharina Gerund, and David Kaldewey. Bielefeld: Transcript Verlag, 2015. 245–78.

Forceville, Charles J., and Eduardo Urios-Aparisi, Eds. *Multimodal Metaphor*. Berlin: de Gruyter, 2009.

Foucault, Michel. *Discipline & Punish: The Birth of the Prison*. 1977. New York: Random House Inc., 1995.

Foucault, Michel. *The Birth of the Clinic*. 1973. Translated by A.M. Sheridan. Abingdon: Routledge, 2003.

Foucault, Michel. *Power/Knowledge: Selected Interviews and Other Writings 1972–1977*. Brighton, UK: Harvester Press, 1980.

Gleeson, Sinéad. 'Second Mother.' *Constellations: Reflections from Life*. London: Picador, 2019. 221–35.

Hartung, Heike. 'Introduction.' *Embodied Narration: Illness, Death and Dying in Modern Culture*. Ed. Hartung. Bielefeld: Transcript Verlag, 2018. 9–19.

Henning, Michelle. 'Media: From Things to Experiences.' *Museums, Media and Cultural Theory*. New York: Open UP, 2006. 90–8.

Kontos, Pia C. 'Ethnographic Reflections on Selfhood, Embodiment and Alzheimer's Disease.' *Ageing and Society* 24.6 (2004): 829–49. https://doi.org/10.1017/S0144686X04002375

Krizan, Zlatan, and Omesh Johar. 'Narcissistic Rage Revisited.' *Journal of Personality and Social Psychology* 108.5 (2015): 784–801.

Lakoff, George, and Marc Johnson. *Metaphors We Live By*. 1980. Chicago: UP of Chicago, 2003.

Lakoff, George, and Marc Johnson. *Philosophy in the Flesh: The Embodied Mind and its Challenge to Western Thought*. 1999. New York: Basic Books, 2015.

Li, Aijun. *Encoding and Decoding of Emotional Speech: A Cross-Cultural and Multimodal Study between Chinese and Japanese*. New York: Springer, 2015.

'percept.' *Collins Dictionary*, www.collinsdictionary.com/dictionary/english/percept [22 May 2020].

"The Problem of Perception" *Sanford Encyclopedia of Philosophy*, 8 march 2005, plato.stanford.edu/entries/perception-problem/. Accessed 12 Aug. 2021.

'Rorschach test.' *Encyclopedia Britannica*, 23 May 2018, www.britannica.com/science/Rorschach-Test [22 May 2020].

Rudmann, Laurie A., and Kris Mescher. 'Of Animals and Objects: Men's Implicit Dehumanization of Women and Likelihood of Sexual Aggression.' *Personality and Social Psychology Bulletin* 38.6 (June 2012): 734–6.

Staszak, J.F. 'Other/Otherness.' *International Encyclopedia of Human Geography*. Eds. N. Thrift and Rob Kitchen. Elsevier, vol. 8, 2009. 43–7.

Viki, G. Tandayi, and Raff Calitri. 'Infrahuman Outgroup or Suprahuman Ingroup: The Role of Nationalism and Patriotism in the Infrahumanization of Outgroups.' *European Journal of Social Psychology* 38.6 (2008): 1054–61. *Interscience*, doi: 10.1002/ejsp.495

Part Two

The poetics of dementia and masculinity: Between eulogy and negation

4

Living oblivion: Poetic narratives of dementia and fatherhood in Pia Tafdrup's *Tarkovsky's Horses*

Katharina Fürholzer

1. Poetic narratives of dementia and loss

In 2006, Danish poet Pia Tafdrup wrote a eulogy in honour of her father who had just died of dementia. Her intimate text laid the ground for the cycle of poems *Tarkovsky's Horses* (Tafdrup 2010; originally published Tafdrup 2006),[1] which can be understood as a poetic portrayal of the 'existential metamorphosis' (Seng 2017, my translation) dementia may cause. Tracing a father's final stages of dementia, his death, and its aftermath, the book's fifty poems – framed by an additional intro and outro poem – depict the continuous changes this disease had forced on the family: from being a father to a sick and eventually a dead person, and from being a daughter to a relative and eventually a surviving dependant. *Tarkovsky's Horses* confronts the reader with experiences of human existence that go beyond the familiar. When Tafdrup states that the book's 'poems narrate the drama it is to be human' (Semmel 2010, 44), this abrogation of genre borders seems like an analogy to the borders we may be forced to cross when being confronted with dementia. Accordingly, Tafdrup's book allows the poems to be read both as individual texts and as joint parts of an overarching metanarrative about the disease of dementia, the biography of the father, and the autobiographical experiences of a daughter who has slipped her father's mind.

---

[1] For the book's background see Semmel 2010, 44–7.

The specific presentation of these narratives is inseparably shaped by the book's specific genre: poetry hints to what is in and beyond a word, opening up unknown perspectives on the hidden dimensions of language as a central medium with which we try to fathom the world and the phenomena within it. By being able to sensitize us for the plurality of a word's possible de- and connotations, poetry is hence a means to approach and ponder also health-related issues from a different angle.[2] American poet Patricia Traxler's reaction to her father's Alzheimer's diagnosis demonstrates this quite impressively; 'Aphasia is an oddly beautiful word, like the name of a flower. I imagine it blue, with slender petals and delicate filaments, breaking through hard winter soil, because each word my father manages to speak is like a tender blossom struggling into the air' (Traxler 2007, 16).

By allowing us to express our experiences not only through language but also through form, poetry may vent both what can and what cannot be said. After all, language and form are inextricably intertwined in this genre. As Tafdrup once said, a poem 'must demonstrate' its topic in its 'choice of words, [...] and all the way into the sentence construction. [...] The poem's being must be realized in its figure. I find that poetry is a unique linguistic possibility in order to be what is being spoken about' (O'Callaghan 2013, 102). This way,

> [p]oems are able of something neither science, philosophy, psychology, sociology, religious teachings nor any other institution can do. Poems are no better, but by their means they are able to move and disturb in a specific way. [...] Where science, philosophy, psychology, sociology and religion each have their discourse to speak *about* reality, poetry differs by not primarily pointing, but *being*.
>
> Tafdrup 2017 [1991], 108, original emphasis, my translation[3]

When it comes to dementia, poetry's potential of 'being' instead of 'pointing' may instantly make visible what it means to lead a life marked by oblivion – a state that Timo Brandt quite beautifully describes as follows:

---

[2] In this regard, note also Hanna Zeilig's (2014, 172) observation that '[t]hrough its appeal to our imaginations and empathy, poetry brings into focus those slant truths that lie to the side of our vision'.

[3] The genre's openness towards the grey area between what a person wants to say and is able to say is also used in the work with patients suffering from dementia, with the goal to prevent patients being excluded from communication because of their symptoms. See: The Alzheimer's Poetry Project (undated); see also Garrie et al. 2016; Janson 2005, 655.

We are cast from memories and you can notice, you can feel the cast rusting, becoming brittle in some places, but it can also happen that everything suddenly melts away in a heat one cannot do anything about. Gaps built between memories and present and past merge in the defluent flow of memory, a dreadful variation on the symbol of Heraclitus.

Brandt undated, my translation

In *Tarkovsky's Horses*, the poems' condensed[4] and fragmentary form which time and again cause voids in need of interpretation ultimately seems like a mirror of the demented person's jagged state of memories and narratives. Next to that, also the poetic narrative's macrostructure can be read as a link between clinical symptom and poetic style, in which the gutters between the individual poems can be understood as a visual portrayal of the demential gaps of memory and narration. By visually mirroring the demential game of lost and not-found, Tafdrup's poems not least correspond with the genre's tendency

> to focus on particular moments, individuals and details in order to illuminate the general experience. The business of poetry is distinct from prose, it hopes to show rather than 'tell' us about a state or condition and searches for insights that are not obvious, in order to make us 'feel'. It works upon us subtly. Poetry extends our understanding through the force of emotional logic and therefore helps us to feel that dementia sufferers are more than a host of objectified medical symptoms.
>
> Zeilig 2014, 173

In this regard, the fractures in poetic language and form – the symbols and metaphors, the enjambments and stanzas, the blank spaces between the texts[5] – cannot only express the demented person's aphasic or even mute search for words, memories, and persons but can also shed light on the psychosocial 'symptoms' dementia may cause in relatives. One may just think of the gaps in the storyline of *Tarkovsky's Horses*, which make this book a loosely connected account of beginnings and endings: childhood memories from a far distant past alternate with glimpses of a presence coined by disease, dying and death; stories from the father's youth contrast with his age and ageing; love stories are

---

[4] As Tafdrup once said: 'Poetry is the most concentrated form of language, the most sublime, human beings have developed' (Tafdrup 2016, my translation).
[5] All of which can be found in quite similar form both in the Danish original and the English translation.

narrated by the poles of beginning love and final separation – but where is the middle in all of this? What about school, education, work? Engagement, marriage, (grand-)children? Celebrations, farewells, rituals, daily routines? Cultural or global events that impact one's life? Instead of showing the in-between, the fractured storyline of *Tarkovsky's Horses* displays the lapses of memory that cannot only be noted in the sick person him- or herself, but also in a relative trying to grasp a ceasing present by its apparently opposed origins.[6]

2. Language, literature, and dementia

With regard to Tafdrup, her father's death caused a sudden caesura in the daughter's work: 'My father died on 3 June 2005. It had been arranged a year in advance that I would spend one month in Berlin in July 2005 to write. The only thing that came out of my pen was "FATHER ..."' (Tafdrup 2011, 10, original emphasis, my translation). The poet is bereft of language, only left with one word, a word, however, that expresses the essence of what the deceased meant to her, regardless of his medical condition. The quote's focus on words and writing is also in line with the poetic portrayal of fatherhood in *Tarkovsky's Horses*. For throughout the book, the lyrical speaker selects memories where a shared affinity for language and literature can be seen as one of the building blocks of the father–daughter relationship: it was the father who taught the lyrical speaker the power of words, who introduced her to the world of literature, and who encouraged her first philosophical thoughts.[7] Constantly interspersed references to, e.g., literature and mythology give additional weight to this emphasis on issues of intellect as a joining bond between parent and child, which ultimately cumulated in the daughter's vocation as a writer. That

---

[6] This phenomenon can also be noted in other approaches to dementia. In Edward Hirsch's (2009 [2003], 132) poem 'Wheeling My Father through the Alzheimer's Ward' (2003), for instance, a son's visit to his demented father triggers childhood memories that contrast the nearing end of their relationship.

[7] See, e.g.: 'I read stories / my father once gave me' (Tafdrup 2010, 124); '– *The body has at least one wound* / is the first whole sentence I remember / my father addressing to me, / in those days when I had just begun / to get to know the world. / I was four years old / and took part / in my life's / first philosophical discussion' (142, original emphasis); 'Beloved was my father, / and the first person in the world / to whom I gave a name –– / in the form of a self-ignited / sound, / before I could utter the word / "father"' (153). For the biographical background of this emphasis see Tafdrup 2011, 10–11.

the father's former affinity for language and literature is eventually irretrievably impaired by the demential decrease of his mental power and language faculty,[8] stands in harsh contrast to this portrayal. This is further strengthened by the fact that this portrait is not written in prose but in the form of poetry, a genre commonly associated with a most elaborated linguistic and literary proficiency.

With that said, it seems standing to reason that the emphasis on language, literature, and intellect sheds immediate light on core features of the sick person's personality, values, or mindset. However, when it comes to illness narratives – not only with regard to those written in poetic form –, the impact clinical symptoms may have on aesthetic representations calls for a certain aloofness: after all, topoi, motifs, or techniques that are either particularly close or opposed to the disease in question may inevitably make us wonder in how far this depiction emanated from certain – witting or unwitting – aesthetic norms or ideals: does a pathography present us with a 'realistic', wholistic portrayal of a person or are the traits that were most changed by the disease highlighted out of proportion? Would a character be attributed to different professions and affinities if the respective book or movie were centred on a different disease? For instance, how strongly would aspects like sports be emphasized if limited motor skills were the most central symptom of Alzheimer's? How many musicians would one find in literary or filmic dementia narratives if hearing loss were one of the disease's key clinical signs?

Be it non-fictional or fictional, be it in poetic or narrative form, be it a book, a movie, or a play, the aesthetic of illness narratives can usually not be separated from the clinical symptoms in question. The narrative *is* the disease, it is 'infected' by its symptoms in language, imagery, and form. By highlighting language and literature in the context of dementia, *Tarkovsky's Horses* inevitably inscribes itself in a topos common in both the fictional and non-fictional discourse of dementia. Lisa Genova's novel *Still Alice* (2007) or Felix Mitterer's drama *Der Panther* [The Panther] (2007) are, for example, both centred on Alzheimer's patients who are former professors of linguistics or literature, respectively. In Alice Munro's short story 'The Bear Came Over the Mountain' (1999) and Jonathan Franzen's novel *The Corrections* (2001), it is again one of

---

[8] See, e.g.: 'My father doesn't remember how well-read / he is.' (p. 107); 'The mouth is open, the words / sleepless circles in the water: / The things I can neither / ask my father about / any more / nor please him with' (Tafdrup 2010, 152).

the relatives who held a professorship in literature. Also in non-fiction one can notice a distinct focus on language, literature, and intellect, e.g., in *Demenz. Abschied von meinem Vater* [*Dementia. Farewell to My Father*] (2009), a pathography written by journalist Tilman Jens about his father, the philologist, literary historian, professor of rhetoric and writer Walter Jens, or John Bayley's remembrance of his wife, the famous writer Iris Murdoch, in *Elegy for Iris* (1999). In *Der alte König in seinem Exil* [*The Old King in his Exile*] (2011), Arno Geiger's homage to his demented father August Geiger, the reference to literature can again be understood as part of a narrative technique, in which a plethora of intertextual quotes contrastingly demonstrates the pathological rhetoric of Alzheimer's while at the same time creating an upvaluing closeness to the rhetoric of high literature. Against this backdrop, the idea suggests itself that when it comes to narratives of Alzheimer's and dementia, matters of language, literature, and intellect serve as a contrast medium to the disease and its symptomatic loss of memory and linguistic mastery, in which the antithetical topos of former ability vs. current inability creates a drastic, instantly comprehensible – and, when speaking from a strictly literary perspective: aesthetically satisfying – imagery inevitably linked with one of the central clinical signs of dementia.[9]

3. Intertexts as side narratives

When it comes to narratives of diseases like dementia, a focus on language, literature, and intellect may thus tell us more about the disease itself than the people affected by it, be it the patients, relatives or health care providers. Therefore, when trying to get a better understanding of the individual story hidden behind the clinical symptoms, one has to take a closer look at the particularities of such foci. In *Tarkovsky's Horses*, it is most notably the poems'

---

[9] Even though this chapter is not the place to develop further on it, one might argue that the (pop-cultural) play with such an antagonism may contribute to the distorted perception of dementia as a disease of intellectuals, while at the same time disregarding the plight of patients from different backgrounds. Apart from this, the focus on the 'demented intellectual' may also evoke the implicit notion that the clinical symptoms of dementia may weigh more heavily on some persons than on others; as a result, there is not least the risk that respective literature or movies cause some sort of an elitist compassion topos that goes hand in hand with a hierarchizing re- or devaluation of certain patient groups linked to specific sociocultural and socioeconomical backgrounds.

intertextual, symbolically charged side narratives that give insight into the lyrical speaker's specific perspective on dementia and fatherhood. Not all of these references can and must be dealt with here; there are however three intertexts that require a closer look in the context of this paper: the reference to the character of the (stupid) Auguste, to Russian filmmaker Andrei Tarkovsky and associated concepts of masculinity, and eventually to the mythological bond between Orpheus and Eurydice.

3.1 Stupid August(e): Common connotations of Alzheimer's

In *Tarkovsky's Horses*, intertextual references are oftentimes found almost inconspicuously, as if incidentally interspersed in the poems, as the following excerpt may illustrate:

> The house has collapsed,
> the doorbell doesn't work,
> the coat is gone from the hook.
> *Ach, du lieber Augustin* . . . [O, you dear Augustin]
> [. . .]
> Walks and walks
> to meet the endless beginning.
> THE TONGUE IN FLAMES.
> *Alles ist weg, weg, weg* . . . [Everything's gone, gone, gone . . .]
>
> 121, original emphasis[10]

The poem depicts a situation familiar to those acquainted to life with dementia: the disease has ravaged the once guarding shelter of the private home, and everyday objects are constant reminders of the apraxic impotence caused by dementia, which does, however, not protect the father from losing himself in the inside and the outside, to go astray, until his relative wanders the streets as well, anxiously calling his name, so long, so loud, until the tongue seems to be in flames. Two verses from the Austrian folk song 'O du lieber Augustin' (text

---

[10] Both the Danish poem and its English translation deviate from the original wording of the Austrian folk song 'O du lieber Augustin' quoted here: while the song's stanzas end with the line 'Alles ist hin,' which translates not only as 'Everything is gone' but also bears the notion that everything is 'kaputt' or 'broken,' the change of adverb ('Alles ist *weg*' / 'Everything is *gone*') puts a stronger focus on the aspect of loss – and thus on one of the core symptoms of dementia.

ca. 1679, composition ca. 1800) have lost their way into this everyday chaos of dementia, bringing the father into sudden closeness with someone who – right down to the song's last stanzas – is constantly chased by bad luck:

> Every day's been a feast
> Now all is plague diseased
> Just one big corpse's feast
> Everything's ceased.
> Augustin, o come on,
> Now your grave's close upon,
> Augustin, o come on,
> Dear, all is gone.
>
> Hauptmann et al. 2010, 96, my translation

In the context of dementia, the name Augustin opens up a sombre innuendo to Alois Alzheimer's famous patient Auguste D., who played a pivotal role in the understanding and definition of this disease. Through the link between the ill and the ill-fated alluded to, the father becomes indirectly associated with someone whose lot is hopeless: once happy, he is now doomed to fail, and only death will put an end to his misery. The image is further strengthened by the homonymity of Augustin, Auguste D., and the Auguste, a type of clown that always fails, a warm-hearted, but foolish, silly character, haunted by bad luck. As both in the poem's Danish and English version the song's lyrics are quoted in the original language, this connotation receives further weight by the fact that in German the clown's name is usually called with the epithet – less *ornans* than *humilians* – 'Dummer August' ['Stupid Auguste']. Nevertheless, the reference to the ever so ill-fated character(s) – or rather caricature(s) – of Augustin/Auguste adds a surprisingly humoristic side to the poem's depiction of the father. After all, originally written in major scale, the song does not set the melancholically and bitter counterpoint one might expect in view of the poem's otherwise bleak stance towards a life shaped by dementia. Instead, the song's somehow tragicomical tone connotes its poetic context with a grim sense of humour as if to say – in an almost sarcastic way – to make the best of this demential catch-22. At the same time, in light of the great popularity 'O du lieber Augustin' enjoys as a children's song, the reference also seems like a reminiscence to the daughter's blithe days of childhood, where she could think herself safe in the protecting care of the father.

But these happy days are now gone, gone, gone ... Now it is the child calling out for the father, searching for him, taking care of his safety, while being constantly aware of the threat of his impending death. The image of a child's care for a father, who due to his disease is no longer able to fulfil roles formerly associated with fatherhood, evokes common perceptions of dementia as an inversion of both familial roles.[11] The demented father's childlike clumsiness, his ill-fated situation that is doomed to result in his downfall, is ironically increased when considering the origins of the name 'August', with which the father is connoted in the poem: Deriving from Augustus (lat. 'the esteemed, the venerable'), the traditional male title of Roman emperors, the name attributes an aura of inherent dignity and majesty to the father.[12] By the intertextually triggered allusions to the hapless Augustin, the clown 'Stupid Auguste', the historic patient Auguste D., and the ancient emperor's title Augustus, the father is thus characterized by a complex interplay of connotations that can ultimately be encapsulated in the image of the pitiable downfall of the erstwhile majestic: once the noble and grand emperor in the child's kingdom, a dignitary she admiringly looked up to, who was almost invincible in his power when protecting her from harm and hardship, the previously august father has now turned to a demented Auguste.

3.2 Tarkovsky's horses: Cruelties of dementia

The ironic image of the downfall of a former majesty is turned to an extreme by the book's linkage of dementia with Russian director Andrei Tarkovsky and his movie *Andrei Rublev* (1969). Explicitly cited in the titles of Tafdrup's book and its very last poem (2010, 159), and accompanied by additional allusions throughout the book, the intertextual reference to Tarkovsky, 'the poet of apocalypse', (Quandt 2018) and this movie is one of the most highlighted in Tafdrup's poetic illness narrative – and ultimately connects it with gender-based images of male cruelty in times of vulnerability. This is particularly

---

[11] In this regard, note also the comparison of dementia narratives with a '*Bildungsroman* in reverse' (Hartung 2016, 170–220).
[12] Arno Geiger's *Der alte König in seinem Exil* [*The Old King in his Exile*] entails a similar comparison, which is evoked by the explicit reference to the demented father, whose first name is indeed August, as an 'old king'.

triggered by one of the most violent and controversial scenes in *Andrei Rublev*, a (film) shot of a horse falling down a flight of stairs, overturning several times, and eventually, when lying injured on the ground, being stabbed to death by soldiers. The gruesomeness of the cinematic picture is increased by the scene's real background, as Tarkovsky had the animal fetched from a slaughterhouse, shot in the neck for the filming, this way causing the fall of the once majestic creature that was finally stabbed and killed with another headshot (Fenech undated; Lipkov 1967). In the context of Tafdrup's poetic dementia narrative, the reference to Tarkovsky's horses thus evokes an image of male exercises of power, where strength is ostentatiously demonstrated by a – presumably self-proclaimed – right to torture and even to decide on life and death.[13] What makes this even more cruel is the fact that the brutal behaviour is not directed against an equal opponent, but a vulnerable being, an 'innocent victim [] of [its] association with man', (Johnson and Petrie 1994, 214) as Tarkovsky once described his symbolic perception of horses.

In Tafdrup's book, this image of (male) demonstrations of power is intertwined with the disease of dementia, which is depicted as an almost human agent charged with stereotypical male attributes: like a personified attack against allegedly core attributes of masculinity, dementia forces a once-powerful dignitary – Augustus – to his knees, takes the sick man's power and strength, and continues to fight him despite his defeated vulnerability. The connotation of the disease with stereotypical male attributes such as aggressiveness, cruelty, and mercilessness is juxtaposed with the book's otherwise striking focus on female care and compassion: apart from the father and his only briefly mentioned brother and son, hardly any male characters, e.g. physicians, friends, or colleagues, can be found in the poems; instead, the father is primarily shown in relationships to women, in particular his – already deceased – mother, his wife, and his daughter, the lyrical speaker.[14] As both his

---

[13] Also with regard to Andrei Tarkovsky himself; after all, Tafdrup's book is not titled *Rublev's* or *Andrei's Horses* and thus focused on the movie or its characters, but explicitly emphasizes the name of the director.

[14] In correspondence to the book's general emphasis on intertextual references, the men mentioned in the poems are mostly writers, e.g. Gunnar Eklöf, T.S. Eliot, Lars Norén, and Rainer Maria Rilke. The lack of a portrayal of family members does not have to be seen as something negative; in view of the book's biographical roots, such an exclusion can rather be understood as a means to protect their private sphere; see Fürholzer 2019, 105–52, in particular 123–34.

wife and daughter are portrayed as assuming a caring role for the vulnerable and weak father, the idea suggests itself that the book presents us with gender-bound concepts of nursing care. However, despite several allusions to this image, *Tarkovsky's Horses* does not seem to play with any sort of reverse 'paternalization' or 'femininization' of the demented father. Instead, by constantly redirecting the reader's view to the disease itself, the reference to Tarkovsky's horses rather seems like a symbol for the – almost human or even super-human – power and viciousness of a disease that may, out of nowhere, strike us from ambush, cause us to stumble and fall, until we lie helpless on the ground, humiliated in our former majesty, suffering a cruel and painful end of life.

Fortunately, neither Tarkovsky's film nor Tafdrup's poetic illness narrative end with such a gloomy connotation. Instead, in analogy to the last scenes of *Andrei Rublev*, the book's outro poem reveals an imagery of peace and serenity:

> In that beauty a horse
> displays,
> standing in sun
> on a grassy field
> [...]
> With the same exalted peace
> Tarkovsky's horses
> in *Andrei Rublev*
> radiate
> in the film's final images,
> my father is present,
> resting in himself.
>
> Tafdrup 2010, 159

The intertextually sustained symbolic view of horses evoked in this final stanza of the book re-associates the dead father with an erstwhile majesty, grandeur, and beauty that had temporarily fallen into oblivion. As a result, the child's earliest memories of her father as someone powerful, strong, and majestic are depicted as attributes that may be forgotten and – deliberately or not – trampled on, but remain nevertheless an inalienable part of a sick person's self – which ultimately shows them as being more powerful than the ferocity of dementia.

3.3 Orpheus: Relatives in the underworld

In *Tarkovsky's Horses*, the disease's gruesomeness that may strike both the father and his relatives are inevitably linked with the experience of loss: 'The book narrates two kinds of loss: partly the loss my father experienced in form of oblivion, and partly the loss I, his daughter, experienced, as in a way one loses his father while he is still alive. And yet at the same time, one doesn't, as there are only new pages emerging' (Tafdrup 2011, 10, my translation). The association with dementia as a sort of living death concerns both the sick and his relatives – as poet Ragan Fox once stated in light of his father's Alzheimer's disease:

> I suppose I have spent the last 10 years mourning the loss of my father. Each time he forgot my name, I mourned. When he forgot to attend my college graduation and said he never remembered being invited, I mourned. When he stopped eating solid foods, I mourned. The tears I expect at the death call have already been spent. I mourned a *dying* father so much that I have no idea how to respond now that he is actually dead.
>
> Fox 2010, 4, original emphasis

According to Jonathan Franzen (2001, 89), 'the most common trope of Alzheimer's: that its particular sadness and horror stem from the sufferer's loss of his or her "self" long before the body dies' is not least fuelled by medial and scientific representations of this disease. Against this backdrop, it will come as no surprise that within the scientific literature, Alzheimer's dementia is sometimes referred to as a sort of 'psychosocial death', (Zarit et al. 1985; Doka and Aber 1989; Furlini 2001) as due to the changes dementia usually evokes, friends and family may encounter patients as if they are already dead despite being still physically alive.

In *Tarkovsky's Horses*, this experience of the living death that can both hit the sick person and his or her relatives is embedded into the repeated reference to Orpheus and Eurydice. Cited both in the book's intro and outro poem, this ancient legend forms the narrated frame for the lyrical speaker's poetic approach towards dementia and her relationship with her father. As an epitome of the doomed search for a lost love, the myth stresses the book's emotional focus on the two poles of despair and love, a love that can, however, not even be broken by – demential – loss. At first glance, Orpheus's loving search for

Eurydice seems like a contrasting juxtaposition of the gender-bound image of male-like power and cruelty evoked by the reference to Tarkovsky. The book's stance on the ancient myth shares, however, a significant commonality with Tarkovsky's apparently opposed counter-text, which is, once again, its focus on the cruel downfall of the innocent, vulnerable, majestic. This connotation is already evoked in the introductory poem 'Darkroom on Immanuelkirchstrasse', in which the lyrical speaker tries to convey her grief into a poetic tribute in memoriam of the deceased father. Like some kind of author's prologue, the poem depicts the challenging writing scene the lyrical speaker is faced with in this regard:

> one night in Berlin,
> and a piece of paper, filled
> with *something* that wants to be called
> forth.
>
> Tafdrup 2010, 94; original emphasis

In light of his dementia, however, the search for the father – his personality, his identity, his meaning for her and for others – becomes inextricably linked to a search for her own identity: for what is a daughter when dementia has eliminated the father's memory of his child? Given the cruelty of being dead while still alive, the lyrical speaker in 'Darkroom on Immanuelkirchstrasse' finds herself in the perverted role of Eurydice:

> Will Eurydice fetch
> her dead father –
> like Orpheus sing
> of what's lost?
> Eurydice, memory,
> the eruption.
> [...]
> Eurydice did have a life, after all.
>
> Tafdrup 2010, 94

In *Tarkovsky's Horses*, dementia perverts relationships. The daughter is looking for her father, but no matter how close she gets to him, the disease condemns them to remain separated. Although among the living, the daughter is already stuck in the underworld of her father's oblivion. In an inversion of the ancient myth, it is not Orpheus but Eurydice herself who is calling for the loved one, until 'the tongue' is 'in flames' (see above).[15] But despite the poet's particular linguistic and artistic competence, her calling 'song' cannot create a connection between them, no matter how hard she tries to reach the father. Orpheus, still among the living, but nevertheless irreversibly separated from Eurydice, can no longer look out for her. In his world, Eurydice does no longer, or rather: does not at all exist, as, what is worse, she is not dead but inexistent. As in perverted cruelty, dementia can extinguish a life as if this person, this shared relationship, had never existed: 'Eurydice did have a life, after all' – but in contrast to the myth, the dementia-caused death of a relative can be absolute.

In an intense manner, Tafdrup's poems thus broach the anguish dementia's 'psychosocial death' may cause both the sick person and the relatives, as the poem 'Flames Freeze' impressively demonstrates:

> – Here is a picture of you,
> my father says, handing me
> an unfamiliar photo
> of my mother, naked, and quite young.
> [...]
> – And here is our mother,
> my father adds cheerfully
> handing me a picture
> of my grandmother.
>
> Tafdrup 2010, 110

Due to dementia, the daughter becomes the wife, the wife becomes the sister ('our' mother: 'yours and mine').[16] This image confirms common assumptions about dementia: 'Caregivers assume, for example, that when a father does not appear to recognize his daughter, the daughter becomes bereft of a father;

---

[15] Next to that, transferring the myth to the parent–daughter constellation invokes oedipal resonances (my thanks to Rüdiger Kunow for his intriguing observation of Freudian references notable in various parts of Tafdrup's poetic volume).

[16] An again quite Freudian image. See also 'Whether it's me or my mother / sitting in the chair, / what does it matter? / Whether it's my sister or me, / does it change anything' (Tafdrup 2010, 98), 'but the woman / he loved / has turned into his mother, / and he into the son of his beloved --' (101). While the daughter is buried alive, the wife is married, divorced: when her sick husband is transferred to a nursing home, the spouses' separation is equalled to a divorce, both for the father ('he wants out and away, / wants to go HOME. / [...] / HOME is, / where my mother is', 106, original emphasis) and for the mother, considering that dementia can invert an 'Until death do us part' into a premortal 'Until oblivion do us part.' See, e.g. 121, 110 in this regard.

'fatherhood' is defined as an overt social interaction, a performance, rather than an emotional state that may not be expressed' (Simon 2014, 9). In this regard, the notion that there are a lot more facets to a father that go beyond the roles of a biological begetter, legal guardian, or social parent, is also notable in 'Flames Freeze': for even though his family members' specific relation to him is forgotten, the father is nevertheless still able to recognize their emotional ties. As it is stated a few verses later:

> I still remember
> everyone I love – – –
>
> Tafdrup 2010, 110[17]

Although dementia may assail familial roles, they are not erased but only changed. Even in cases where a father suffering from dementia is no longer able to maintain the legal or social aspects associated with fatherhood, even if the father–child relationship undergoes changes – the father's neurons may be coated in plaques, but both the plaque-resistant genetics and the emotional ties are able to survive dementia's oblivion.

4. Conclusion

In a complex interplay of biographical memories and intertextual side narratives that embed the poetic cycle in a broader context, Tafdrup's poetic illness narrative both confirms and revokes the fictional and non-fictional dementia discourse: while the image of the child taking care of the parent corresponds to certain conceptions of dementia as a disease of loss and inverted roles, there is no suggestion that this change in the relationship leads to a paternalistic form of sick-care nor to an infantilization of the father. Neither does the book attribute the sick man with any sort of femininization: while the book – not least due to its intertextual references to director Tarkovsky and his movie *Andrei Rublev* – implicitly personifies dementia by attributing it with male-like violence and cruelty that forms a contrast to the compassionate care of the father's female relatives, the family members are not

---

[17] See also 'there is only one body in the room, / – – and it is ours, / a family body' (Tafdrup 2010, 140).

characterized by (stereo-)typically 'male' or 'female' attributes. After all, the father never corresponded to traditional concepts of fatherhood as for example a stern, authoritative father figures such as the *pater familias* or *auctoritas*. Concepts of aggressive or cruel forms of male demonstrations of power and strength are rather contrasted with the power and strength of a father's loving care for his child.

While the disease inevitably changes the father's self and his relationship to his daughter, the poems demonstrate that there are nevertheless facets that are immune to dementia. For despite dementia's destructive impact on the father's love for language and literature, an attribute that is central to the lyrical speaker's understanding of her father and her relationship with him, and despite the disease's gruesome threat to bring down the once majestic, powerful emperor of the child's private realm and turn him into a humiliated, ill-fated clown, doomed to fail, eventually separated by a gap of oblivion from his family, *Tarkovsky's Horses* makes aware that there are aspects of fatherhood that cannot be infected by this illness. As notwithstanding the destructive power of dementia and the losses it may cause, the father will always remain someone who loved and was loved – the emotional ties between parent and child thus continue to exist, regardless of age, gender, or physical state.

Bibliography

Brandt, Timo. 'Die endlichen Sätze der Erinnerung. Rezension: Pia Tafdrup: *Tarkowskis Pferde* [The Finite Sentences of Memory. Review: Pia Tafdrup: *Tarkowkis Pferde*].' *Signaturen. Forum für autonome Poesie* (Undated). https://signaturen-magazin.de/pia-tafdrup--tarkowskis-pferde.html [25 February 2020].

Doka, Kenneth J., and Rita A. Aber. 'Psychosocial Loss and Grief.' *Disenfranchised Grief: Recognizing Hidden Sorrow*. Ed. Kenneth J. Doka. Toronto: Lexington Books, 1989. 187–99.

Fenech, Freddy. 'Animals Were Harmed: A Brief History of Animal Cruelty on Film.' *The Bloody Show* (Undated). https://thebloodyshow.com/animal-cruelty-on-film [29 February 2020].

Fox, Ragan. 'Re-membering Daddy: Autoethnographic Reflections of My Father and Alzheimer's Disease.' *Text and Performance Quarterly* 30.1 (2010): 3–20.

Franzen, Jonathan. 'My Father's Brain. What Alzheimer's Takes Away.' *The New Yorker* (10 September 2001): 81–91.

Fürholzer, Katharina. *Das Ethos des Pathographen. Literatur- und medizinethische Dimensionen von Krankenbiographien* [Ethics of Pathography. Ethical Dimensions of Illness Biographies from the Viewpoint of Medical Humanities]. Heidelberg: Winter Verlag, 2019.

Furlini, Linda. 'The Parent They Knew and the "New" Parent: Daughters" Perceptions of Dementia of the Alzheimer's Type.' *Home Health Care Services Quarterly* 20.1 (2001): 21–38.

Garrie, Alaina J., Shruti Goel, and Martin M. Forsberg. 'Medical Students" Perception of Dementia after Participation in Poetry Workshop with People with Dementia.' *International Journal of Alzheimer's Disease* (2016). http://dx.doi.org/10.1155/2016/2785105 [25 February 2020].

Hartung, Heike. *Ageing, Gender and Illness in Anglophone Literature: Narrating Age in the Bildungsroman*. New York: Routledge, 2016.

Hauptmann, Cornelius et al. Eds. *Volkslieder*. Stuttgart: Carus/Reclam, 2010.

Hirsch, Edward. 'Wheeling My Father through the Alzheimer's Ward. [2003].' *Beyond Forgetting: Poetry and Prose about Alzheimer's Disease*. Ed. Holly J. Hughes. Kent: Kent State UP, 2009. 132.

Janson, C.G. 'White Daisies on My Mind (Requiem for an Alzheimer Patient).' *Neurology* 65.2 (2005): 654–6.

Johnson, Vida T., and Graham Petrie. *The Films of Andrei Tarkovsky: A Visual Fugue*. Bloomington and Indiana: Indiana UP, 1994.

Lipkov, Aleksandr. 'The Passion According to Andrei: An Unpublished Interview with Andrei Tarkovsky, conducted February 1, 1967.' Translated by Robert Bird. *Nostalghia.com*. https://web.archive.org/web/20120813182721/http://people.ucalgary.ca/~tstronds/nostalghia.com/TheTopics/PassionacctoAndrei.html [28 February 2020].

O'Callaghan, Ruth. '"The Body Has At Least One Wound": Pia Tafdrup in Conversation.' *Critical Survey* 25.1 (2013): 99–110.

Quandt, James. 'Andrei Tarkovsky. The Poet of Apocalypse.' *Tiff* (1 October 2018). https://www.tiff.net/the-review/andrei-tarkovsky-the-poet-of-apocalypse [26 February 2020].

Semmel, K.E. 'A Daughter's Story: An Interview with Pia Tafdrup.' Translated by David McDuff. *World Literature Today* 84.2 (2010): 44–7.

Seng, Joachim. 'Ein Regenbogen unter der Glocke der Dunkelheit. Die Gedichte der dänischen Dichterin Pia Tafdrup sind eine Entdeckung.' *literaturkritik.de* 11 (2017). https://literaturkritik.de/tafdrup-tarkowskis-pferde-ein-regenbogen-unter-glocke-dunkelheit-gedichte-daenischen-dichterin-pia-tafdrup-sind-eine-entdeckung,23850.html [28 February 2020].

Simon, Linda. 'Battling the "Invincible Predator": Alzheimer's Disease as Metaphor.' *The Journal of American Culture* 37.1 (2014): 5–15.

Tafdrup, Pia. *Tarkovskijs heste. Digte* [Tarkovsky's Horses. Poems]. Copenhagen: Gyldendal, 2006.

Tafdrup, Pia. *Tarkovsky's Horses*. Translated by David McDuff. Highgreen: Bloodaxe Books, 2010.

Tafdrup, Pia. *Over vandet går jeg: Skitse til en poetik* [Over the water I walk. A poetic sketch] [1991]. Copenhagen: Gyldendal, 2017. E-Book.

Tafdrup, Pia. 'Mit liv med demens [My life with dementia].' *Livet med demens* 21.4 (2011): 10–11.

Tafdrup, Pia. 'Poesi. Et nyt blik at se med [Poetry. A new look to see with].' *Literatursiden* (4 January 2016). https://litteratursiden.dk/artikler/poesi-et-nyt-blik-se-med [24 February 2020].

The Alzheimer Poetry Project (Undated). http://www.alzpoetry.com [29 February 2020].

Traxler, Patricia. 'I'm Still Listening for My Father's Words; Alzheimer's Stole My Dad's Vocabulary. But He Never Needed Language to Show Me that He Cared.' *Newsweek* 149.23 (2007): 16.

Zarit, Steven H., Nancy K. Orr, and Judy M. Zerit. *The Hidden Victims of Alzheimer's Disease*. New York: New York UP, 1985.

Zeilig, Hannah. 'Gaps and Spaces: Representations of Dementia in Contemporary British Poetry.' *Dementia* 13.2 (2014): 160–75.

5

Anne Carson, dementia and the negative self

João Paulo Guimarães and Daae Jung

To what extent can one's attitude towards life help mitigate the impact of dementia? In 'Uncle Falling', one of the chapbooks that integrate the *Float* (2016) collection, Canadian poet Anne Carson argues that working against the tendency to exert total control over one's life can provide some protection against the shock of the disease. If the time comes, one should be prepared to let go, or, as the poet points out: 'If you have to fall ... Do your best to fall ... In no time at all' ('Uncle' 37). There is, according to Carson, more continuity than one tends to assume between life before and after dementia, especially in what concerns one's control over language and identity, so it might be possible to find traces of post-traumatic subjectivity in our familiar, supposedly normal, lives, perhaps by paying attention to those aspects of the everyday that undermine our control.

Thus, Carson does not seem to think that dementia entails a radical break with the past. Rather, she suggests that self-knowledge and communication had always been impaired from the start, given that language does not disclose the real in a transparent manner and identity is a perennial riddle.[1] 'Uncle Falling', the poetry chapbook that will be the focus of this chapter (although we will sometimes refer to 'A Lecture on Corners', an essay-form lecture in which

---

[1] The notion that 'all lives are fundamentally opaque' is 'a thread that runs through all of Carson's work' (66), as Joan Fleming points out in her essay about *Nox*. No life is ever normal, straightforward and transparent. In *Nox,* the poet attempts to assemble fragments of her estranged brother's life in order to understand his unexpected death. Wanted by the police, he had left Canada and moved to Europe. From there he would only occasionally contact his family. In the poem, Carson attempts to conjure him by way of letter fragments and remembered phone calls.

Carson talks about her father's dementia), draws extensively on the poetics of Modernist poet Gertrude Stein, indicating that, for Carson, language is not so much a medium of denotative exchange but, more fundamentally, the matrix of memory and subjectivity, a maze of feelings, echoes and questions. Like Stein, Carson foregrounds the slipperiness of the domestic world, at once familiar and strange, a space that both her uncle and father, the central figures of the chapbook, try to master with tragic masculine determination, their desire to hold on to normality paradoxically quickening their descent into dementia.[2] In this essay, we will put Carson's text in conversation with the work recently done by French philosopher Catherine Malabou and psychoanalysis scholar Slavoj Žižek on the topic at hand, our aim being to ascertain to what extent the strange worlds of Carson and Stein can make more navigable the domain of dementia, often cast as radically unfamiliar.[3]

'Uncle Falling' is the longest of the twenty-two chapbooks that compose *Float* (2016), Anne Carson's most recent print release. The title of the project comes from the chapbook 'Cassandra Float Can', which features the Greek prophetess Cassandra as a central character and in which 'floating' thus appears as a symbol of artistic and philosophical insight, by way of prophecy ('Everywhere Cassandra ran Cassandra found she could float (. . .). Everywhere Cassandra ran she found she was already there': 1–2). Prophetic language, with its tautologies, its enigmatic incoherence and playful logic, is one of the key

---

[2] 'Uncle Falling' and 'A Lecture on Corners' are not the only places where Carson has written about her father's dementia. In 'The Anthropology of Water', Carson compares her relation to her sick father to that between a pilgrim and a saint. In her article about the poem, 'The Pilgrim and the Riddle', Tanis MacDonald notes that Carson sets up an analogy between the demented parent's elliptic speech and the indecipherable speech of a shrine's divinity. Her father had always been private (his puzzling silence is something Carson insists upon in the two works we analyse here), so in 'The Anthropology of Water' the poet places him in the domain of the sacred. Her father's remoteness makes it impossible for her to mourn him in a satisfactory manner. About this MacDonald says: 'The father remains beyond the reach of the narrator's love, even as she strives to read him as an untranslated (and ultimately untranslatable) text that will not yield traditional consolation' (1).

[3] In her book entitled *The New Wounded: From Neurosis to Brain Damage*, Catherine Malabou mounts a strong attack on psychoanalysis through her neurobiologically informed reading of patients with brain traumas such as dementia, post-traumatic stress disorder, and brain injury. The philosopher argues that the psychoanalytic notion of the unconscious is inadequate to account for these types of brain traumas and becomes theoretically redundant in the face of the neurobiological affirmations of the emotional brain and neuroplasticity. In a critical review of *The New Wounded* entitled 'Descartes and the Post-Traumatic Subject', Žižek claims that in her otherwise robust reading of Freud, Malabou misses out the fact that what she calls, the 'new wounded' – the subject profoundly transformed by a brain trauma – is already implicated in the psychoanalytic account of the death drive.

themes of *Float* as a whole, including 'Uncle Falling', which can, as we will see, be seen as a meditation on the potential poetic qualities of dementia patients' cryptic speech. But we also find echoes of the main title of the collection in another chapbook called '108 (floatage)', a term that refers to assorted objects that float on the water and which thus epitomizes Carson's encyclopaedic, omnivorous, and paratactic approach to poetic composition. *Float* contains a bit of everything: humorous rewrites of ancient Greek myths and plays ('Zeusbits', about the Olympian's escapades in modern capitalist society, and 'Pinplay', a brief postmodern/absurdist take on Euripides' 'Bacchae'), paeans to the memory of lost family members ('Powerless Structures Fig II', about her aimless brother and the Danish wife he left behind, and 'Uncle Falling'), texts that put a spin on traditional poetic forms ('Possessives Used as Drink: A Lecture in the Form of 15 Sonnets') or follow a miscellaneous list format ('Stacks' and 'Maintenance'), tributes to other artists ('Eras of Yves Klein'), and poems that reflect upon different kinds of discrimination towards women ('Pronoun Envy', 'Contempts' and 'Variations on the Right to Remain Silent'). Of greatest interest to us are 'How to Like "If I Told Him: A Completed Portrait of Picasso" by Gertrude Stein' and 'Nelligan', the first because it is a humorous instruction manual on how to appreciate the work of Gertrude Stein, a figure who has a prominent role throughout 'Uncle Falling', and the second because it collects a set of translations of poems from French-Canadian author Émille Nelligan, who was diagnosed with dementia praecox when he was twenty, a tragic event which foreshortened his artistic life, which ended up lasting less than a decade.

It is important to make clear from the beginning that Carson does not set out to challenge the prevalent view of dementia as a disease that robs the person of his or her identity. The perspective she offers us is that of a relative who sees her father and uncle get progressively worse and thus unable to communicate or recall their past lives. This is an angle that lies in stark contrast with that which, for example, Ulla Kriebernegg explores in her paper about Arno Geiger's *The Old King in His Exile*.[4] There Kriebernegg argues that Geiger tries to develop an improvisational relationship with his father as he adopts a

---

[4] For a reading of Geiger's dementia memoir in the context of ageing masculinities, see Michaela Schrage-Früh's chapter in this volume.

new kind of self, changing his habits and his personality. The scholar figures this as a more humane and productive kind of relationship (the son chooses not to insist on the father's past identity) with a person with dementia. Although Carson mentions, in passing, a few adjustments she had to make in order to accommodate her father's condition (in 'Corners' she says they communicate most successfully when they speak in 'word salad'), she mostly seeks to describe and understand the latter's cognitive decline. She does not seem to think that it is possible to develop more than a mere surface-level relationship with a person with dementia.

Towards the end of the chapbook, Carson suggests that the most one can hope for when it comes to dementia is a kind of prophylactic protection, something that softens the blow (40). The metaphorical example she uses is Achilles' legendary helmet, whose 'exceptionally fine and close-textured' (38) lining (made with a rare kind of sponge) appears to mirror the poetic mesh Carson evokes throughout the piece with her continuous references to the style of Gertrude Stein. The stories and reflections that make up 'Uncle Falling' are interspersed with a series of chorus sections in which four voices, all belonging to Gertrude Stein, comment on the progressive unravelling of the mental health of Carson's father and uncle. Riffing off Stein's penchant for colourful wordplay, these sections unfold as a string of puns, tangents and gnomic statements that might constitute an attempt, on Carson's part, to evoke, albeit in a benign and humorous fashion, the state of confusion that dementia patients find themselves in.[5]

With its chorus, use of masks, different speaking parts and references to ancient myth, Carson frames the chapbook 'Uncle Falling' with reference to Greek drama. Madness is one of the central themes of 'Uncle Falling', not only

---

[5] In her 'Two Stein Talks' (a print version of which was released in her essay collection *The Language of Inquiry*), American poet Lyn Hejinian claims that the dynamism of Stein's poetry is not so much that of the traditional 'stream of consciousness'. Rather, because it is jerky, discontinuous, filled with stops and starts, her writing is closer to bird flight, the alternative metaphor that William James uses to describe the motions of thought in his groundbreaking essay 'Stream of Thought': 'As we take (...) a general view of the wonderful stream of our consciousness, what strikes us first is [the] different pace of its parts. Like a bird's life, it seems to be made of an alteration of flights and perchings. The rhythm of language expresses this, where every thought is expressed in a sentence, and every sentence closed by a period' (qtd. in Hejinian 121). Stein studied psychology under William James in her youth and, as Steven Meyer reminds us in his book about the poet, her writing attempts to capture what James called 'knowledge of acquaintance' (Meyer 14) i.e., the imprecise but nonetheless rich experience one has when one interacts with an object without attempting to describe it (which James calls 'knowledge about').

because both its male characters are mentally ill but also because the chorus speaks in the 'mad' style of Gertrude Stein. In ancient tragedy, the chorus was composed by members of some group that was outside of mainstream political life (slaves, foreigners, women or old men that no longer could participate in warfare). The chorus was tasked with commenting on the action, suggested how the audience might react to this or that scene, and expressed certain hidden fears of the main characters. In 'Uncle Falling', the multiple Gertrude Stein parts, with their wordplay, nonsensical asides and gnomic pronouncements, at once convey how far Carson's father and uncle have moved from the realm of everyday discourse and voice their and our confusion when confronted with the damage done by dementia.

Both Carson's uncle and father are depicted throughout the book as having a fondness for orderliness and a need to map and understand the world. Ironically, this compulsion, Carson notes, becomes more pronounced as their disease progresses. For example, we are told that, before falling ill, her father had the habit of keeping a record of his transactions and of making lists (for example, of wines and recommended pairings or of words he had to look up in the dictionary while reading). For his part, Carson's uncle Harry was an avid collector of the *National Geographic*: 'Living for Harry was knowing how things work' (7), the poet notes. As he starts getting worse, her father's need to control his environment intensifies. For example, he began writing down everything he did during the day. As Carson points out in 'Corners', he started

> to pin down every moment of his day by writing little scribbled notes to himself, mapping out almost simultaneously with his life, the landscape of every action, responsibility or fear. 'Turn out the lamp; Put the keys in the drawer; Go eat supper.' We found these notes all over the house after he was gone, in books, in his pockets, under the cat's dish, behind the clock. He was going for control.
>
> n. p.

When he moves in with Carson, he becomes possessive towards her:

> I had begun to wake up earlier and earlier in the morning to avoid dad. No sooner did he hear me in the kitchen then he appeared, dressed in pajamas and fedora, to begin the barrage of questioning that was his defense against

inner chaos. He needed to control something. And if I were going for a walk, he needed to know every twist and turn of the route I would take.

'Corners' n.p.[6]

The references to her uncle and father's graspingness are offset, throughout 'Uncle Falling', by the sections that evoke the spirit of Gertrude Stein. Stein stands for the uncertain, partial or provisional, that which eludes categorization and control. Stein's poems do not so much describe the real as they open it up for exploration, testing the boundaries between objects and individuals by blending them with things and people with which they maintain perceptual, mnemonic or conceptual affinities.

Consider, for example, the first poem from *Tender Buttons*, 'A Carafe, that is a Blind Glass', perhaps the most cited piece from that book:

> A kind in glass and a cousin, a spectacle and nothing strange a single hurt color and an arrangement in a system to pointing. All this and not ordinary, not unordered in not resembling. The difference is spreading.
>
> 26

Here Stein takes a familiar domestic object – a carafe – and renders it strange: she invites us to see it as an abstract shape or a class of objects ('a kind') which, when decontextualized, might be geometrically comparable to other objects of the same family ('a cousin'), perhaps other bottles or types of glassware. Although she is describing a carafe, Stein thus diverts our attention to an unspecified array of other objects ('the difference is spreading'). A carafe looks like other things but, at the same time, it is also a unique object ('not unordered in not resembling'), marvellous in its irreducible specificity. The phrases 'A blind glass' and 'a single hurt color' tell us that the carafe is full – with red wine, possibly, dark and opaque – but the adjectives ('blind' and 'hurt') Stein uses to convey this endow the scene with a strange emotional quality.

---

[6] Carson also suggests that, because it compromises their ability to take care of themselves, dementia deprives her relatives of their masculine habits, or at least makes them depend on someone else's judgement, turning them into matters of permission or negotiation. For example, once his sister becomes his caretaker, she effects 'a reordering of [uncle] Harry's life. Three meals a day. Clean underwear. No cursing. There were points on which they agreed to disagree like Harry's admiration for starting the day with a tot of whiskey' ('Uncle Falling' 9).

According to American avant-gardist Charles Bernstein, Stein's poems 'elide past and future in favor of continuous presents. As when paintings collapse figures onto ground so that the action of the painting occurs on the same page, without the subordination of perspective, Stein's compositional space, in her most radical works, collapses the separation of viewing and viewed, seer and seen' (85).[7] In other words, her poetry is not 'realistic', in the conventional nineteenth-century sense of the term; it does not try to describe reality objectively. Rather, Stein's objects are constellations of sense and memory impressions. Bernstein notes that 'Meaning [in *Tender Buttons*] is not something to be extracted or deciphered but rather to be responded to (...). The more readers can associate with the multiple vectors of each word or phrase meanings, the more fully they can feast on the unfolding semantic banquet of the work' (88). *Tender Buttons* is not, that is, a mass of information that the reader needs to process but a sort of playground where we can lose ourselves, with very little in the way of fixed rules of engagement. Stein shows us that even the things we think we know best, namely domestic objects and spaces, often dismissed, then as now, as belonging to the sphere of the feminine, are ultimately rich and elusive.

However, if, as Carson points out in her lecture on 'Corners', 'the lure of the abyss can be domesticated' and one does not 'have to hit the ground to experience cornerless space', we can say that in Stein's poetry we encounter at once the abyss of the domestic and a domesticated abyss. While Stein's work may indeed confuse us, hers is nonetheless a controlled sort of confusion, not to be mistaken, as Carson warns in her poem, with a truly traumatic mode of experience, such as that occasioned by dementia. In 'Uncle Falling', the poet brings up the work of choreographer Elizabeth Streb to make the point that the kind of danger we find in art, no matter how extreme, is ultimately very different from that of real life. Streb's dancers practise falling from a great height but, despite the daring and risky nature of their craft, their experience is of a highly controlled sort:

> Elizabeth Streb is a Brooklyn choreographer who teaches her dancers to fall straight down from a height of thirty-two feet, flat on their faces or flat on

---

[7] As we will see, according to Carson, there are similarities between the language of Stein and that of dementia patients. Similar to what happens in a Stein poem, dementia patients are not able to correctly differentiate subject and object: 'Demented people do not seem to experience the self as a shelter. There is some basic animal certainty – that you are who you are and it's ok – that is deleted from them. No more dialectic of inside and outside. You are simply exposed' ('Corners').

their backs or sideways through the air as if flying. They fall as fast as stars and look like gods in an instant. They redeem the shame of falling, an act we usually associate with being very young or very old or very lost or not master of oneself. They bounce beautifully and regather control of their bodies and motions almost at once. To watch them fall fills you with an inexpressible odd longing. Perhaps it is the longing for what Streb calls 'a real move.' Her dancers do not perform this, they imitate it only. 'A real move would rip the flesh off your bones,' she says, 'a human being could not inhabit it.'

35

Carson thus appears to be making the claim that the experience of dementia is of a radically different kind from what we find in works of art that attempt to capture it. This argument is similar to the one philosopher Catherine Malabou makes in her book *The New Wounded*. There Malabou considers patients with various types of brain traumas from Alzheimer's disease and autism to brain injury as 'the new wounded'. According to Malabou, in spite of their different etiological origins, 'they all display permanent or temporary behaviors of indifference or disaffection' (10). Malabou asserts that degenerative brain diseases such as dementia generate a new kind of subject, one that is governed by the death drive and thus by the gradual obliteration of memory and identity.[8] The new subject forged by dementia, she contends, lives death as a form of life. Contra Freud, the philosopher figures traumatic events like dementia as meaningless intrusions of external reality on subjectivity (Freud argued that such events always resonate with our internal reality, namely, in this case, our masochistic desires).[9] According to Malabou, the brain in no way anticipates the possibility of

---

[8] While Malabou's approach is largely informed by the recent development in brain studies, she simultaneously points out that neurobiology fails to sufficiently theorize what she calls the 'destructive plasticity' of the brain – a type of plasticity that destroys its existing form and assumes the very form of this destruction. According to Malabou, clinical works by such neurologists as Alexander Luria and Oliver Sacks fall short of accounting for the radical *rupture* that patients with dementia or brain injury undergo. For Malabou, these scientists cling too much to the idea of 'narrativizing' the disease as she explains, 'Neurology, then, must become a "romantic science" by defining itself as neuropsychology – which would take into account the "biography" of its patients' (186). While commending these scientists for their humane effort, Malabou nonetheless insists upon the necessity of theorizing a 'plasticity without remedy' to fully confront the 'incursion of the negative' that new wounded subjects embody (188).

[9] According to Malabou, contemporary neurobiology fundamentally calls into question Freud's hypothesis that every external shock is 'translated into the language of endogenous events' (Malabou 7) through the intervention of the psychic apparatus governed by a libidinal economy. Contrary to what Freud affirms, the philosopher argues, cerebral damages that affect dementia patients or trauma victims do not take hermeneutic detours through a pre-existing sexual conflict or fantasy. In contrast to sexuality as an aetiological origin of neurosis, Malabou writes, 'cerebrality is thus the causality of a neutral and destructive accident–without reason' (9).

its own destruction. The person that suffers from dementia thus undergoes a transformation that nothing could have prepared him or her for.

In his response to Malabou's theory, Slavoj Žižek argues that that is not the case. To be sure, the demented self may lose all libidinal investment in the world, as Malabou contends, but the subjectivity that results from dementia is not something radically new. Rather, Žižek maintains, it is a more primal/foundational form of selfhood, one defined by negation, albeit not a positive kind of negation (meaningful or formative) like that which makes up the frustrating desires that drive traditional neurotic subjects (I desire not this, not that, but always something else). In his own words: 'The de-libidinized subject effectively is the pure subject of the death drive: in it, only the empty frame of death drive as the formal condition of libidinal investment survives, deprived of all its content' (23). Žižek reproaches Malabou for focusing too much on the traumatic 'content' (a cerebral wound that erases one's memories and personhood) and neglecting the very *form* of subjectivity that in the first place entails the radical negation of any substance (27). There is, nevertheless, some continuity between these two types of negativity, which explains why Žižek opposes Malabou's neat opposition of the pleasure principle vis-à-vis the death drive.[10] For Žižek, a form of pleasure that is purely positive (like, say, a dementia patient's enjoyment of a certain food) is of a different nature from what he calls desire, which always involves an element of negation.

This latter form of positive negativity is visibly on display in Gertrude Stein's poetry, especially *Tender Buttons*, marked as it is by the constant variability of its object of focus, the discontinuity of the observer's attention and her tendency to digress. The syntactic (dis)order of Stein's world, however, has very little to do with the kind of 'word salad' Carson uses to communicate with her sick father. As Malabou points out, the speech of a dementia patient has no revelatory meaning, despite its being mangled and cryptic and thus similar to

---

[10] While Freud speculates about whether there is a 'beyond' of the pleasure principle, as documented in his 1920 essay, 'Beyond the Pleasure Principle', Malabou claims he ultimately fails to formulate it because of his inability to conceive of a pure destruction, what she calls, a 'death of the drive' within the psychic economy. As Malabou explains, 'The limit of psychoanalysis is its failure to admit the existence of a beyond of the pleasure principle. This beyond, which would also be the beyond of all healing, of all possible therapy, never appears in Freud's text' (189). Yet, Žižek responds to Malabou on this point by highlighting that for Freud, the death drive is not another opposing force with regard to the libido or the pleasure principle but it rather indicates a constitutive impasse of the pleasure principle that governs human sexuality.

what we find in an avant-garde text like Stein's. Dementia patients may indeed speak the language of prophecy, but it is of a malignant kind, its negativity no longer a creative and constructive force. As Malabou asserts, dementia's negativity is destructively plastic, in the explosive sense of the word. According to Žižek, patients are reduced to shells of their former selves. Carson makes a similar statement in her abovementioned lecture, highlighting how, although a gradual but nonetheless radical and irreversible transformation has taken place, on the surface everything remains the same:

> The starving brain is surprised. It doesn't know itself or know the world. It keeps arriving at difficulty. Difficulty is dealt with in different ways by different brains. And all of this happens bewilderingly gradually. A common feature is to keep pretending everything is normal as long as possible. You know what daily life is supposed to sound like and look like and taste like. You can put that surface together, keep it running, long after there stops being anything inside. You can act the parts.
>
> 'Corners' n.p.

Contrary to the majority of humanities scholars that do research on dementia, Carson does not appear to see a silver lining in terms of how the disease affects older people and their caretakers. For her, the central issue is not so much how to live with dementia but how to prepare for it, loosening our grasp over those things that provide us with a secure sense of self, the kind of (masculine) fixation with control that is, in 'Uncle Falling', emblematized by the father and the uncle. It is here that Stein's poetry, unpredictable, whimsical and disorienting, might provide a model. If the floor might crumble beneath our feet at any moment, then, at least, as denizens of her fallen feminine world, we might learn how to be better prepared when the time comes to take the plunge.

Bibliography

Bernstein, Charles. *Pitch of Poetry*. Chicago: Chicago UP, 2016.

Carson, Anne. 'Uncle Falling.' *Float*. New York: Knopf, 2016.

Carson, Anne. 'A Lecture on Corners.' CUNY, The Graduate Center, 10 May 2018, New York. Via: https://www.youtube.com/watch?v=CYiMmCLRIQ0 [Accessed March 2021]. Unpublished Lecture.

Fleming, Joan. "'Talk (Why?) with Mute Ash': Anne Carson's *Nox* as Therapeutic Biography." *Biography* 39.1 (2006): 64–78.

Hejinian, Lyn. *The Language of Inquiry*. Berkeley: U of California P, 2000.

Kriebernegg, Ulla. "'I'll never be closer to him than I am in that moment': Dementia and Intersubjectivity in Arno Geiger's *The Old King in His Exile* (2011)." Trent Aging 2019, Trent University, Peterborough, 29 May 2019, Peterborough. Unpublished Paper.

MacDonald, Tanis. 'The Pilgrim and the Riddle: Father-Daughter Kinship in Anne Carson's "The Anthropology of Water".' *Canadian Literature* 176 (2003): 67–81.

Malabou, Catherine. *The New Wounded: From Neurosis to Brain Damage*. New York: Fordham UP, 2012.

Meyer, Steven. *Irresistible Dictation: Gertrude Stein and the Correlations of Writing and Science*. Redwood City: Stanford UP, 2003.

Stein, Gertrude. *Tender Buttons*. Mineola: Dover, 1997.

Žižek, Slavoj. 'Descartes and the Post-Traumatic Subject: On Catherine Malabou's *Les nouveaux blessés* and other Autistic Monsters.' *Qui Parle* 17.2 (2009): 123–47.

Part Three

Masculinity and dementia in film: Between laughter and violence

6

Of bees, boobies and Frank Sinatra: Masculinity and Alzheimer's in contemporary European film comedies

Stefan Horlacher and Franziska Röber

This article examines how masculinity, sexuality, Alzheimer's and older age are conceived of and intertwined with one another in a selection of film comedies, both mainstream and non-mainstream, produced for European and American markets. We ask whether and how traditional Alzheimer's and gender stereotypes are used (but also questioned), what this tells us about hegemonic but also implicit, unacknowledged, and probably alternative concepts of masculinity, and whether there is a trend in films on Alzheimer's away from the perspective of those caring for patients towards narratives that prioritize experiences of the persons living with dementia.[1] If the scripts of traditional hegemonic masculinity are no longer suitable for male Alzheimer's patients, we inquire which alternative scripts are offered, how the relation between Alzheimer's, masculinity/gender identity, maleness, age and sexuality is presented and how the films deal with the paradox that men with Alzheimer's, too, define themselves mainly 'through the most available and accessible avenues legitimated' in heteronormative patriarchal societies, i.e., 'sex, sexuality and male dominance of women' (Hope qtd. in Jackson 2016, 81).

---

[1] Like most scholars, we use the terms Alzheimer's and dementia interchangeably. Dementia is an umbrella term for a variety of symptoms that affect 'memory, other cognitive abilities' as well as '[behaviours] that interfere significantly with a person's ability to maintain their activities of daily living' (WHO 2019). Among various forms of dementia, Alzheimer's is the most common form, contributing to 60–70 per cent of cases (WHO 2019). However, there are no clear-cut lines between the set of symptoms that constitute Alzheimer's or other forms of dementia. As some of the films analysed in this article do not clearly state which form of dementia their protagonists suffer from, we generally assume that the protagonists are suffering from Alzheimer's.

One reason why we focus on the intersection of film comedies, Alzheimer's, sexuality, and masculinity is that comedies have been largely overlooked in gerontological research, given that most films dealing with Alzheimer's belong to the 'serious' and more prestigious genre of drama; a genre which seems to naturally go along with the disease, given that the 'dominant dementia discourse is decline, loss and negativity' (Sandberg 2018, 26). Films on Alzheimer's seem to favour a tragic tone and, more often than not, focus on female protagonists.[2] Portrayals of male dementia patients seem to be few and far between; a tendency which echoes the 'feminization' of Alzheimer's by representing women as the centre of the illness, both as carers and as patients.

The second reason for our focus pertains to the genre itself: While some basic research has been done on the vast majority of films featuring Alzheimer's, i.e., movies such as *The Notebook* (2004), *Iris* (2001), *Mr Holmes* (2015), or *Happy Tears* (2010), films that tackle the motif of Alzheimer's from a decidedly different, i.e., comic perspective, are still the exception. In the face of the (often tragic) portrayal of dementia on screen, however, we argue that the apparent unsuitability of comedy might be the very reason why different and more affirmative approaches to dementia may be found in 'funny' films, as these films, for instance, can invite the audience to adopt a 'laughing-with' and as its consequence a 'suffering-with' position based on inclusion and the notion of our shared humanity.

Forcing audiences to assess characters with Alzheimer's and their situations may help to overcome binary understandings of the illness so that the Alzheimer's patient ceases to be an object to be pitied or even laughed at. Here, again, it is the genre of comedy which lends itself to critical analysis, especially if one takes into consideration that, more than drama or tragedy, comedy (at least theoretically) allows the films to shift away from portraying the illness as a burden which seeks to rob the patients of their agency, and to offer alternative perspectives.

We argue that because of its inherent logic and unique perspective, comedy[3] has the power to challenge hegemonic discourses of stigmatization, isolation,

---

[2] Notably some of the more commonly known and critically acclaimed films such as *Iris* (2001), *Still Alice* (2014), and *The Iron Lady* (2011) are first and foremost dramas, focusing on the struggles and loss of agency faced by those suffering from the illness.

[3] Parts of the following paragraphs are based on Horlacher and Röber 2020; for a more elaborate discussion of comedy and the comic, see Horlacher 2009.

and exclusion. Viewing the often-crushing diagnosis and illness in a humorous light may help to dismantle negative stereotypes by employing 'a special type of communication impossible in everyday life' that 'involves a temporary suspension of everyday norms and anarchically subverts established boundaries', thereby unsettling power structures, 'often making them visible in the first place' (Kamm and Neumann 2016, 6). This unsettling might also help to remove 'the horror and the embarrassment associated with dementia [...] in order to avoid stigma and discrimination' (Medina 2018, 3).

If we differentiate between two fundamental aspects inherent to the comic, firstly denigration or exclusion, which works with the help of contrasts and incongruencies, and secondly, valorization or inclusion, which is liberating and often has recourse to the grotesque, thereby emphasizing the corporeal and the creaturely, then, at least theoretically, comedy can offer the possibility of valorization and inclusion of the repressed, of the marginalized, i.e. of the Alzheimer's patient. Through humour and laughter, comedies can function as powerful instruments of inclusion that challenge and subvert the established orthodoxies, authorities, and hierarchies (Horlacher 2009, 18). Thus, they may reformulate 'for a temporary period at least, socially sanctioned power relationships, bringing the margin to the centre, making it visible and giving it voice' (Stott 2014, 35).

1. Introducing the corpus of analysis

By far the most successful production discussed here is Til Schweiger's *Honig im Kopf* (2014). The film grossed $78,127,384, was seen by 7.19 million viewers, was the most successful movie in Germany in 2014, and ranks as number six among the most successful German movie productions since 1968 (insidekino.com). In this, it fundamentally differs from its American remake *Head Full of Honey* (2018), which was pulled from distribution in the US after only six days (grossing $12,300 in the US and $138,844 in total[4]) and which was lambasted by critics and audiences alike. Though *Honig im Kopf* and *Head Full of Honey*

---

[4] All following box office numbers and grossing numbers are taken from the respective imdb.com pages.

are essentially the same film, albeit with slightly different cultural and national angles, Schweiger's US-remake was derided as 'stunningly awful' (Buck 2019), with an 'idiotic plot' (ibid.), i.e., a 'wildly implausible, overlong jumble' which would have 'required a scalpel, but saw the blunt end of a sledgehammer instead' (Goldstein 2018).[5]

La Finale (2018), directed by Robin Sykes, grossed $4,742,293 worldwide and received mostly positive reviews which lauded its script and intergenerational focus. At the 21st 'Festival du film de comédie de l'Alpe d'Huez', *La Finale* won the 'Grand Prix' and its protagonist, Thierry Lhermitte, the 'Prix d'Interprétation masculine'. The fourth film analysed here, *Vater Morgana* (2010), was directed by Till Endemann and grossed $7,609, rendering it more of a niche film.[6] It was deemed pleasant entertainment (Engel 2010), with the performances of Michael Gwisdek and Christian Ulmen receiving approval overall, while it was criticized for its lack of emotional depth (Schwickert 2010). From a technical perspective, it is probably the most conventional of the films analysed here, relying mostly on slapstick and over-illustrated physical humour.

The films analysed are rather similar in their choice of male protagonists[7] who are 'third agers', i.e., male retirees who, at the onset of their disease, are active, healthy, autonomous, and engaged with and in society, or who have just lost their wives and are confronted with a new and demanding situation. This holds true for Amandus/Amadeus (Dieter Hallervorden/Nick Nolte) in *Honig/Honey*, who is a veterinarian and after his wife's death moves in with his son Niko's/Nick's (Til Schweiger/Matt Dillon) family, and for Roland (Thierry Lhermitte) in *La Finale*. Roland had to give up his brasserie in Paris about one

---

[5] This difference in reception of Schweiger's films could be due to the fact that *Honig im Kopf* retains its provincial character and is not cosmopolitan'. This, together with its overly moralistic undertone and its focus on retaining an uncritical status quo, both of which also characterize its remake, spelled trouble as it became obvious that German audiences were too parochial and 'undemanding' in what they watch. Thus, the film, contrary to how German critics argued, was not 'too demanding for US audiences' (Decker in Landsberg 2019) but simply not sophisticated, innovative or critical enough.

[6] The numbers for *Vater Morgana* might seem, in comparison to the previous examples, extremely low. This is mostly due to its limited release. While *Honig/Honey* and *La Finale* were released in most cinemas nationally and, in terms of *Honey*, internationally and were preceded by a large-scale advertising campaign, both the advertising and the subsequent release of *Vater Morgana* was smaller in scale, with *Vater Morgana* being only released in selected cinemas in Germany before being made available by syndication (programmkino.de).

[7] Given that all of the films analysed focus on a very limited number of specific masculinities which are embodied by male protagonists, and given that this is only a first foray into the field of masculinity and Alzheimer's, this article does not take concepts such as female masculinity or transgender masculinities into account.

year before the main action of the film is set and now lives with his daughter Delphine (Émilie Caen) and her family in Lyon. Though Walther (Michael Gwisdek) in *Vater Morgana* is placed in a nursing home and the use of props such as a cane denote him as 'old', he is nevertheless perceived as an active 'showman', using the nursing home rather as a hideout and more for his criminal and sexual activities than as a place in which he is actually being cared for.

Thus, none of the films follow traditional representations of frail, pitiable Alzheimer's patients in dire need of care; instead, the films feature active and mobile protagonists. With the exception of *Honig* and *Honey* (and both films only devote very few scenes to the final stages of the disease), none of the movies go into any detail on what severe cases or deterioration might look like; presumably both for dramatic reasons and due to the perceived 'intrinsic unwatchability' (Williams et al. 2007, 2) of the later stages of the disease, they rather choose to end on positive or at least harmonious notes.

2. Hegemonic masculinity (revoked), the trickster, and the ability to voice feelings

Raewyn Connell's concept of hegemonic masculinity seems best suited to explain how, in the comedies analysed, the male Alzheimer's patients deal with their predicament, why they adopt certain strategies, and to which degree these strategies mirror extratextual realities. Though 'masculinity varies with both time and place, creating a multitude of masculinities', Bethany Coston and Michael Kimmel argue that 'generally, a dominant model exists – a "hegemonic" definition of masculinity, to which men are expected to adhere' (2013, 192). For the United States, they trace the dominant image of masculinity back to the nineteenth century and identify it as 'the self-made man' who, they argue, is generally known 'for manly stoicism and fierce resolve, he was emotionally impenetrable, an armour-plated machine who showed no weakness' (2013, 192).

These characteristics of what could almost be called an archetypal version of traditional masculinity are by no means limited to the United States and correspond to what Robert Brannon and Deborah S. David define as 'the four basic "rules" of manhood' (Coston and Kimmel 2013, 192; Brannon and David 1976, 1–48). In their rather reductionist categorization, they characterize masculinity as being defined by distance from what is considered to be feminine, and as being characterized by wealth, power, and success, by reliability and stoicism, as well as by risk-taking behaviour and aggression.

For healthy men, but also for men with dementia, concepts of personhood and self are often based on a continuity and stability of gender and sexual identity over the life course; a continuity that is perceived as 'natural' and desirable. While the categories above, thus, still function as guidelines for older men affected with Alzheimer's, in the following we will focus on sexuality as one of the staples of the construction of later life masculinity. Not only do people, at least in the early stages of dementia, 'continue to regard themselves as sexual beings' (Sandberg 2020, 2), but many conceptions of later life masculinity are also traditionally understood 'to be linked to the penis and the ability to gain an erection' so that the loss of virility (and thus sexuality) 'is consequently commonly understood as [...] a threat to masculinity' (Sandberg 2011, 19). As such, older men, in order to be perceived as 'real men', are tasked to conform to a 'play hard, stay hard' mentality which corresponds to a rather Manichaean view, similar to binary understandings of the illness (before/after), of gender (masculine/feminine), and of sex (male/female).

Indeed, sexuality and the expression thereof seem to be a cornerstone in constructing later life masculinities in the films analysed: In *La Finale*, we encounter a *sportif* and good-looking male protagonist who used to run his own business, is used to driving a Porsche 911, and openly alludes to sexuality when his daughter gives him his medication and he jokingly asks whether this is Viagra (00:04:52). Sexuality is also, more implicitly, addressed when Roland is introduced to Juliette, another Alzheimer's patient, three times in a row, with both of them starting to flirt after each successive meeting. On the one hand, the film uses this to create laughter and to make fun of the situation, on the other hand, there is also an openness and a candid quality involved which at least hints at an alternative reality symbolized by the community of Alzheimer's patients on their bus tour. Roland can join them only for a few hours, but the film implies that this is probably where he belongs. Though the film hints at the possibility of a romantic relationship, this is finally negated – as is sexuality, which not only in the logic of this but also in Schweiger's films is still a taboo for the old, the sick, the handicapped.

The funny, but to a certain degree surreal or dreamlike sequence of falling in love three times with the same person and of joining an alternative community is balanced with moments that reveal another side of Roland's character: a side characterized by racist and misogynist tendencies. What becomes evident here is a kind of behaviour already shown in the very first scene of the film when, in his brasserie, Roland thinks that a customer has not paid his bill and he – in a rather unfriendly tone – shows him 'le carton rouge' (00:01:22). Roland clearly stands, or rather stood, for a traditional form of hegemonic masculinity. He is used to being in control, to give orders and to monitor others, and is shown checking his ledgers long after he has sold his restaurant – a scene that mirrors the beginning of the film, thus harking back to his life 'before' the illness.

This configuration of masculinity and the power it comes with is also evident when he explains to his nephew that you have to fight for your right, that power has to be taken ('le droit ne se donne pas, il se prend' 00:40:37). However, 'his right' is linked to his subject position as a functioning male in a patriarchal socio-symbolic order. The moment his disease sets in, Roland starts to lose his specific hold on reality and power until he does not even recognize himself in the mirror and is reintegrated – almost as a child – into the fold of the family, taking over the room of his nephew Jean-Baptiste (Rayane Bensetti), who leaves for Paris.

From the few scenes in which Roland is shown in his brasserie in Paris and the few moments of insight (if they can be called such) where old prejudices resurface, we can conclude that before his illness, Roland represented a rather traditional, white middle-class model of hegemonic masculinity which is now slowly disintegrating. Though he does not show bodily frailties and though there are not many awkward or really embarrassing scenes, he comes across as confused, as losing his grip on reality, as not being in control anymore, not even of himself. His joke on Viagra can be read as a way of dealing with his loss as he has to give up all the symbols which stand for hegemonic masculinity – on his way to Paris he even forgets how to change gears and has to hand over his Porsche to his grandson.

This symbolic 'emasculation' is counterbalanced by misogynist outbreaks, the most noticeable being in a police car where, in the presence of Jean-Baptiste and a male police officer, he starts to guess what kind of sports an accompanying female police officer practices because of her looks and her body. He comes up with a barrage of stereotypes (including badminton, figure skating, and synchronized swimming), and is completely shocked when he learns that she plays football: 'et vous faites comment pour les amorti poitrine? Enfin le foot, faut des couilles' ['and how do you stop a ball – with your chest? Football, well, you need balls to play football'] (00:36:05–00:37:08). However, this outburst does not lead to male bonding, there is no patriarchal dividend, no complicity the men (and the audience) share. Roland's misogynist outburst only speeds up his further isolation so that in Sykes's film, this form of masculinity discredits itself as outdated, racist, chauvinist and vanishing, which, due to Alzheimer's, it indeed is.

Walther, the protagonist of *Vater Morgana*, is one of the few characters who live (more or less) together with a female partner and supposedly retain an active sexuality. He is presented as the 'Frank Sinatra of the nursing home', where he sings to entertain the patients. While Walther is, on the surface, functioning well by, for instance, being dressed elegantly in white, his introductory scene clearly sets up his illness as he forgets the lyrics to the song 'My Way' (00:08:54). This lapse is symbolic and stands for both the setting in of Alzheimer's as well as for a growing dependency on Britta (Ulrike Krumbiegel), his nurse who is also his lover. Though the illness resurfaces again and again in Walther's verbal slips and his lapses in memory, it does not impede him in any other way. Throughout the film, Walther is revealed to be a charming fraud, an elegant womanizer without scruples who flirts with the female patients in the nursing home.

At first glance, Walther's masculinity is in no way subdued or changed by Alzheimer's. Though he becomes less sure of himself and is conscious of his lapses, he is still able to enjoy life, for instance by ordering champagne and oysters for consumption in a bathtub when hiding in a hotel with his son Lutz (Christian Ulmen). Moreover, he is also able to functionalize his illness, i.e. by using his Alzheimer's diagnosis to feign incontinence in order to avoid having to defend himself against his son. Even at the very end of the film, he does not appear as the suffering patient but as the same trickster and charmer he has been right from the start, even making fun of Alzheimer's and celebrating his romantic relationship (01:21:03–01:21:22).

Walther is all shine and very little substance, a charming conman changing from one personality to another, all performance but no core. As long as he performs and is on stage, he is alive, the very embodiment of Pierre Bourdieu's habitus of an 'old school' seductive heterosexual masculinity. This phallic image, however, is perforated and slowly starts to crumble at the margins when the first symptoms of his disease show. This tension between the active womanizer and the vision of the passive recipient of care the film hints at, between being able to plan and commit a crime only to forget where the loot has been hidden, characterizes the film right from the start when Walther, realizing his health problems, alludes to Britta's double function as lover and as nurse:

Walther   Passt du auch auf mich auf wenn ich nicht mehrr ... [Will you take care of me, even when I ...]
Britta   ... auch wenn du mich vergessen hast? [...even when you've forgotten about me?]

Vater Morgana 00:09:15–00:09:25

Walther embodies a very traditional heteronormative masculinity which is conscious of being threatened, transformed, and probably erased. *Vater Morgana* does not really offer an answer to these problems but leaves Walther's fate (as he enters a submarine to flee to Cuba in the end) – just as the consequences of his Alzheimer's diagnosis – ambiguous and ultimately unexplored.

However, there is also another aspect of masculinity and Alzheimer's in this film: Similarly to *Honig* and *Honey*, the disease is functionalized to enable men to talk about their feelings and create a bond between estranged fathers and sons. Right from the beginning of *Vater Morgana*, it is obvious that Walther has been an uncaring and absent father who has the tendency to appear only in order to wreck his son's life. From this perspective, Walther is a threat to his unadventurous, slightly boring son Lutz who is fully aware of this, and almost throughout the entire film refuses to call Walther 'father'. This changes only in the very end when the threat of Alzheimer's combined with – or even symbolized by – Walther's disappearance in a submarine makes it possible for the two men to openly declare their feelings, declare their love: 'Ich liebe Dich, mein Sohn' ['I love you, my son']; 'Ich liebe Dich auch, Papa' ['I love you too, Dad'] (01:19:45–01:20:00).

This is similar to scenes in *Honig* and *Honey* where Alzheimer's virtually destroys power structures and hierarchies linked to hegemonic masculinity and sets men free to give voice to their emotions. Only in moments of acute crisis are Niko/Nick and Amandus/Amadeus able to open up, to acknowledge their feelings, and thus their love for one another: Niko is in tears when his father says:

> **Amandus** 'Ich liebe dich' ['I love you'] (00:58:11).
>
> **Niko** 'Weißt du denn gar nichts mehr?' ['Don't you remember anything anymore?']
>
> **Amandus** 'Nee, alles weg, da ist nur noch n' Loch' ['No, it's all gone, there is only emptiness'] (00:59:08–00:59:25).

Amandus cries and both men embrace, reduced to their bare being and shared humanity, as if the disease enables them to break through the carapaces of their masculinity. Or, in Sarah's (Emily Mortimer) words: 'He's always loved you. But now he can say it' (*Honey*, 01:10:41–01:11:00).

This is somewhat paradoxical since it is finally a disease affecting language and memory that enables the subjects to speak; at least in some of the films, Alzheimer's opens a bridge into the semiotic, the emotional, the non-rational and makes it possible for both, patients and relatives, fathers and sons, to acknowledge and to voice their innermost feelings. In other words: Alzheimer's becomes a means to transfer some kind of 'inner truth of the (male) subject' into the symbolic and thus creates not necessarily a new but an explicit and more conscious kind of knowledge for all concerned.

3. Instead of alternative masculinities: Functionalizing stereotypes

If the episodes in which voice is given to the unspoken are notable in *Vater Morgana*, *Honig*, and *Honey*, it is no less notable that Schweiger's films contain more sexual connotations, and even denotations, than any other of the films analysed here. Especially in *Honig* and *Honey*, sexual connotations are obvious markers of a traditional but outdated kind of masculinity: When Amandus/Amadeus is forced to move in with his son and his daughter-in-law Sarah

(Jeanette Hain/Emily Mortimer), it soon becomes clear that he fancies her, for example when he makes strange – one could also say lewd – clicking sounds every time he regards her photo. Amandus/Amadeus does this while the entire family is present, and later shows the same kind of behaviour when Heidi Klum and, in the US version, Melania Trump are shown on the TV screen. Though Sarah takes offence at his leering, no one else in the family seems to mind, both Tilda/Mathilda (Emma Schweiger/Sophia Lane Nolte) and Niko/Nick even going as far as laughing at his antics, rather than sympathizing with Sarah.

Amandus's/Amadeus's sexually offensive behaviour resurfaces several times, i.e., when he and his granddaughter Tilda/Matilda spend a night in a nunnery on their way to Venice. Not only can Amandus/Amadeus not resist making a dirty (and silly) joke with a cucumber (*Honig* 01:43:40), but when the nuns seemingly do not understand the joke, he insists on explaining it, which Tilda/Mathilda only barely manages to prevent. However, the film alludes to Amandus's/Amadeus's obsession with sexuality and the phallus again when they take leave and he gives one of the nuns a cucumber as a present (*Honig* 1:49:28). What becomes obvious is that this kind of behaviour is not conscious, but rather suggests that his social skills and awareness of societal 'rules', i.e., what is acceptable and what is not, are slowly vanishing. This stereotype of the unrestrained, even lewd Alzheimer's patient is reinforced several times and the film even suggests that this is a common problem for carers and relatives of Alzheimer's patients: When Niko visits a nursing home to find a place for his father, he is chatted up by a female Alzheimer's patient who seems to have worked as a 'dancer' and makes very explicit propositions if Niko were to agree:

Hildegard Wollen wir zusammen ein bisschen ficken? So'n, so'n ganz kleines bisschen? (...) Kannst Du Dir ja mal überlegen. [How about the two of us have a bit of a fuck? Just a teensy-weensy one? Just think about it.]

(...)

Manager Auch der Wunsch nach Sexualität ist ein großes Thema im Umgang mit Alzheimerpatienten. [Yes. Sexuality is a big issue with Alzheimer's patients.]

Honig 01:01:47–01:02:10

Here, in an act of labelling and containment by explanation, the American film version is more explicit than the German version, featuring a scene where the manager explains that this is not only about sexuality but also about 'inappropriate sexual behaviour' which 'can be an issue with Alzheimer's' (01:06:28–01:06:31). When the manager goes on: 'And we would ensure your father is shielded from female attention as far as possible', Nick answers: 'Well. That's the last thing he is going to want, trust me. You might want to shield them from him' (*Honey* 01:07:10). What is troubling here is less that Amandus/Amadeus is – again – presented as a lascivious old man, but the fact that the more obscene suggestions come from a female Alzheimer's patient, casting her in the role of seductress and creating the highly problematical ideological subtexts of 'dancer equals whore'[8] and 'once a whore, always a whore'.

The last impression the film gives of Amandus's/Amadeus's sexuality is him back at home with his family, groping the caretaker's breasts (*Honig* 02:01:56) who finally leaves because of his continued sexual harassment – a mirror image of a scene on the night train to Venice when Amandus/Amadeus enters the wrong compartment of the sleeping car and fondles the breast of an unknown woman (*Honig* 01:19:55) who then shrieks and complains but whose complaint is ultimately dismissed and not taken seriously. This obsession with breasts is introduced early in both movies when, during the church ceremony at the funeral of Amandus's/Amadeus's wife, he openly talks about her big bosom (*Honig* 00:05:16) and, in the American version of the film, jokes 'What bees make milk? Boobies' (*Honey* 00:05:24–00:05:28).

All of these scenes play into the question as to whether the sexual behaviour(s) of Alzheimer's patients are, somewhat categorically, 'inappropriate' or 'improper'. Given Amandus's/Amadeus's tendency to sexually harass nuns as well as nurses, it paradigmatically raises the question of policing and regulating sexuality. What is important for the political subtext of both films is that neither Amandus's/Amadeus's nor the sexuality of the female Alzheimer's patients represents a 'gendered performativity, where the expression of an inappropriate (queer) sexuality challenges or transgresses a heterosexual matrix' (Sandberg 2018, 27). To the contrary, there is nothing new to the sexuality presented here, which never surpasses the unimaginative heteronormative repetition of the *topos* of the dirty old man.

---

[8] The film makes it quite clear that the word 'dancer' is used as euphemism for prostitute, in that it highlights that 'dancer' is only the way Hildegard's daughter paraphrases her mother's seemingly colourful past (*Honig*, 01:02:02–01:02:31).

If Schweiger's films pretend to challenge the discourses of an asexual old age, it is neither to advance the sexual rights of older people nor should the characters' sexual overtures be understood as sincere manifestations of 'embodied selfhood, where masculine and heterosexual styles that have materialised over time persist and shape interactions and continue as a means of expression' (Sandberg 2018, 27). Unless, of course, we argue that Amandus/Amadeus has always been a closet breast fetishist and is now simply acting on it, much in the same way as he enjoys urinating in the family fridge instead of the toilet (*Honig* 00:37:55). Since this interpretation is rather unlikely, it follows that Schweiger's films do not assert the right of Alzheimer's patients to sexuality, but make fun of it by going out of their way to portray Amandus and Amadeus as breast-grabbing dirty old men who flirt offensively, covet their daughters-in-law, harass nuns with 'naughty' jokes, publicly tout the qualities of their wives' breasts and fondle sleeping women. Not only are these actions brushed or laughed off with Alzheimer's being cited as the only possible explanation for such behaviour, but moments which start out as intimate and emotional, such as Amandus/Amadeus searching for his wife while staying in the aforementioned convent, are also ridiculed, as offensive sexual behaviour seems to take precedence over questions of intimacy, love and grief.

While identity, masculinity, and sexuality are social constructs that, with the onset of Alzheimer's, are subject to change so that different and alternative forms of masculinity or sexuality might come to the fore, what *Honig* and *Honey* offer is the resurfacing of old stereotypes – the repeated use of which is revealing about the kind of humour and the misogynist subtexts that pervade the films, but does little to closely examine the male protagonists, their psyches, their suffering, or their need for intimacy.

4. Conclusion

Even if the comedies analysed do break with some of the traditionally negative portrayals of Alzheimer's, i.e., in portraying patients as people with social or sexual needs that transcend care settings, or in representing largely independent, socially-engaged older adults who are neither objects to be ridiculed nor 'lesser men' who are to be pitied, the films nevertheless fall prey to binary and problematic conceptions of older men living with dementia.

In *Vater Morgana*, Walther is portrayed as a sexual being, presenting audiences with another 'sexy oldie' who is more of a playboy than a dirty old man. His behaviour is not inappropriate; instead, he is in a relationship with his carer, and while sexual activity is not foregrounded as it is in Amandus's/Amadeus's case, it is certainly implied to be still taking place. In this case, it is not only the implied sexuality that reaffirms Walther's masculinity but also his choice of partner, as Britta is a much younger woman. This choice of a younger partner is not only a strategy to keep ageing at bay, but also implies that Walther is still able to 'keep up' and stay 'forever functional'. Furthermore, Britta's willingness to stay in a relationship with him, despite age and illness, suggests that she is sexually satisfied and romantically content. However, this stability in their partnership is treacherous, endangered, and probably short-lived. Britta's transformation from lover to nurse and a shift away from a traditional phallic sexuality is hinted at by Walther's significant memory lapses, his symbolic submerging in a submarine, but even more by him asking her whether she will take care of him when he has forgotten her.

At least at first sight, *La Finale* seems to be a little more ambiguous. From time to time, remnants of Roland's former gender identity resurface when his masculinity discredits itself as outdated, racist, and chauvinist, yet the film does not use this to create male complicity or bonding but exposes racist and misogynist tendencies for what they are. *La Finale* does imply Roland's continued attractiveness to women by having a woman who is also afflicted with a form of dementia develop a crush on him. Though this reaffirms his masculinity, the interlude is brief, has a dreamlike quality, and relegates both potential lovers to the sphere of the Alzheimer's community, which is somewhat separate from society. Sexuality is not denied but seems only possible, if at all, in segregation or in a dream world given that the triple falling in love scene is so improbable that it threatens to revoke itself. Since Roland is not (yet) part of this Alzheimer's community symbolized by the bus tour, he re-enters his family by taking up the position, not of the *pater familias*, but of the son. Roland moves into Jean-Baptiste's room and, in the last scene, together with his family and his grandson's peer-group, is watching 'la finale' between France and Brazil and is convinced it is 12 July 1998. Identity, maleness, or masculinity is not a 'problem' anymore if one takes the original TV commentary given in this scene seriously: 'On peut mourir tranquille!' [You can die in peace!] (01:17:44).

Of all the protagonists, Amandus and Amadeus are the most concerned, if not obsessed, with sexuality. However, neither *Honig* nor *Honey* uses the creative space Alzheimer's offers for alternative concepts of maleness or masculinity. Instead, the films reinforce pejorative stereotypes, be it of the lascivious old female 'dancer' or the dirty old man. The predominance of sexuality and (sexual) performance as a constitutive part of later life masculinity, whereby men have to stay 'forever functional and forever willing' (Sandberg 2011, 252), is a notion which has led critics to argue that later life masculinities have at times been exclusively constructed around the struggle for and loss of potency and sexual satisfaction. In accordance with this, the comedies demonstrate that Amandus/Amadeus, Walther, and to a lesser degree Roland (though he explicitly mentions Viagra) are still very much sexual beings, thus perpetuating the idea that sexuality and, by extent, virility are defining features of ageing males dealing with Alzheimer's.[9]

As such, all four protagonists are shown to conform to notions of autonomy, trying to retain most of their capabilities in the face of the illness, and simultaneously serve as examples of how the neurodegenerative impacts of Alzheimer's 'constitute a direct threat to male identities underpinned by the value placed on independence and instrumental competence' (Tolhurst and Weicht 2017, 35). If critics argue that Alzheimer's patients often 'compensate for their perceived loss of manhood by emphasizing other dimensions of that traditional role' (Coston and Kimmel 2013, 195), Amandus's and Amadeus's increasing fixation on breasts, their insistence on telling sexist jokes, and their sexually aggressive behaviour, just as Roland's misogynistic diatribes against women's soccer, could be seen as an expression of this overcompensation which ultimately covers a lack they are only subconsciously aware of.

Though the films analysed portray sexual activity and interest as continuous in spite of dementia, they nevertheless reinforce the idea of such sexual

---

[9] The fact that most of the attributes of maleness the films use refer to stereotypical notions of a very traditional kind of hegemonic masculinity is not really surprising, given that the socialization into masculinity of Alzheimer's patients usually dates back more than half a century. Moreover, most of the comedies analysed are geared towards the European and North American mass market where rather traditional understandings of masculinity prevail, so that a certain conservativeness of their concepts of masculinity should not come as a surprise either.

expression being ultimately ridiculous, mostly inappropriate, somewhat improper, or hypersexual, all of which are terms that are also 'used in scientific accounts and everyday discourses to classify and describe intimate sexual behaviours of people with dementia' (Sandberg 2020, 1). Whereas all films make the point that the scripts of traditional hegemonic masculinity are no longer suitable for male Alzheimer's patients, they are simultaneously presented as the only scripts available for older men. Thereby, the films not only demonstrate the importance of gender identity and sexuality for the protagonists but also their necessity to adapt and to rewrite male gender scripts to better sustain their evolving selves in dementia.

If Alzheimer's undermines 'the traditional equation of masculinity with phallic prowess', it simultaneously points 'to alternative models of being a man' (Armengol 2018, 364). This might be experienced as a challenge, but can also be seen as a unique opportunity for Alzheimer's patients 'to rethink themselves as men' (Armengol 2018, 364). Or, as Richard Ward and Elizabeth Price argue, 'the experience of dementia may actually generate an emancipatory space in which to explore hidden, forgotten, or quite new aspects of self and identity in ways that may not previously have been possible' (2016, 67). But if Alzheimer's may lead to new kinds of agency, to new gender identities and forms of sexuality, this is exactly where the films fall short.

If the comedies portray their protagonists' sub- or unconscious battles with their changing sexual needs and gender identities, this does not become a topic for discussion in the films but is functionalized to conjure up surreal romantic moments or to create laughter and awkward situations: an awkwardness, however, which never veers towards the grotesque or towards black humour but safely stays within the realms of light and easily consumable comedy. Though Walther, Amandus, Amadeus and Roland realize that their health, their living conditions, their subject positions, and also their identity and sexuality are undergoing significant changes, and though they are shown experiencing processes of emasculation, feminization, and infantilization,[10] they are not allowed to seriously reflect on this or to gain insight into what is happening to them. On the contrary: On a deep structural level and without openly acknowledging it, the films make sure that the audience does not

---

[10] See Horlacher and Röber 2020.

identify too closely with the protagonists, lest audiences be confronted with their own potential memory loss and thus, by extent, their own mortality – a thought which could be deeply uncomfortable and potentially distract from the plights and shenanigans of the patients' wider, and ultimately healthy, social network in the films. As such, scenes where serious topics such as memory loss or the ability to voice feelings of love are discussed remain an exception or are bookended by situations that, through their use of humour and laughter, diminish the potential negotiation of intimacy and emotion.

From this it follows that the comedies analysed are more interested in staging the disease than in adequately representing or understanding it. Instead of fathoming the possibilities of what humour and laughter are capable of, the movies prefer to functionalize the early stages of Alzheimer's to spark off laughter and to create comic relief and a 'feel-good' mood for the entire family who might watch *Honig, Honey, Vater Morgana* or *La Finale* on a Sunday afternoon. Repeatedly, the protagonists are kept at a distance so that laughing-at becomes possible while their masculinity is reduced to some sort of awkward phallic sexuality (Amandus/Amadeus). This process follows traditional scripts and stereotypes and is neither productive nor conducive to new insights. Thus, what the films refuse to tackle is the underlying paradox that older men or men with Alzheimer's, that is '[men] with limited or no access to true power or resources', too, define their maleness and/or masculinity/gender identity through 'sex, sexuality and male dominance of women' (Hope qtd. in Jackson 2016, 81).

However, the comedies analysed do not only give away the tragic dimension of their protagonists' predicaments, they also fail to probe the creative potential Alzheimer's as well as the genre of comedy does offer.[11] Neither Sykes's nor Endemann's or Schweiger's films take the risk of inviting the audience to adopt a 'laughing-with' and as its consequence a 'suffering-with position'. As such, they refrain from exploring the possibilities of alternative sexualities, gender identities and narratives for men who are barred from traditional scripts of hegemonic masculinity but are tasked, if not condemned, to perform such scripts nevertheless. Finally, neither later life nor traditional dementia

---

[11] Therefore, the films do not fail because comedy as a genre is unsuited for the topic of Alzheimer's or because of (potentially limiting) generic conventions but because of their conservative conventionality – and probably also because of their being directed at a mass market.

narratives nor, indeed, the comedies analysed here offer persuasive, differentiated representations of – or new scripts for – ageing men, or, even worse, ageing men with Alzheimer's.

Bibliography

Armengol, Josep M. 'Aging as Emasculation? Rethinking Aging Masculinities in Contemporary U.S. Fiction.' *Critique: Studies in Contemporary Fiction* 59.3 (2018): 355–67.

Brannon, Robert, and Deborah S. David. 'The Male Sex Role: Our Culture's Blueprint of Manhood, and What it's Done for Us Lately.' *The Forty-Nine Percent Majority: The Male Sex Role*. Eds. Robert Brannon and Deborah David. Boston: Addison-Wesley, 1976. 1–48.

Buck, Mathew. 'Head Full of Honey.' Letterboxd.com, https://letterboxd.com/film_brain/film/head-full-of-honey-2018/ [17 October 2019].

Coston, Bethany, and Michael Kimmel. 'Aging Men, Masculinity and Alzheimer's: Caretaking and Caregiving in the New Millennium.' *Aging Men, Masculinities and Modern Medicine*. Eds. Antje Kampf, Barbara L. Marshall and Alan Petersen. Routledge: London and New York, 2013. 191–200.

Engel, Thomas. 'Vater Morgana'. *Programmkino: Kinomagazin der deutschen Arthouse- und Programmkinos*, 2010. https://www.programmkino.de/filmkritiken/vater-morgana/

Goldstein, Gary. 'Review: Head Full of Honey is a Sticky Sweet Mess of a Family Drama.' *Los Angeles Times*, 2018. https://www.latimes.com/entertainment/movies/la-et-mn-head-full-of-honey-review-20181130-story.html

Horlacher, Stefan. 'A Short Introduction to Theories of Humour, the Comic and Laughter.' *Gender and Laughter: Comic Affirmation and Subversion in Traditional and Modern Media*. Eds. Stefan Horlacher et al. New York/Amsterdam: Rodopi, 2009. 17–47.

Horlacher, Stefan, and Franziska Röber. '"On peut mourir tranquille!" Functionalizing Alzheimer's Disease from *Wellkåmm to Verona* (2006) to *La Finale* (2018).' *Acta Universitatis Wratislaviensis* 58 (2020): 35–71.

Jackson, David. *Exploring Aging Masculinities: The Body, Sexuality and Social Lives*. Basingstoke: Palgrave Macmillan, 2016.

Kamm, Jürgen, and Birgit Neumann. 'Introduction'. *British TV Comedies: Cultural Concepts, Contexts and Controversies*. Basingstoke: Palgrave Macmillan, 2016. 1–20.

Landsberg, Torsten. 'Why was the German comedy *Head Full of Honey* a total flop?' 2019. *DW. Made for Minds*. https://www.dw.com/en/why-was-the-german-comedy-head-full-of-honey-a-totalflop/a-47856170 [15 January 2020].

Medina, Raquel. *Cinematic Representations of Alzheimer's Disease*. Basingstoke: Palgrave Macmillan, 2018.

Sandberg, Linn. *Getting Intimate: A Feminist Analysis of Old Age, Masculinity & Sexuality*. Gender Studies, Dept. of Thematic Studies, Linköping University, 2011.

Sandberg, Linn. 'Dementia and the Gender Trouble? Theorising Dementia, Gendered Subjectivity and Embodiment.' *Journal of Aging Studies* 45 (2018): 25–31.

Sandberg, Linn. 'Too Late for Love? Sexuality and Intimacy in Heterosexual Couples Living with an Alzheimer's Disease Diagnosis.' *Sexual and Relationship Therapy* (2020). doi: 10.1080/14681994.2020.1750587

Schwickert, Martin. 'Kritik zu Vater Morgana.' *EPD-Film*, 2010. https://www.epd-film.de/filmkritiken/vater-morgana

Stott, Andrew. *Comedy*. London: Routledge, 2014.

Tolhurst, Edward, and Bernhard Weicht. 'Preserving Personhood: The Strategies of Men Negotiating the Experience of Dementia.' *Journal of Aging Studies* 40 (2017): 29–35.

Ward, Richard, and Elizabeth Price. 'Reconceptualising Dementia: Towards a Politics of Senility.' *Lesbian, Gay, Bisexual and Trans* Individuals Living with Dementia: Concepts, Practice and Rights*. Eds. Sue Westwood and Elizabeth Price. Routledge: London and New York, 2016. 65–78.

World Health Organisation. 'Dementia'. *who.int*, 2019, https://www.who.int/news-room/fact-sheets/detail/dementia

Williams, Angie, Virpi Ylanne, and Paul Mark Wadleigh. '"Selling the Elixir of Life": Images of the Elderly in an Olivio Advertising Campaign.' *Journal of Aging Studies* 21.1 (2007): 1–21.

Filmography

Head Full of Honey. Dir. Til Schweiger. Barefoot Films, 2018.
Honig im Kopf. Dir. Til Schweiger. Barefoot Films, 2014.
La Finale. Dir. Robin Sykes. Production Co.: 2425 Films and Union Générale Cinématographique, 2018.
Vater Morgana. Dir. Till Endemann. Prod. Douglas Welbat, 2010.

7

Writing the past to fight Alzheimer's disease: Masculinity, temporality, and agency in *Memoir of a Murderer*

Raquel Medina

Memoir of a Murderer is a 2017 South Korean thriller film directed by Won Shin-yun and adapted from the 2013 fiction novel by South Korean writer Kim Young Ha, *A Murderer's Guide to Memorization*. The film tells the story of Byung-soo, a 70-year-old veterinarian and former serial killer, who lives a quiet life with his daughter Eun-hee, who has cared for him ever since his Alzheimer's disease diagnosis. When Eun-hee brings her new boyfriend home, the young policeman Tae-joo, Byung-soo realizes that Tae-joo is a serial killer as well. To save his daughter, Byung-soo must fight both Tae-joo as well as his forgetting. Therefore, the film's story is constructed and structured around two narrative levels: the film's narrative and Byung-soo's diary writing in which he inscribes his memories (and narrates himself). In addition, embedded within the narrative of the film, Alzheimer's disease becomes a plot device to create suspense by erasing or blurring the limits between reality and fiction. Hence the Alzheimer's disease experience of the main character is used to shape the viewing experience itself; the viewer is never sure if what is presented on screen is Byung-soo's imaginative rewriting/remembering of the past and present or the events as they happened and are happening in the present. The film, with the goal of getting the viewer to identify with the main character, makes the viewer experience memory loss as Byung-soo is experiencing it, adding thereby another degree of uncertainty about reality.

Film and TV series in which dementia is a plot device have shown a clear tendency to masculinize crime narratives as spaces in which the forgetting minds of the detectives or criminals still shelter the intelligence and agency to resolve a crime or to redeem themselves (Cohen-Shalev and Marcus 2012; Medina 2018). There is a vast discussion among film scholars about the differences between mystery and crime film, their subgenres (Rafter 2000), the viewer's expectations (Leitch 2002), and the difference between crime, a metaphor for social unrest, and thriller, in which an isolated event takes place (Clarens 1997). The same problem occurs when trying to define thriller or film noir. Frank Krutnik (2001,17) stresses the trans-genre quality of film noir, hence his preference for using the term 'tough' thriller, which is used for those films centred on a male hero who is involved either in the investigation of a crime or in the crime itself (Krutnik 2001, 24). Likewise, the 'tough' thriller 'reveals a particular obsession with the representation of masculine identity and male cultural authority' (Krutnik 2001, 25). Within this 'tough' thriller term, the psychological 'tough' thriller is also found (Krutnik 2001, 18), which can be succinctly defined as a story usually told from the point of view of characters experiencing psychological problems and thus depicting their mental state and perceptions.

Nikki J. Y. Lee and Julian Stringer (2013) pin down the post–Second World War period as the time when many US and European genre films were finally released after the hiatus occurring during the Second World War. Following this trend, South Korean filmmakers started to make films with thriller elements to distance themselves and their films from melodrama, the most popular genre of the period. From this point onwards, crime/action-thrillers became very popular in South Korea. Since the 1960s, thrillers in all their subgenres have been produced in great numbers, in all subgenres, and with big box-office success. In fact, as Jinhee Choi (2010) points out, thrillers allowed the advent of the blockbuster phenomenon in South Korea at the turn of the century and after the 1997 IMF crisis.[1] As will be discussed, thrillers were conceived as a means for restoring masculinity in Korean cinema and subsequently in South Korean national identity.

Among the most recent filmmakers combining thriller and masculinity is Won Shin-yun. His first horror film was *The Wig* (2005), followed by action-thrillers such as *A Bloody Aria* (2006), *Seven Days* (2007), *The Suspect* (2013), and *Memoir of a Murderer* (2017). His last two films, *Fifth Column* (2020) and *The Battle: Roar*

---

[1] South Korea signed an agreement with the IMF to address the financial problems resulting from the 1997 Asian financial crisis that affected much of East Asia and Southeast Asia in July 1997 and lasted until the end of 1998.

to Victory (2019), combine period action and the military along with crime plots. Following the path of the recent Korean thriller success, Won Shin-yun directed *Memoir of a Murderer*, where he employs one of the aspects of the psychological thriller: to follow the state of mind of the character, thus focusing on the individual's subjectivity and not so much on the plot. *Memoir of a Murderer* is an example of a thriller in which masculinity, male authority, and the individual's state of mind and subjectivity are core for the understanding of the film within the context of the remasculinization of South Korean cinema (Kyung Hyun Kim 2004) after the so-called 'IMF crisis' in 1997.

In this chapter, I examine *Memoir of a Murderer* from three perspectives. First, the film is analysed as an ethical reflection about violent masculinity (Peberdy 2011) within the context of the remasculinization of South Korean cinema. This ethical reflection is deployed through the remembering and then writing about the crimes that the retired serial killer committed with the intention of justifying the ethical (and patriarchal) reasons behind those killings (his father's sexual abuse of his sister and physical violence against him; the adulterous wife; etc.) and trying to redeem himself by stopping Tae-joo's killings of innocent women. That is, Byung-soo's masculinity and the patriarchal role men have in South Korea are reflected through his role as both the protector and punisher of women. Secondly, the paradoxical effect Alzheimer's disease has on the retired serial killer will be explored: memory loss allows him to first remember his past and then to memorize it through writing, which in turn permits him to narrate himself. Finally, this chapter will show how this memorization, as reflected in the circularity of the film and its ambiguous ending, acknowledges that forgetting that something has happened can help to maintain one's temporality: Byung-soo's forgetting of having killed Tae-joo (recent past) drives him to preserve his own life (present), instead of committing suicide because his goal is still to hunt down Tae-joo (future).

1. Violent masculinity and the concept of the 'eternal recurrence of the same'

The Korean War (1950–3) resulted in an image of an emasculated and weak Korean male. This emasculation was fought with the implementation of a state-enforced public discourse that presented a militarized masculinity (Chungmoo Choi 1998). During Park Chung-hee's dictatorship (1961–79) and the Vietnam War, a concept of masculinity that was anchored in the notions of nation and duty in both the military and economic spheres was created. This masculinization of the Korean male was later reinforced by a buoyant labour market that allowed men to become successful and empowered (Elfving-Hwang 2017). The masculinization of employment defined Korean men as the family providers, hence strengthening the Korean patriarchal social system and relegating women to the domestic sphere.

However, the 1997 Asian financial crisis severely affected South Korea and produced a high rise in unemployment rates and consequently a crisis of patriarchy. The loss of employment evolved in a new emasculation of the Korean male and family provider that, in return, according to Joanna Elfving-Hwang,

> was used to legitimate the perceived necessity of supporting the existing gendered structures, which in turn repositioned women into the domestic support roles or into 'flexible workforce' thought to benefit the nation and society at large by safeguarding the normative family.
>
> 2017, 57

Elfving-Hwang notes how by the early 2000s a new type of 'soft' masculinity surfaced in Asia that popularized the so-called 'flower boy': androgynous males who became very popular among young and middle-aged women. This new kind of 'soft' masculinity, according to Elfving-Hwang, was perceived by the political and social establishment as a threat to Korean masculinity (2017, 58).

The tension just described between masculinization and emasculation seems to have defined the role of men in South Korea in the last seventy years. As a result of the historical traumas that South Korea as a nation experienced, Miyoung Gu argues that South Korean cinema has embraced the representation of a post-traumatic father that is characterized mainly as violent and sacrificial, and emerges as a metaphor of national identity in films produced in the last fifteen to twenty years (2020, 73). Gu classifies the different types of father presented in these films: the poor father, the homemaking father, the desperate father, the gangster father, the salaryman father, the brutal father, the criminal father, and the sacrificial father, among others (2020, 75). Similarly, Gu claims that 'Korean films exhibit a trend of strengthening the position of the father, thereby increasing male solidarity by representing the crisis of masculinity in terms of men who have lost their patriarchal authority' (2020, 75).

Y. N. Kim (2010) has analysed the figure of the violent father in South Korean film as the method of representing the collapse of the family and the victimization of the patriarchal figure due to either social injustice or the deceit of the state. Nonetheless, as Gu highlights, violent males, instead of directing their violence in the direction of the state (the perpetrator of their trauma), direct it towards female figures: mothers, wives, daughters, girlfriends, etc. (2020, 78), whose disobedience to patriarchy is highly sexualized and needs to be punished.

Memoir of a Murderer presents on screen at least three generations of male characters whose commonality resides in their innate violent behaviour towards women. Thus, the thriller offers from the beginning a conscious depiction of a reflection about violent masculinity. Through the writing of his memoirs, the retired serial killer starts remembering his crimes and aims to justify the ethical (and patriarchal) reasons behind those killings: the constant sexual abuse by their father that Byung-soo's sister has to endure; the brutal physical violence against him and the mother; his adulterous wife; and the danger his daughter, Eun-hee, is in by befriending the young policeman Tae-joo, whom the 70-year-old Byung-soo believes to be a serial killer as well.

The viewer learns in the opening scenes of the film that Byung-soo's father came back home from the Vietnam War in 1971. The military boots, as well as his characterization as a ferocious domestic abuser against all the members of the family, directly link his violent masculinity not only to the masculinization of war but also to the transposition of brutal violence from war to home. The opening scenes introduce a young Byung-soo who suffers and witnesses the violent abuses of his father against all members of the family. The father's characteristic violent personality is based on his military status by showing both his boots and his uniform (he wears it even while asleep) as prominent symbols. In clear contrast to the violent masculinity symbolized by the muddy and stiff military boots, Byung-soo's soft white sneakers embody the gentle and non-violent masculinity that he wishes for himself. The white sneakers, later worn first by his daughter Eun-hee, and then by Byung-soo himself at the end of the film, turn out to be a symbol of a desired but unachievable male purity. Although Byung-soo has witnessed the brutal abuses against his mother and sister and has also been viciously abused, he loses his tolerance when he finds out that his father has destroyed his white sneakers. That is, the trigger of Byung-soo's killing of the father is not an episode of domestic violence but the destruction of his white sneakers, which symbolize his future aspirations.

Although the killing of the father seems to be justified in Byung-soo's mind as the consequence of the former's violence against wife and daughter, it is also important to highlight that placing the ultimate motive of the killing into a material object enhances the perpetuation of violent masculinity. Even more, this motive displaces domestic violence and portrays it as a family and private matter[2] (Heo 2010, 227). Tae-joo's depiction follows the same pattern with regard to the reification of the motive that impelled him to kill, but a generation later. In his case, this third generation seems to place on the mother the cause of the killings. Tae-joo's mother assaulted him when he tried to kill his father in order to stop him from physically abusing her. The mother, contrary to any expectation, defended her husband and attacked her son, causing Tae-joo to lose part of his head after being hit with an iron. Despite the unrealistic touch surrounding the character of the young policeman (he has a prosthesis to cover the missing part of his head that can be removed anytime), the iron comes to symbolize femininity and therefore equates it to violence as well, but violence in a domestic space dominated by the female figure. The violent nature of Tae-joo is shown as justifiable by presenting it as the consequence of his mother's abuse. Moreover, Tae-joo's physical appearance follows the androgynous pattern of the 'flower boy' that is only overcome and masculinized when violent behaviour occurs.

Memoir of a Murderer presents killing as something innate to some men. For Byung-soo killing his father made him realize that 'obligatory murder existed in our world. I continued to kill after that day. That was not murder; let us call it cleansing. There were plenty of people who deserved to die, and I started to clean them from this world.' Saving the world from depraved people is Byung-soo's ethical justification for his serial killings which he remembers in

---

[2] It was not until 1997 that the South Korean government passed the Prevention of Domestic Violence and Victim Protection Act and the Special Act on the Punishment of Domestic Violence Crimes.

short and fragmented sequences. Although Byung-soo's memory is failing and he cannot remember many things about his past, he claims that 'my head may be losing its memories, but my hand remembers like an old habit'. By locating killing as a habit that survives in the body, the film associates murder with an embodied instinct that allows the old serial killer to recognize and hunt down other serial killers despite memory loss.[3]

From this point onwards, memory loss due to Alzheimer's disease becomes a twofold plot tool: on the one hand, it serves the purpose of creating tension and doubts around what is, in fact, real or just the product of Byung-soo's imagination and memoir writing; on the other hand, it enables the character to reflect on the ethics of killing in a corrupted society. In addition, and related to writing, Byung-soo attends poetry lessons in which he is capable to express the sublime emotions of killing. Within this context, Nietzsche's famous lines from *Thus Spoke Zarathustra*, 'all that of which you speak does not exist. There is no devil and there is no hell. Your soul will be dead even sooner than your body: fear nothing henceforth!' (2003, 13) recited by the poetry teacher[4] infuse the film with Nietzsche's discussions around concepts such as the *Übermensch*, 'God is dead', and the 'eternal recurrence of the same'. Thus, these three concepts are the philosophical pillars that sustain the thriller both at the formal and content levels. On the formal level, the circularity of the film connects with the concept of the eternal recurrence of the same, whereas the main character, despite his illness and old age, is constructed as a person who can overcome his deficits and infinitely returns to murder. On the content level, Nietzsche's concepts permeate the ethical reflections deployed by the film, as well as the actions narrated: Byung-soo is depicted as an *Übermensch* whose memory loss permits him to save his daughter from the hands of another serial murderer to continuously redeem himself and to project himself in the future regardless of

---

[3] Drawing on Bourdieu's habitus, Pia Kontos and Wendy Martin (2013) consider the body as the place where discourse is inscribed, and subjectivity is constituted. Eric Matthews (2006) indicates that aspects of identity are sedimented in the body's habits and consequently persist despite severe cognitive impairment.

[4] Eun-hee enrols his father for adult poetry lessons because she has read that poetry helps people with dementia to engage with others and to keep focused. In fact, it is interesting to note that poetry also becomes a focal point in other South Korean film, *Poetry* (2020) by Lee Chang-dong. Beyond the middle-age flirting male poetry teacher, both films illustrate the corruption of the police force, the patriarchal nature of society, and the violent masculinity impregnating South Korea. Likewise, both films highlight poetry as an intense and emotional way of communication that people with dementia seem to master.

the circularity of time. Like Zarathustra, Byung-soo acknowledges that all events in one's life will happen again and again. Within this context of the eternal recurrence, Byung-soo wishes the return of his murderous instinct embodied in his hands and symbolized by the white sneakers. As shall be explored later, his will allows him to emerge victorious (at least in his mind) from his fight against a young and healthy Tae-joo, while his memory loss warrants him to return to the beginning. In consequence, stopping Tae-joo from killing again, as well as exposing the corruption and the inefficiency of the police force, become some of the ethical justifications for Byung-soo to resume killing.

2. Memorizing and forgetting the past

Reacting to his daughter's request to use a voice recording device to remember the things he needs to do, or the things he has already done, the first words spoken by Byung-soo in the film are: 'That is why I write in my journal. Remembering yesterday is pointless.' Through his writing, the audience, and Tae-joo within the film itself, learns that he had been diagnosed with Alzheimer's disease three months before he had started writing the journal. As will happen many times in the film, Byung-soo's voice-over is telling the story while he is shown typing it into the computer. The viewers can read his writing on the screen as he types, action that is quickly followed by the images of the scene as he is recalling it: that is, the audience is made to follow the process of (volatile) remembering, making it permanent (writing), and then re-imagining the past.

Byung-soo's decision to write his memoirs does not seem to respond to the need of changing any intradiegetic readers' attitudes towards him and the horrific crimes he has committed. Although he explains the reasons for becoming a murderer, the goal is to capture his long-term memories to narrate himself, to maintain his identity, and to not forget his acts. Contrary to what scholars have highlighted about confessing murderers' life-writing (Lovitt 1992), the 70-year-old veterinarian has no intention to re-enter society as he had already done so by stopping killing seventeen years before he starts writing his memoirs. In addition, he shows very little remorse and, therefore, the only judgement he fears is that of his daughter. Byung-soo's life-writing has not the intention to present a justification of his killing beyond his beliefs that his killings responded to innate male instincts, social corruption and vulgarity. Life-writing in this film allows the person living with Alzheimer's to memorize his long-term memories when they start to disappear, so he does not commit any unnecessary mistake and kill again. In the same way, the voice recorder is employed as a short-term memory aid that assists him with his daily life and his investigations of Tae-joo's murders. Hence, the journal and the voice recorder machine become both a sort of prosthetic memory that permits him to keep long and short-term memories at hand and, as a result, to maintain his agency. Similar to what Martina Zimmermann has argued with regard to dementia patients' life-writing, this film proposes an 'illness presentation that matches their attention span, live within their remaining abilities, and, thus, authoritatively claim their continued independence' (2017, 21).

Byung-soo's journal writing becomes a tool to emphasize the lack of correlation between words and actions. When a new killing is covered in the TV news, Byung-soo quickly reacts by checking if his white sneakers are dirty, a sign that could mean that he has started killing again and he does not remember. For instance, after stating that he is glad to be able to work as a veterinarian even with dementia, he unwillingly kills a cat with an overdose of medication. Immediately after the scene of the poetry lesson, Byung-soo tells/writes about and shows the viewer his last killing, seventeen years before the time of the narration. He claims not to remember why he killed that woman, but he remembers burying her and then having a car accident, which he considers to be the reason for his dementia. His memory then seems to be affected not by forgetting the vivid details but by losing the reasoning behind his actions. The latter assigns credibility to Byung-soo's dementia, but this credibility is many times neutralized by other moments in which his cognitive impairment does not seem to be a problem for understanding/justifying his behaviour. This constant play between remembering and forgetting, and between reasoning and not understanding the motive of his actions, drives the viewer slowly not to trust the old man's narrative. Thus, every single element in the film is directed towards creating disbelief of Byung-soo's storytelling. His memories are fragmented and unreliable, but the viewers do not know if the cause is truly dementia or if he is deceiving them through his journal writing.

Curiously enough, the old veterinarian's killings and lack of emotions work to write poetry about killing. As he will say, 'killing is poetry'. His poem about killing flawlessly describes his actions when dismembering the bodies and the stains caused by the blood of his victims. Asked by one of his classmates what metaphor is, he replies by saying 'it is a comparison'. At this point, the viewer understands that the old man's way to narrate himself is based on the comparison he makes between himself and those other men around him. The three generations of men presented on screen are comparable to each other because they are all inherently violent; they are all killers. In Byung-soo's mind, Tae-joo's murders are comparable to his: women are normally the victims, they are dismembered and buried in the woods. Tae-joo's killings are comparable to his; similarly, Byung-soo's violence against women resembles the actions of his father.

As the cognitive impairment progresses, the character of the daughter, Eun-hee, becomes pivotal to the plot, thus standing as not only the enhancer and subject of her father's memory loss and the resurgence of the killing habit linked to the memory of the hand, but also of his final 'redemption'. Byung-soo's fragmented memories become even more disjointed as the film progresses, with short-term memory gaps that last longer and make him violent towards his daughter. Likewise, he starts to experience hallucinations which complicate furthermore the plot and the viewer's understanding of what is happening; the viewer can only guess their true nature when the same scene is shown from the perspective of another character. As his memory vanishes, Byung-soo's killing habits reappear stronger and more frequently; he even tries to strangle his daughter because in his mind (a mind living in his long-term past) she was a loose woman. But paradoxically, dementia is also presented as the retrieval of traumatic memories, such as happens with the suicide of his sister whom he has kept fictionally alive as a nun in his hallucinations. The same goes for his last killing, which he finally remembers as that of his unfaithful wife, a moment in which he also learns that he is not the biological father of Eun-hee.

The traumatic memories retrieved make Byung-soo believe that he is the perpetrator of the recent killings in the area, subsequently confessing his past murders to the police. His attempt to change the role of the killer for that of a detective while having all the above-mentioned memory problems is exploited by Tae-joo, who has covered up his killings as the ones by Byung-soo after reading his memoirs. This role reversal is the turning point for Byung-soo's change in terms of cognitive skills as presented to the audience. More importantly, this reversal of roles intensifies the audience's doubts about Byung-soo's memory. On the one hand, the old veterinarian is now capable of remembering very specific details such as the precise time and place of some events, the blood type of the blood recovered from Tae-joo's car after the accident, etc., although he still needs to record them in the voice recording device. On the other hand, after the audience learns that Tae-joo has found Byung-soo's journal in the computer and is reading its content loud while keeping Byung-soo captive, both the audience and Byung-soo are made to wonder if Tae-joo has somehow altered the memoirs or if all the memories that the 70-year-old man has been writing have already been distorted due to his memory loss and hallucinations. Once more, however, his daughter and the voice recorder become crucial elements in restoring Byung-joo's agency and self: on the one hand, she finds in the voice recorder that Tae-joo confesses to having covered up his killings and that she is his next victim. On the other hand, listening to her recorded voice stops Byung-joo committing suicide and, by doing so, allows her father to hunt down Tae-joo.

The ending of the film takes the audience to the very beginning of it and without making explicit if Byung-soo has killed Tae-joo or if it has just been his imagination/hallucination. Tae-joo's picture is not only carried by Byung-soo, but he (and the viewers) can see Tae-joo looking at him while Byung-soo's voice-over says 'Do not trust your memory. Min Tae-joo is still alive.' If Tae-joo is still alive, Byung-soo has a purpose to live for and to continue to narrate himself, and therefore memory and agency are preserved – despite Alzheimer's disease.

3. Dementia: Time and temporality

Repetition and recurrence are two aspects of temporality that *Memoir of a Murderer* aesthetically and thematically presents, hence departing from the definition of time as a progressive structure that establishes a linear ordering of past-present-future. This linearity determines that time is usually experienced and understood in its chronicity. From a philosophical perspective, temporality has been explored from many perspectives but always as a notion of how time is understood. McTaggart in 'The Unreality of Time' in 1908 claimed that time is unreal and the notion of time as a continuum is an abstraction. However, he also stated that our perception of temporal order is based on a linearity that conceives the past as being always earlier, the future as being always later, and the present as being always a temporal position that is at all times earlier or later than some other temporal position. Close to the conception of time is Paul Ricoeur's (1984) understanding of the narration of a story: the story progresses sequentially by starting frequently in the past, continuing to the present, and normally arriving at a resolution while moving on to the future. Hence, in order for a story to make any logical sense, the reader/viewer has to be able to perceive the cohesion of the story and to believe the conclusion.

The film seems to be formally constructed around a structure that replicates the memory deterioration of the person living with dementia. Thereby, flashbacks, circularity, repetition of events, white and black screens and abrupt cuts are all used to parallel symptoms of the disease such as repetitive behaviour, memories that are constantly recollected, memory gaps, loss of short-term memory, achronological storytelling (among others). In addition, all these techniques and themes are employed in the film to create not only suspense but also to impel the viewer to identify with the main character's loss of temporal orientation. However, this loss is finally transformed into temporality by employing repetition as a temporal indicator of time progression instead of time stasis.

For instance, repetition is the main structural factor in the film. Sequences are repeated across the film in no chronological order, although in some cases they add an element to assist the viewer in understanding Byung-soo's psychological state of mind. Likewise, repetition of a concrete body response to a psychological state of mind is used for instance with the main character's nervous twitch of his right eye every time his embodied memory of a killer takes over his cognitive functioning. Although this twitching is presented in the first scene of the film, the audience will not realize that it is used to warn them that Byung-soo's killer persona has taken over until he recalls wanting to kill his daughter after the car accident. The repetitive and fragmented nature of the film makes of it a sort of jigsaw puzzle that the viewer, along with Byung-soo, is impelled to solve in a progression of time. Solving this puzzle is what generates a possible future.

Fragmentation of memory and achronological storytelling in people with dementia is one of the main issues explored in the film. Hence, the notion of time and temporality in *Memoir* permeates everything, from characters to objects and spaces; everything and everyone is charged with temporality or its problematization. In the film, contrary to general understanding, forgetting that something has happened is to maintain one's temporality: Byung-soo's forgetting having killed Tae-joo (recent past) drives him to preserve his own life (present) instead of committing suicide because his goal is still to hunt down Tae-joo (future).

As the previous analysis of the fragmented nature of memory in the person living with dementia has shown, the temporality deployed in *Memoir of a Murderer* problematizes the sequential character of temporality. In this sense, the film addresses the culturally and socially constructed notion of dementia as a condition of progressive decline, thus predicting an unavoidable absence of the future. As has been addressed earlier on in this chapter, Nietzsche's concept of the eternal return is not only made explicit in the film during the second poetry lesson but seems to have been consciously used as the structural element of the storytelling: the film starts and finishes at the same point in time and place. This recurrence, whether triggered by Byung-soo's dementia or not (repetitive memories) confers to the old veterinarian's existence by generating his subjective impression of time passing. Byung-soo's journal writing indicates both the inscription and understanding of the past from a present in which the progression of time towards a future seems to be vanishing. Therefore, in order to maintain temporality and consequently his existence, Byung-joo's repetition of memories always leads him to return to the same starting point. However, this return makes possible the concept of future, even if repetitive, and Byung-joo's own existence. That is, his forgetting murdering Tae-joo grants Byung-soo the possibility of continuing to hunt him down and, as a result, generates a recurrent future time that can repeat indefinitely.

The repetitive character of memory and of time in a person living with Alzheimer's disease are also replicated at the formal level with the use of the same type of camera angles, shots, light, and colours. Similarly, mirroring the fragmented nature of memory in a person living with dementia, the film is constructed in fragments that sometimes do not follow a chronological order or which are showing Byung-soo's disjointed perspective and subjectivity. These sudden jumps recreate the memory gaps of the person living with Alzheimer's disease and are normally either presented through long fades to black or just instant cuts. The editing enables switching from the subjectivity of the character to an objective camera that shows what is happening, and thus has a double effect: on the one hand, it creates confusion in the viewers, who are subsequently unable to distinguish between reality and imagination; and, on the other hand, viewers are prompted to also experience the subjectivity of the character emotionally.

4. Conclusion

Memoir of a Murderer is a complex film that brings together different cultural and social issues related to contemporary South Korea. Following the conventions of the psychological thriller, the film presents a story that revolves around violent masculinity in patriarchal South Korea and the limitations of memory. The three generations of men presented in the film are all depicted as inherently violent due to their dependence on a patriarchal society that influences their actions and social roles. All three men are defined by their violent masculinity that resulted from the effect of social and political matters: Byung-soo's father's violent behaviour is presented as a result of the Vietnam War, while Byung-soo's violence is justified by himself as the normal consequence of his father's abuse. His subsequent killings are justified to himself based on the corruption that permeates society: prostitutes, adulterous women, womanizers, alcoholics, etc. Despite this explanation of his killings, Byung-soo also admits that killing has become a habit linked not to the mind but to the memory of the body. In Tae-joo's case, he adheres to the new look of feminine or soft masculinity, although this new look only disguises the existence of a violent masculinity. In fact, his killings are again justified by the harm made by an abusive father and a mother who accepted the abuses as normal behaviour.⁵ His soft masculinity is shown to be at odds with his profession, his killings, and his sadistic behaviour. Hence, with respect to both characters, the audience is positioned to make moral judgements about whether some killings are acceptable due to the traumatic events that impelled the killers to commit them. In doing so, the film places the audience in a very contentious position as empathy towards Byung-soo may be felt by some viewers. This empathy is constructed through the comparison and contrast between Byung-soo and Tae-joo. Byung-soo, despite all his killings, is depicted as a weak old person with memory loss and hallucinations who requires his diapers to be changed and his shoes to be laced. The weakness of this character due to age and cognitive impairment is contrasted with Tae-joo's youth, strength, and beauty. However, the unequal fight between the two murderers makes evident that youth and strength are not sufficient qualities to be a good killer, and therefore it makes the viewer feel empathy towards the older character.

Alzheimer's disease is employed in this film both as a plot device and as a philosophical discussion around the notions of time and temporality as experienced by the person living with dementia. In accordance with societal expectations of what a person living with dementia can and cannot do, the successful narrative articulation is positioned as 'central to the perception of identity, social assertion and self' (Zimmermann 2017, 75). Memory loss due to Alzheimer's generates suspense because of the absence of a 'normal' narrative articulation. It also makes the viewer take an active role in discerning whether what is shown on screen is real or just a defective memory or a hallucination. Similarly, the limitations of memory presented in the film as lived by Byung-soo are depicted at two levels: firstly, forgetting long-term memories prompts the old veterinarian to write his memoirs, while short-term memories are captured in a voice recorder. Secondly, it makes the character and the viewer question whether recollections are based on hallucinations and therefore

---

⁵ It will be important that future research on this film addresses the place and roles assigned to women. A feminist approach to the film would most probably uncover a clear patriarchal concept of the role of women in South Korean society and the dangerous influence that capitalism may inflict on them. Therefore, despite being sexually, physically, and psychologically abused by men, women are either depicted as adulterous, flirtatious, and highly sexualized, or as mothers, daughters, and nuns. Similarly, this film can also be approached from the role played by carers of people living with dementia.

faulty. By writing his memoirs, Byung-soo is not only inscribing his past but also allowing himself to narrate himself within time, as well as assigning temporal status to his lived experience. Likewise, repetition is employed as a temporality notion linked to Nietzsche's concept of eternal return. It is this notion that warrants temporality to Byung-soo's existence, regardless of his forgetting the past.

Memoir of a Murderer places the audience in a very unstable position in terms of understanding what is real and what is just the product of Byung-soo's cognitive impairment. It is this unpredictability about twists and turns of the plot that not only creates suspense, but also reflects the lived experience of the person with Alzheimer's disease and those caring for them. In this way, the person living with Alzheimer's disease in the film claims his independence and his quality as an authoritative narrator who emerges victorious despite his cognitive impairment.

Bibliography

Choi, Chungmoo. *Dangerous Women: Gender and Korean Nationalism*. London and New York: Routledge, 1998.

Choi, Jinhee, *The South Korean Film Renaissance: Local Hitmakers, Global Provocateurs*. Middletown, CT: Wesleyan UP, 2010.

Clarens, Carlos. *Crime Movies*. Ed. Foster Hirsch. Boston: Da Capo Press, 1997.

Cohen-Shalev, Amir, and Esther Marcus. 'An Insider's View of Alzheimer: Cinematic Portrayals of the Struggle for Personhood.' *International Journal of Ageing and Later Life* 7.2 (2012): 73–96.

Elfving-Hwang, Joanna. 'Aestheticizing Authenticity: Corporate Masculinities in Contemporary South Korean Television Dramas.' *Asia Pacific Perspective* 15.1 (2017): 55–72.

Gu, Miyoung. 'Paternal Masculinity in Korean Films.' *Transcommunication* 7.2 (2020): 73–92.

Heo, MinSook. 'Women's Movement and The Politics of Framing: The Construction of Anti-domestic Violence Legislation in South Korea.' *Women's Studies International Forum* 33.3 (2010): 225–33. https://doi.org/10.1016/j.wsif.2010.01.005

Kim, Kyung Hyun. *The Remasculinization of Korean Cinema*. Durham, NC: Duke UP, 2004.

Kim, Y. N. 'Salvation and Punishment, the Arrival of New Father [Gu wongwa eoung jing, saelowon abeojieui deung jang]'. *Cine Forum* 11 (2010): 5–36. Available from: http://www.dbpia.co.kr/journal/articleDetail?nodeId=NODE01651782

Kontos, Pia, and Wendy Martin. 'Embodiment and Dementia: Exploring Critical Narratives of Selfhood, Surveillance, and Dementia Care.' *Dementia* 12.3 (2013): 288–302.

Krutnik, Frank. *In a Lonely Street: Film Noir, Genre, Masculinity*. London: Routledge, 2001.

Lee, Nikki J. Y., and Julian Stringer. 'Film Noir in Asia.' *A Companion to Film Noir*. Eds. Andrew Spicer and Helen Hanson. London: Blackwell, 2013. 477–95. DOI: 10.1002/9781118523728.ch28

Leitch, Thomas. *Crime Films*. Cambridge: Cambridge UP, 2002.

Lovitt, Carl. 'The Rhetoric of Murderers' Confessional Narratives: The Model of Pierre Riviere's Memoir.' *Journal of Narrative Technique* 22.1 (1992): 23–34.

Matthews, Eric. 'Dementia and the Identity of the Person.' *Dementia: Mind, Meaning and the Person*. Eds. J. C. Hughes, S. J. Louw and S. R. Sabat. Oxford: Oxford UP, 2006. 163–77.

McTaggart, J. Ellis. 'The Unreality of Time.' *Mind* 17.68 (1908): 457–74. JSTOR, www.jstor.org/stable/2248314 [23 October 2020].

Medina, Raquel. *Cinematographic Representations of Alzheimer's Disease*. Basingstoke: Palgrave, 2018.

Merleau-Ponty, Maurice. *Phenomenology of Perception*. Translated by Colin Smith. London: Routledge and Kegan Pau, 1962.

Nietzsche, Friedrich Wilhelm. *Thus Spoke Zarathustra: A Book for All and None*. Translated by Thomas Wayne. New York: Algora Publishing, 2013.

Peberdy, Donna. *Masculinity and Film Performance: Male Angst in Contemporary American Cinema*. Basingstoke: Palgrave, 2011.

Rafter, Nicole. *Shots in the Mirror: Crime Films and Society*. Oxford: Oxford UP, 2000.

Ricoeur, Paul. *Time and Narrative*. Translated by Kathleen McLaughlin and David Pellauer. Chicago: Chicago UP, 1984.

Zimmermann, Martina. *The Poetics and Politics of Alzheimer's Disease Life-Writing*. Basingstoke: Palgrave, 2017.

Filmography

Memoir of a Murderer. Dir. Won Shin-yun. Green Fish Pictures, 2017.

Part Four

Perspectives on masculinity and dementia in memoirs and fictional narratives

8

Stories of exile and home: Dementia and masculinity in Arno Geiger's *Der alte König in seinem Exil* and Ian Maleney's *Minor Monuments*

Michaela Schrage-Früh

1. Introduction

Dementia epitomizes the cultural fear of old age since its typical symptoms of cognitive decline are often equated with the loss of personality and a person's 'social death' (Hartung 2016, 179; cf. also Trevitt 2006, 109). This fear is illustrated by Sinéad Gleeson's drastic comments in an essay about her aunt's dementia: 'I fear losing my mind more than I do dying. I'd take a shark attack and falling from a height and being stabbed before I'd take my mind being hijacked and replaced with clouds. I would take another round of cancer over untreatable dementia. [...] I'd take that over my family watching my personality, my memory, me drift – unreachable – to the bottom of some sea' (Gleeson 2019, 223–4). Gleeson's essay poignantly articulates the widespread horror that a diagnosis of 'untreatable dementia' equals death in life. Hers is the perspective of a grieving family member comparing her cognitively impaired aunt to the person she was '[b]efore illness stole her from us' (Gleeson 2019, 224). Gleeson's view, however, is surely also shaped by the predominantly negative 'sociocultural construction of dementia' (Zeilig 2013, 258), including popular metaphors that dehumanize and stigmatize people living with the disease as mindless zombies or 'living dead' (cf. Behuniak 2011, 71), turning them into 'strange, and even frightening, others' (DeFalco 2010, 54). Yet, as Arno Geiger notes, 'Kein Demenzkranker ist wie der andere, oft sind Verallgemeinerungen heikel, jeder ein Einzelfall mit eigenen Kompetenzen, Empfindungen und eigenem Krankheitsverlauf' (96). ['No two people affected by dementia are alike, and any generalisations are problematic. Those affected by the illness remain essentially unfathomable, each of them a particular case with his or her own abilities or feelings, in whom dementia takes a different course' (94)].[1] Accordingly, a number of recent memoirs seek to provide more nuanced accounts of the impact the disease can have on both the person living with dementia and their closest relatives. While not eschewing the pain, struggle and loss entailed by a family member's cognitive decline, Austrian writer Arno Geiger and Irish writer Ian Maleney strive to document an older man's progress into Alzheimer's disease by foregrounding his unchanged personhood, gendered self, and embodied, relational subjectivity.

Written from the son's and the grandson's point of view respectively, Geiger's *Der alte König in seinem Exil* (2011) [*The Old King in His Exile* (2017)] is set in rural Austria, while Maleney's *Minor Monuments* (2019) is rooted in the rural region of Ireland's Midwest. In view of their respective father's and grandfather's dementia, both authors share the need to preserve in memory and writing 'something that cannot be replaced' (Maleney 2019, 95). Their concern is not only for the personal loss of their respective father's and grandfather's individual life stories, but also for a vanishing communal, rural way of life which, as the narratives suggest, facilitates person-centred care. In taking on the roles of chronicler, and, to a lesser extent, carer, they also embark on a self-exploratory quest for identity, facilitated by their renewed, changed and intensified relationship with their respective father and grandfather. In both texts Alzheimer's disease is metaphorically linked to experiences of exile and emigration and is explored in the contexts of home and place, shifting family, community and gender constellations, and the authors' own search for identity and belonging in a world unsettled by a paternal figure's cognitive decline. Their accounts also shed light on constructions of hegemonic masculinity embodying 'ideals of physical ability, independence and self-reliance and the dominance of doing rather than being, activity rather than passivity' (Ribeiro et al. 2007, 304) as these ideals collide with older men's realities of living with

---

[1] References from Geiger's and Maleney's texts are incorporated in brackets in the running text. With regard to Geiger, the German original from 2011 is cited first, followed by Stefan Tobler's official translation into English (2017) in square brackets.

dementia and relying on care. Both authors find value in caring for their parent or grandparent and in their self-assigned roles as chroniclers of their father's or grandfather's life story in terms of both its individual and cultural significance. In doing so they write against 'the cultural mainstream narrative of Alzheimer's disease', which is a narrative 'heavily loaded with stigma, as it centres on fears of caregiver burden, dependence, passivity and vulnerability' (Zimmermann 2017, 4). They thus counterbalance the narrative of decline as epitomized by the public image of age-related dementia with much-needed person-centred stories and images that engender emotional connection, identification and empathy rather than fear, alienation and distance.

2. Arno Geiger's *Der alte König in seinem Exil*

Arno Geiger's memoir starts out with a childhood memory of his grandfather, who, when Arno was six years old, stopped recognizing his grandson. It is significant that Geiger notes how he *forgot* this memory until, many years later, his own father was diagnosed with Alzheimer's disease. Forgetting is natural, it is human, yet certain forms of forgetting are stigmatized more than others. And, indeed, in Geiger's account of his own father's slowly and at first almost imperceptibly advancing dementia, the disease is presented in terms of a hostile takeover (20). This image of a patient's defencelessness resulting in inevitable defeat seems incompatible with the son's image of his father's personality and social role: 'Jahrelang war mir dieser Gedanke nicht einmal gekommen, das Bild, das ich vom Vater gehabt hatte, war dieser Deutung im Weg gestanden. So absurd es klingt, aber ich hatte es ihm einfach nicht zugetraut' (25). ['For years the thought hadn't even crossed my mind. My childhood image of my father blocked it out. As absurd as it sounds, dementia was the last thing I expected from him' (25)]. His father, August Geiger, seems to share this perception of himself as he initially glosses over his forgetfulness, preferring his family's increasing irritation with him to their sympathy or help. The disease contradicts everything August Geiger stands for, personality traits such as his self-reliance, skilfulness and work ethic as well as his role as a parent, and inevitably reshapes the father–son relationship. And yet, in his account of the continually evolving relationship with his father, Arno Geiger challenges the widespread notion that the illness destroys a person's self, thereby reversing his initial view expressed early on in the book: 'Die Persönlichkeit sickert Tropfen für Tropfen aus der Person heraus' (12) ['A person's personality trickles out, drop by drop' (13)]. Instead, he gradually comes to realize that his father's personality remains largely intact, untouched by the disease, even though his memories slip away. As Geiger notes, his father 'hatte seine Erinnerungen in Charakter umgemünzt, und der Charakter war ihm geblieben' (73) ['had transformed memories into character, and his character remained' (72)]. Geiger's account thus provides a compelling testimony to 'the father's unbroken identity within dementia' (Zimmermann 2017, 63) and subtly redefines the widely accepted notion that we are the sum of our *memories* by suggesting that we are really the sum of our *experiences* – regardless of whether we remember these experiences or not. This realization is in accord with the view that 'a basic subject of experience exists apart from memory, perception, language, intelligence and that this self continues to exist even in the presence of the depredations of dementia' (Oyebode and Oyebode 2017, 113). As Elizabeth Barry explains, '[h]abit and embodied memory can allow for forms of sociality that can, among other things, express attachment and sympathy, produce situational humour, tease, clown, and follow quite complex conversational conventions, even in the absence of autobiographical memory' (2020, 134). The insight that a person's self is embodied and not necessarily tied to his or her autobiographical or narrative memory is also reflected in the book's structure, for, as Zimmermann notes, 'Geiger's decision to alternate chapters relating the father's past with those telling of current cognitive difficulties frames his view of the coherence maintained between the father's past personality and in his present illness' (2017, 67). Geiger thus refuses to conflate the patient with his or her illness and challenges the view that a person living with dementia is merely a shadow of their former self, an empty shell or, as Gleeson puts it, 'a grainy facsimile of who [they] used to be' (2019, 222).

In doing so, Geiger does not ignore the pain and distress caused by a disease that leaves his father periodically disoriented and upset as he fails to recognize his son, forgets how to eat, believes himself to be a stranger in his own house or feels threatened by and acts out against his well-meaning carers. Early on in his memoir Geiger acknowledges: 'Da mein Vater nicht mehr über die Brücke in meine Welt gelangen kann, muss ich hinüber zu ihm' (11). ['As my father can no longer cross the bridge into my world, I have to go over to his' (13)]. This realization implies an attitude of empathy, imagination and open-mindedness on the son's part which, in turn, facilitates insight into a condition that seems to epitomize (self-) alienation and decline. Recognizing the unchanged personhood of a person living with dementia requires meeting them on their own terms, regardless of society's norms and expectations, or as Geiger puts it with respect to his father, 'innerhalb der Grenzen seiner geistigen Verfassung [wo] er noch immer ein beachtlicher Mensch [ist]' (11) ['within the limits of his own mental state [where] he is still an impressive man' (13)]. Accordingly, as Heike Hartung notes, Geiger 'depicts his father's decade-long suffering from Alzheimer's disease in an empathetic way that focusses on his fashioning a new relationship with the father rather than concentrating on the losses' (2016, 212). However, despite narrating his father's life story and journey into Alzheimer's disease from the point of view of a son and partial caregiver, Geiger avoids appropriating his father's voice, instead filling the pages in between chapters with short dialogues between father and son, in which his father's personality and wit shine through without requiring further comment, analysis or interpretation. The father's self is thus recognized and sustained 'in social interactions with others' (Sandberg 2018, 27) and he is at least to some extent afforded the role as co-author of his life narrative (cf. Sandberg 2018, 27).

Nonetheless it is the son who takes on the roles of chronicler and interpreter of his father's life and mental condition. His father's life story is thus inevitably filtered through the son's perceptions and narrative choices and the images he draws on to illuminate his father's mental condition seek to bridge the gap between those living with dementia and those not afflicted with the disease.[2] If the zombie metaphor dehumanizes the person living with dementia as a mindless and emotionless walking corpse, precluding empathy or even sympathy, the analogy between dementia and exile has the opposite effect. The human need for a home is a universal experience that most people will share

---

[2] While exile is the central metaphor in the text, Geiger offers other ways to facilitate an imaginative and empathetic understanding of the disease by comparing the condition to temporary states such as the moment between sleeping and waking or the immersion in absurd fictional worlds such as those created by Franz Kafka.

and be able to relate to. For August Geiger this need is particularly poignant as his formative experience is his trauma of war captivity as a young man. According to his son, this traumatic experience determined his father's life choices and priorities based on his central concerns: 'Zuhause, Sicherheit, Geborgenheit' (82) ['home, safety, security' (81)]. The family home that he started to build in the 1950s and that he continued to expand and improve throughout his life bears testimony to this deeply rooted need. According to Geiger, his father decided to get married to his mother primarily to provide her with a home. The house as his life-long project also testifies to the father's self-taught and idiosyncratic skills as architect and carpenter, which in turn signify his masculine self-image as his family's protector.[3] The book's title describes the father as an exiled king, thus suggesting that his – in this case – benevolent rule has been forcefully ended, that he has been deprived of his power to protect his family and himself behind the walls of his 'castle'.

Recent studies emphasize the importance of acknowledging the unchanged gender identity of people living with dementia (cf. Ribeiro et al. 2007; Boyle 2017; Tolhurst and Weicht 2017; Sandberg 2018). While Geiger repeatedly emphasizes his father's lack of paternal authority – 'Trotz des Altersunterschieds spielte sich der Vater nie als Herr- und Haushaltsvorstand auf' (84) ['In spite of the difference in my parents' ages, my father made no pretence about being the head of the family' (84)] – as well as his lack of ambition to assert his masculinity (78), he also points out how August Geiger remained faithful to the values of the tight-knit rural community in which he grew up and where he spent all his life, favouring stability and security over opportunity and happiness (77). As Geiger notes, 'Er war fest davon überzeugt, dass es Männer- und Frauenarbeit gibt' (84) ['He firmly believed that there was man's work and woman's work' (84)], and he was content to be stuck in 'den alten Gewohnheiten seines dörflichen Daseins' (87) ['the old habits of his village life' (86)]. This includes the father's firm refusal to take his family on holidays or even to accompany his newly-wed wife on a walk in the woods in lieu of a honeymoon (82). Geiger provides psychological explanations for his father's refusal to travel by referring to the trauma of his war captivity, yet his father's lack of consideration for his

---

[3] Geiger describes how his father repeatedly goes in search of his four young children he fears have disappeared from their beds or asks whether he will be able to take his family with him when he goes 'home'.

wife's and children's wishes is clearly in line with the characteristics typically attributed to traditional notions of masculinity according to which a father provides a home and income for the family rather than emotional care. The reader learns that, in line with ideas of masculine self-reliance and toughness, it was not in August Geiger's emotionally withdrawn character to open up to his family about his fears caused by the first signs of dementia (21). This also indicates a masculine personal strategy of stoical 'acceptance of circumstances' (Tolhurst and Weicht 2017, 31). Even in the later stages of his disease, August Geiger is presented as being preoccupied with expectations around performance, self-reliance and productivity, all of which would be associated with hegemonic masculinity. In conversations with his son, he repeatedly comments on his sense of failure in old age and his resigned, apologetic exasperation about his lack of strength and performance is a recurrent theme throughout the text: 'Weißt du, bei mir ist nichts mehr los, ich bin schwach, ich bin leistungsschwach, das hat sich so ergeben. [...] Ich bin leider einer, der nicht mehr tüchtig ist.' Dann setzte er sich zu mir an den Tisch und legte den Kopf auf die am Tisch verschränkten Hände' (116–17). ['You know, nothing's going on with me. I'm weak, I achieve little. [...] Unfortunately, I'm no good at anything anymore'. Then he sat down at the table and lowered his head unto his folded arms' (111)]. And yet, the father's recurrent concern with and emphasis of his past strength and achievements also serve 'as an assertion that he has met the moral standard of economic distribution to wider society over his lifespan' (Tolhurst and Weicht 2017, 33). This assertion of a sense of masculine continuity between his former and present self is illustrated best in the playful activity of arm-wrestling in which August Geiger puts all his strength to show his son that while he may not be as strong as he used to be, he is not a '*Pappenstieler*' (136) ['peanut' (129)] either.

Nevertheless, Geiger describes how his father, fully aware of his need for assistance and care, welcomes the help offered by his – typically female and Eastern European – carers and has a good rapport with some of them, a compliance which might again indicate a 'reorientation of masculine qualities' in the form of 'stoical' acceptance (Tolhurst and Weicht 2017, 34). However, the relationship between the father and his carers seems to work best whenever he is entrusted with a sense of responsibility and agency. Thus, he acts out violently against carers who treat him like a child or try to enforce his cooperation (132;

125–6). In contrast, his favourite carer Daniela successfully discourages him from leaving the house to 'go home' by arguing that she needs his company (119). As Geiger notes, Daniela also makes a point of thanking his father, even when she is the one doing him a favour, 'das baue ihn auf, dann sei er zufrieden' (120) ['It built him up, left him contented' (115)]. She gives him tasks such as teaching her German grammar or carrying the shopping, a strategy which contributes to the father's sense of well-being. As Trevitt notes and as Geiger's account of successful ways to communicate with his father illustrates, 'there needs to be an emphasis on understanding the world of the person with dementia; on communication that can tap into the "inner core of being" of the person with dementia; and, thoughtful strategies to manage the most disturbing behavioural challenges in a setting that is caring, secure and meaningful' (Trevitt 2006, 109). This is only possible in familiar surroundings, where the person living with dementia is known and his or her personality understood, as is also the case in the care home where August Geiger resides when caring for him at home is no longer possible: 'Dort [im dörflichen Seniorenheim] kennt man den Vater, und nicht erst, seit er krank ist. Dort sieht man in ihm die ganze Person, jemanden mit einem langen Leben, mit einer Kindheit und Jugend, jemanden, der den Namen August Geiger vor mehr als achtzig Jahren bekommen hat und nicht erst mit Beginn der Krankheit' (133–4). ['The village's home for the elderly is staffed by trained professionals, working in good conditions. [...] And they had known our father before he became ill. In the home, they see him as a whole person, someone with a long life, including a childhood and youth, someone who has been August Geiger for more than eighty years and not just since his illness' (127)].

It is presented as a particularly cruel twist of fate that August Geiger, who spent his entire life creating a secure home for himself and his family, comes to experience feelings of exile and homesickness even within the objective safety of his own home. Yet Geiger comes to realize that his father's perpetual feeling of exile is a symptom of the disease that cannot be assuaged by familiar surroundings or reassurances that the place his father does not recognize is still his home (12; 15). Instead, it is '[die tiefe] Heimatlosigkeit eines Menschen, dem die ganze Welt fremd geworden war' (55) ['the utter homelessness of a person for whom the whole world has become foreign' (55)] that prevents him from feeling safe and at home. By making exile the central metaphor of his narrative, Geiger finds a way to make sense of the disease not only in the context of his father's personal life story but also in a broader cultural context, viewing the disease as symbolic of people's disorientation in a globalized world that they may find increasingly difficult to grasp and navigate. Viewing his father's condition through the lens of this shared human desire for a sense of home and belonging on the one hand and the modern condition of living in a disorienting, globalized world on the other facilitates empathy and understanding (57). He also understands that there are ways to provide his father at least temporarily with a sense of home and security regardless of his physical surroundings, for instance by singing familiar folk songs with him, thus creating 'ein Zuhause außerhalb der greifbaren Welt' (14) ['a home outside the tangible world' (15)].

In the course of the memoir, the father's memory loss is attributed with facilitating a caring, emotional and uncomplicated connection between father and son, unburdened by former conflicts (72). The father's vulnerability thus facilitates the emergence of a '[r]elationship of care [...] which is free from the idea of a performance-orientated, dominant or competitive masculinity' (Tholen 2018, 401). August Geiger may not remember that Arno is his son but he reminisces about the importance of his family and his children in particular when he, for instance, refers to the happiest time of his life as the days when his children were young (cf. 75). It appears to be the first time that the father expresses his paternal love for his children in such an open way, a fact in no way diminished by his failure to recognize his adult son. Geiger, too, finds ways to open up to his father, for instance in a poignant scene in which he takes his father's hand and tells him he loves him (184; 177). While the former father–son relationship is described as having been conflict-laden, casual and superficial (99; 97), this relationship is being gradually redefined by the father's advancing illness. As Geiger repeatedly notes, he starts feeling closer to his father and to genuinely enjoy his company. He finds ways to have deeper conversations that do not rely on shared memories but on what Trevitt calls 'spiritual reminiscence' which 'asks questions about meaning in life, joy, sadness, grief and regrets' (2006, 125). This re-acquaintance between father and son also brings to light formerly unsuspected commonalities, for instance when the writer-son marvels at his father's knack for creative and witty wordplay (99).

The importance of Arno Geiger's memoir in counterbalancing narratives of decline, othering, and loss of self cannot be underestimated. There is value, his account reminds us, in even this most cruel of experiences, there is the possibility to experience moments of closeness, content, and happiness, and there is a chance to heal strained, broken or estranged relationships. Despite the changed relationship, in which the son takes on the role as partial carer of his father, he acknowledges and presents his father as a complex and multilayered human being: 'Wenn ich mich frage, was der Vater für ein Mensch ist, passt er manchmal ganz leicht in ein Schema. Dann wieder zerbricht er in die vielen Gestalten, die er im Laufe seines Lebens anderen und mir gegenüber eingenommen hat' (185) ['When I ask myself what my father is like, at first he fits easily into a type. Then he once again splinters into the many shapes that he took on over the course of his life for myself and others' (178)]. His father, then, is valued and acknowledged as a 'self that expands into other lives' (Barry 2020, 132), regardless of his inability to remember and narrate the previous and multiple manifestations of this self.

3. Ian Maleney's *Minor Monuments*

Ian Maleney's essay collection *Minor Monuments* shows many parallels to Geiger's memoir. Maleney's focus is on his grandfather, John Joe, and, as the grandson who only occasionally visits his family, Maleney is even less actively involved in his grandfather's care than Geiger is in his father's.[4] Yet both narratives resort to similar images, most crucially the metaphor of exile, to explore and make sense of a condition that uproots their own and their families' lives. Both focus on their family member's advancing disease in the context of a tightly-knit but vanishing rural community and, in doing so, both embark on a self-exploratory quest for identity, which leads them back, and allows them to reconnect, with the rural home they left behind.

Not unlike Geiger, Maleney struggles with the role reversal implied by the fact that his disoriented grandfather is now in need of his grandson's care and

---

[4] Both authors acknowledge that the actual care work is done by almost exclusively female family members and paid carers.

guidance. Witnessing the effect of his grandfather's beginning dementia for the first time, Maleney recalls: 'John Joe had been, until this point, an authority figure in my life. In some ways, he was *the* authority figure: John Joe could tell even my father to do something and expect it to be done. Seeing him like this – confused, out of place, violent – I no longer had a clear idea where I stood with him. The positions we had always assumed were now reversed' (55). Yet in some ways the disease also brings Maleney closer to his grandfather as he has to relearn the relationship. Like Geiger, Maleney comes to understand that he has to meet his grandfather on the terms dictated by the disease, following him on 'whatever winding paths he was gravelling in his mind that afternoon' (56) in order to create a sense of familiarity, security and home even in an anonymous hospital setting: 'It was my job to recognise him for who he was, and to give him the tools with which to recognise himself in that alien environment. The nurses, for all their strength and kindness, could not make him feel at home. [...] He needed a mirror, someone to say: here you are, I see you' (62–3). John Joe's masculine identity is closely linked to his work as a farmer and it is the conversation about everyday work on the farm, such as bringing in the turf from the bog, that helps him calm down after undergoing surgery and waking up to an unfamiliar hospital setting. In a later scene in which Maleney keeps his increasingly demented grandfather company in his grandparents' kitchen, his grandfather assumes that Maleney works for Bord Na Móna, a turf-processing company, like he did years ago. Maleney describes this misunderstanding as a 'life-saver' (97) as, for a while, his grandfather's interest is kindled, memories are sparked and a lively conversation ensues: 'We could talk as adults about work, and this felt like a miracle' (99). As Tolhurst and Weicht note, '[r]ecalling former endeavours can enable men to assert their former contributions, even when the dementia has limited their current levels of activity' (2017, 33). In fact, John Joe's significant decline in health is captured in a scene that signals a complete loss of interest in his lifetime's work when some cows break out and John Joe, rather than taking charge of the situation, stands at the front door of his house, 'like an oblivious child at a funeral, singing his playful, happy songs like he didn't have a care in the world' (133). This description reveals how the disease has shattered the grandson's image of his grandfather, how, in his perception, the authority figure in his life has been reduced to the image of a carefree child.

Maleney lives a life in Dublin that could not be more remote from his grandparents' and parents' everyday life on the farm in their midlands community. It is through engaging with his grandfather's condition that he is brought back in touch with the rural way of life, if only by writing about it and visiting his family home more often. As he notes, 'I somehow became caught up in my grandfather the way one gets caught in rain. The rural, family life which had seemed before to be a restriction and a limitation became, to my surprise, an opportunity, and then an obsession' (63–4). As in Geiger's memoir, the grandparents' house assumes a central role both in the text and in Maleney's imagination. While his grandfather's disease has upset the securities and certainties of childhood, the house itself becomes a bulwark, 'the strongest shelter I have experienced against time's many corrosions' (41). Unlike August Geiger, John Joe did not build the house but inherited it from his own father, but the fact that he shaped the place with 'his hands' (231), 'lived his whole life in his father's house and never even left the country' (69) provides an important parallel in both life stories. August Geiger and John Joe also share the formative experience of exile, although John Joe's life has been impacted by his siblings' emigration rather than his own. A central memory explored in the text, and one that John Joe retells and treasures as his other memories are fading, is how his sister Chrissy emigrated to America at the age of fourteen. His memory of bidding her farewell turns into the central and most poignant moment of his life. As Maleney explains, if the memory came to his mind, 'he would sometimes be moved to tears' (74). Even though it turns out that Aunt Chrissy's memory of the event and its significance fundamentally differs from and contradicts John Joe's version, the emotional salience of this memory of emigration takes on symbolic meaning in the grandfather's own struggle against a dementia-induced sense of exile and loss. Regardless of the fact that his memory of the event turns out to be 'mostly fiction', it becomes the memory encapsulating 'a life's worth of regret, love, and shame', and a memory that stays with him 'when most other memories had vacated his mind' (77).

The theme of exile is further explored when Maleney describes how John Joe, as his disease advances, clings to folk songs, many of which are about the Irish emigrant experience and most of which he still remembers and sings along to. Just like Geiger, Maleney suggests that the emigrant experience is an apt metaphor for Alzheimer's disease:

As the past grew more distant and foggy in his mind [...] the songs became more important and accurate too. They were a link with that past, that foreign country, even as they dramatised the experience of losing it. John Joe sang like a man whose boat was filling rapidly with water. He had a very wide ocean to cross, one he could not swim over.

128–9

As in Geiger's memoir, the image of exile and emigration, deeply ingrained in the Irish collective consciousness, serves to create a sense of empathy and identification. The songs are also tied to a lifetime of nights in 'the dark and smoke-filled backrooms of local pubs' (128), where community life takes place in the Irish countryside, and while these memories may no longer be verbally accessible to John Joe, the songs still help to anchor him in this familiar social context when, at the end of a song, he asks his grandson 'with as much heart as he could muster, *Get that man another pint!*' (128). While his identity as a farmer seems to vanish, John Joe's 'anchor', until the end of his life, is his wife Kathleen, on whom he relies completely: 'He needed her to be there, and without her he was lost' (79). The grandfather's gendered identity is thus tied to his identity as a husband. Even towards the end of his life when 'he had forgotten almost everything', he still remembers 'scraps of melody' alongside his wife's name, 'hidden in that part of the brain where treasures are kept' (24). These treasures signify his embodied self that persists even in the absence of a narrative memory and that surfaces on certain rare occasions treasured by the family. For instance, a comical remark made by John Joe leaves the whole family 'bent double, crying laughing' (209) in recognition of this glimpse of the grandfather's personality, having reemerged 'from the very depths of his soul' (209). Another poignant instance is the last photograph Maleney takes of John Joe, the last one in which he looks 'himself' and which shows 'the accumulation of life that coheres in the image of the body, the way the past is written into his presence there' (197). Like Geiger, then, Maleney comes to understand the continuity of his grandfather's embodied self even in the more advanced stages of his disease.

Not unlike Geiger's account of his father's dementia, Maleney's essay collection narrates his own quest for identity as deeply intertwined with the exploration of his grandfather's disease. This connection is captured by his realization of the 'uncanny' similarity between John Joe and himself when in the hospital he notices that his grandfather's naked legs, 'almost the legs of a child' (50), look like his own: 'Sometimes I find myself just sitting there, staring at my own feet and thinking of his' (50). His quest to record his grandfather's life, 'to listen hard to his final emergence; to capture his life in the last stage of its becoming – to record that person still forming even as he began, contrapuntally, to unravel' (64), is torn between frustration when his 'hopes of retrieving meaning and significance from the situation were thwarted' (134) and the growing realization of an 'ethical demand' to recognize the person with dementia, to both see and hear them: 'As the usual bonds of recognition and connection are broken – as memories fall away, as activities become impossible, as conversation is reduced to silence – there remains the burden and duty of saying: *I see you*' (214). As Fiona Murphy puts it in a review of the book, 'In the final essay, Maleney suggests community and co-dependency should be valued and cherished. He concludes that to care for someone requires listening – deep, attentive listening – like the red light of a recorder switching on, even when there are gaps and spaces and voids' (2019). This realization implies that, while a person with advanced dementia may be considered 'a person who has no value at all' (177) in a world focused on usefulness and productivity, this person is still very much of value in terms of their relational and intersubjective identity. John Joe remains a valued part of both his family and larger community and he lives on in the communal memory even after his physical death. Thus, on the night of his grandfather's wake, Maleney sees 'the depth of his life reflected in the people who came through the house that evening, the incremental patterning of eighty-three years spent in one place growing richer with every arrival' (228). For Maleney, this realization is bittersweet as he considers that he is no longer an integral part of this vanishing community and has not achieved what his grandfather did during his lifetime: the creation of a home, a place within a community that recognizes and sees a person even if this person can no longer recognize themselves.

4. Conclusion

In both Geiger's and Maleney's memoirs, the journey of documenting the progress of Alzheimer's disease and preserving the rapidly vanishing memories of the person living with dementia yields various insights into the grandfather/grandson and father/son relationship as well as into the complexities of personhood. Both Geiger and Maleney acknowledge and unflinchingly explore the cruelty of the disease and its effect on both the person living with dementia and their carers. At the same time the authors insist on the unchanging personhood of the dementia patient despite and beyond the disease. Even though the men's gendered social roles change due to their dementia diagnosis, as they become dependent on care and largely restricted to a domestic setting, it is obvious that their masculine identity remains an important part of their selves, their assertions of their embodied masculine identity confounding social expectations and repositioning. However, by taking on the role of partial carer and refashioning the relationship to their father or grandfather beyond their role as a paternal authority figure, both Geiger and Maleney gain insight into the self as intersubjective and relational, concepts that would traditionally be aligned with feminine characteristics as well as with life in a close-knit rural community.

By focusing on the person and their life story both authors avoid reducing their beloved family member to a disease, focusing instead on their personhood as being grounded in their embodied, intersubjective, and relational self. In doing so, they also stress the need for person-centred care, as provided in both the Austrian and Irish rural community settings. Moreover, they draw on the metaphor of exile and emigration to facilitate a better understanding of the condition and to create empathy and identification. Both narratives suggest that even in the final stages of the disease the father or grandfather living with dementia can still teach his children and grandchildren valuable lessons about old age and dementia (Geiger 136, 130). In this sense the person living with dementia turns into a mirror to the son's and grandson's own potential future self. It is ultimately the exposure to the realities of ageing and disease, too often hidden away in anonymous institutions, that can facilitate a person-centred approach both in private and public care settings. Moreover, by intertwining their own search for identity with their father's and grandfather's biographies, both Geiger and Maleney invite their readers 'to recognise shared, human vulnerability as well as to attend to the socially situated nature of vulnerability in relationships of care and dependence' (Falcus and Sako 2019, 28–9). In doing so, they provide much-needed counternarratives to popular representations of dementia as narratives of othering and decline.

Bibliography

Barry, Elizabeth. 'Critical Interests and Critical Endings: Dementia, Personhood and End of Life in Matthew Thomas's *We Are Not Ourselves*.' *Literature and Ageing*. Eds. Elizabeth Barry and Margery Vibe Skagen. Woodbridge, Suffolk, UK: Boydell and Brewer, 2020. 120–48.

Behuniak, Susan M. 'The Living Dead? The Construction of People with Alzheimer's Disease as Zombies.' *Ageing and Society* 31 (2011): 70–92.

Boyle, Geraldine. 'Revealing Gendered Identity and Agency in Dementia.' *Health and Social Care in the Community* 25 (2017): 1787–93.

DeFalco, Amelia. *Uncanny Subjects: Aging in Contemporary Narrative*. Columbus: Ohio State UP, 2010.

Falcus, Sarah, and Katsura Sako. *Contemporary Narratives of Dementia: Ethics, Ageing, Politics*. New York and London: Routledge, 2019.

Geiger, Arno. *Der alte König in seinem Exil*. München: Carl Hanser Verlag, 2011.

Geiger, Arno. *The Old King in His Exile*. Translated by Stefan Tobler. Sheffield: And Other Stories, 2017.

Gleeson, Sinéad. 'Second Mother.' *Constellations: Reflections from Life*. London: Picador, 2019. 221–35.

Hartung, Heike. *Ageing, Gender, and Illness in Anglophone Literature: Narrating Age in the Bildungsroman*. New York and London: Routledge, 2016.

Maleney, Ian. *Minor Monuments*. London: Tramp Press, 2019.

Murphy, Fiona. 'The Strangest Architecture: A Review of Ian Maleney's *Minor Monuments*.' The Lifted Brow, 21 September 2019. https://www.theliftedbrow.com/liftedbrow/2019/9/19/the-strangest-architecture-a-review-of-ian-maleneys-minor-monuments-by-fiona-murphy [28 November 2020].

Oyebode, Femi, and Jan Oyebode. 'Personal Identity and Personhood. The Role of Fiction and Biographical Accounts in Dementia.' *Dementia and Literature: Interdisciplinary Perspectives*. Ed. Tess Maginess. London: Routledge, 2017. 103–14.

Ribeiro, Oscar, Constança Paúl, and Conceição Nogueira. 'Real Men, Real Husbands: Caregiving and Masculinities in Later Life.' *Journal of Aging Studies* 21 (2007): 302–13.

Sandberg, Linn. 'Dementia and the Gender Trouble?: Theorising Dementia, Gendered Subjectivity and Embodiment.' *Journal of Aging Studies* 45 (2018): 25–31.

Tholen, Toni. 'Narrating the Modern Relation between Masculinity and Care: Perspectives on a Transdisciplinary Problem.' *Internationales Archiv für Sozialgeschichte der deutschen Literatur* 43.2 (2018): 387–402.

Tolhurst, Edward, and Bernhard Weicht. 'Preserving Personhood: The Strategies of Men Negotiating the Experience of Dementia.' *Journal of Aging Studies* 40 (2017): 29–35.

Trevitt, Corinne. 'Meeting the Challenge: Older People with Memory Loss and Dementia.' *Spiritual Growth and Care in the Fourth Age of Life*. Ed. Elizabeth MacKinlay. London and Philadelphia: Jessica Kingsley Publishers, 2006. 109–28.

Zeilig, Hannah. 'Dementia as a Cultural Metaphor.' *The Gerontologist* 54.2 (2013): 258–67.

Zimmermann, Martina. *The Poetics and Politics of Alzheimer's Disease Life-Writing*. Basingstoke: Palgrave Macmillan, 2017.

Narratives of Parkinson's dementia and masculinities: Jonathan Franzen's *The Corrections*

Teresa Requena-Pelegrí

Recent research in social and cultural gerontology has paid growing attention to intersectionality as an effective theoretical tool to move beyond the observation of difference to an analysis of the social relations of inequality that shape the transition into old age (Calasanti and King 2015, 193; Calasanti and King 2020, 9).[1]

In this chapter, I analyse the ways in which masculinities, old age, and dementia intersect in Jonathan Franzen's *The Corrections* (2001), which features as one of its protagonists, Alfred Lambert, an old man with Parkinson's Disease (PD). To that effect, I draw on Critical Studies of Men and Masculinities (CSMM)[2] and on notions of embodiment and privilege in order to explore the ways in which Alfred Lambert's normative masculine identity as representative of his embodiment of male privilege is transformed by ageing and disease, conditions that place him in a position of vulnerability. I argue that Alfred undergoes a progressive experience of redefinition of his privileged position as a man through the experiences of ageing and PD, which both constitute visible markers on his body. His new nuanced experience of his up-to-then uncontested privilege on account of his gender becomes qualified by ageing and the progression of PD. Thus, I begin by discussing the intersectional

---

[1] Parts of this essay were previously published in 'Negotiating a Masculine Bloc: Jonathan Franzen's *The Corrections*.' *Revista Canaria de Estudios ingleses*, 66, April 2013, 99–109.
[2] The use of the notion of 'Critical Studies of Men and Masculinities' follows Jeff Hearn's definition, i.e. that masculinities are indeed 'critical, are diverse, ontologically, epistemologically, and politically' (2019, 54).

approach to masculinities, ageing, and disease, to later analyse the ways in which these notions are inextricably related to the construction of privilege and embodiment. After this initial section, I analyse *The Corrections* from the point of view elaborated on in the first section. I argue that the representation of Alfred's identity in the text offers a portrayal of the intersections that conform human experience. As a result, the experience of vulnerability derived from age and condition results in a moderate redefinition of male entitlement, thus becoming one of the 'corrections' that the novel explores.

1. Embodying privilege: The intersectional approach to masculinity, old age and dementia

A defining feature of the intersectional approach to age studies fosters an analysis of the specific relations of inequality between groups, thus it does not study groups separately but rather focuses on relating groups 'in terms of institutionalized activities that maintain inequality' (Calasanti and King 2015, 193). To that effect, an examination of the individual and collective differences in relation to age, class, and ethnicity with an intersectional perspective result in views that 'solidify, contest or deconstruct difference' (Hearn and Wray 2015, 206). The incorporation of an intersectional approach entails the realization that it may be not enough to 'add gender to existing frameworks: women are not only women, men are not only men. Instead the challenge is to theorize the interconnections of age, gender(s), sexualities, ethnicities, and other social divisions, and their location in time, place and culture' (Hearn and Wray 2015, 206). From this perspective, intersectionality is in sync with the theorization of age relations, which studies age as a complex amalgam of social relations and may be defined as 'the system of inequality, based on age, which privileges the not-old at the expense of the old' (Calasanti et al. 2006, 13, 17). As these formulations reveal, the notion of privilege and discrimination is part of the structural paradigm of oppression. In Pease's words, 'we cannot understand oppression unless we understand privilege' (ix). Thus, the theoretical articulation of privilege has placed Western dominance, class elitism, white, patriarchal, heterosexual or able-bodied privileges under scrutiny and has contributed to the critique of dominance (Pease 2010, 3). Focusing on those who benefit most from existing social divisions and inequalities and thus emphasizing the structural basis of discrimination, the study of privilege lays bare, among other things, the sense of entitlement that members of privileged groups usually have as to the privileges they enjoy (Pease 2010, 3, 15). In particular, male privilege sustains itself on Connell's concept of 'the patriarchal dividend', that is the advantages that men, as a group, gain from maintaining an unequal gender order, and hence the notion of privileges as being 'unearned', as coming with a 'backpack' of advantages since privilege does not demand the intent of individuals (McIntosh 1989; Pease 2010). Benefits such as money, authority, respect, safety, housing, institutional power or control over one's life are some of the aspects Connell identifies and, as equality grows, the patriarchal dividend is reduced (Connell 2009, 142).

Relevant to my discussion in this chapter is the analysis of privilege in relation to masculinities, age, and disease. The focus on the intersectional approach to these sites reveals the multifaceted position Alfred Lambert, an ageing man with dementia, may occupy in negotiating a position of privilege legitimized by his gender while at the same time experiencing discrimination on the basis of age and disease. In the novel, Alfred constitutes an example of the complex quality of privilege.

Of particular relevance in this network of intertwined subject positions is embodiment, defined as 'our experiences in our bodies as we move through the social and physical world' (Hurd Clarke and Korotchenko qtd. in Hurd 2021, 187). Indeed, it becomes difficult to study ageing, gender and disease as separate processes from that of embodiment since all them entail bodily phenomena (Wehrle 2020). As Pease contends:

> Oppression and privilege are not simply manifested in terms of differential access to resources, they are also embodied. (…) It is important to become aware of how marginality and privilege are experienced in the body because if the body is a site for *doing* privilege, it has implications for how we *undo* it.
>
> 2010, 149

Questions of embodiment have been largely absent from Age Studies (Gullette 2017; Wehrle 2020). This is especially interesting since the visible transformation of the body in the ageing process seems inescapable. However, 'in the study of aging we often lose sight of the lived body' thus diminishing its material presence, tangibility, and visibility (Featherstone and Wernick 1995, 1). A similar opinion has been expressed by Gullette, who has exposed the invisibility of age in embodiment theory:

> Embodiment theory ... increasingly differentiated bodies by gender, race and ethnicity, class, sexualities, and ability, and by their compound intersections. Even so, 'the somatic turn' mostly assumed a body without an age – even when discussing topics that have clear (to me) age-related components: e.g., demography, life-course structures, agency, social stratification, phenomenology, shaming, abjection, subordination, compound stereotypes, care-giving, or rights. Age is a universal intersection, but respected books in body studies may lack any index entry for age, and texts can survey the development of embodiment discourse without even listing age as an etcetera.
>
> Gullette 2017

The absence Gullette refers to has also been present in the study of masculinities and old age despite the fact that the embodiment of masculinity has constituted an ongoing focus of analysis in critical studies in men and masculinities (CSMM). As Connell and Messerschmidt have underscored, hegemonic masculinity is related to particular ways of representing men's bodies, since 'bodies are involved more actively, more intimately, and more intricately in social processes than theory has usually allowed. Bodies participate in social action by delineating courses of social conduct, the body is a participant in generating social practice' (2017, 851). Thus, embodiment is an essential aspect in the construction of gender identity. As Connell has reasoned, the masculine body constitutes the key element in the construction of different masculinities: 'masculinity is, in most cases, thought to proceed from men's bodies ... the body seems to drive and direct action (e.g., men are naturally more aggressive than women) ... or the body sets limits to action (e.g., men naturally do not take care of infants)' (1995, 45). In the case of normative masculinities, the male body has been specifically constructed as physically perfect and whole (Connell 1986, 1995).

The construction of the normative ideal of masculinity based on bodily perfection, health, and youth translate into socially situated forms of dominance, which is another reason that can be put forward in explaining the invisibility of age in discussions of masculinities. As Bartholomaeus and

Tarrant have noted, 'hegemonic masculinity valorises youth or focuses on a middle-age group often perceived to be universal to all ages (or at least the most important)' (2016, 354). The flip side of such valorization is that images of older men continue to be largely constructed in opposition to youthful energy and physicality, an aspect that co-exists with the common 'ghettoization of old age' (Gilleard 2005, 157). As Calasanti et al. argue, old people may feel they have to develop strategies to preserve their 'youthfulness' in light of the physical changes that occur as they age (2006, 16). Such focus on youthfulness also has intersecting consequences in relation to the construction of masculinities and health, since the valorization of youth entails the subsequent detachment of older men from the attributes such as power, control, sports, or the occupational world, typically characterized as belonging to youth. This is the reason why old age continues to be mostly related to a perceived loss of masculinity (Spector-Mersel 2006, 75).

The construction of a normative model of masculinity upon the imperatives of perfection, youth, and health situates the bodies of older men with dementia in a nuanced and contested site of privilege. On the one hand, ageing men may continue to hold on to dominant and unearned positions of privilege derived from the patriarchal dividend while on the other, they occupy a social position of invisibility and discrimination based on ageism and the stigma of disease.

As different scholars have noted, the experience of dementia and its intersections with gender, class or ethnicity still constitute a small amount of the research carried out in dementia studies (Sandberg 2018, 2; Hulko 2009). Sandberg, for instance, argues that this 'dearth of theoretical and empirical work on gender and dementia is surprising since feminist gerontology is a significant strand within social and cultural gerontology, and gender and ageing issues (...) have been discussed by scholars for several decades' (Sandberg 2018, 3).

Different paradigms or narratives have been put forward in cultural and social gerontology that resist the reading of the ageing male body in terms of an inexorable decline. In particular, that of 'successful ageing' seems to have attracted wide notoriety in its refuting of the myth that steep decline was intrinsic to old age by building a notion of success that entailed 'high levels of mental and physical function; avoidance of disease and disability; and engagement through paid or unpaid productive activities' (Rowe and Kahn qtd. in Calasanti and King 2020, 2). This model has been questioned for its reliance 'on personal responsibility to control aging through health and lifestyle choices' (Calasanti and King 2020, 2). As such, the successful ageing model fosters the problems that affect old people as concerns that are essentially personal, thus undermining the effect of age relations that needs to be addressed at the collective or institutional level (Calasanti and King 2020, 2). A derived aspect in the critique to successful ageing is the fact that it is a narrative that continues to maintain a relational quality of ageing male bodies to young bodies, in that the assumption is that 'old people can minimize their difference from youth so long as they age successfully' (Calasanti and King 2020, 4).

A different approach that eschews a successful ageing narrative is the one promoted by later life embodiment research, which has explored the ways that bodily changes derived from disability and illness impact old people's everyday lives and sense of self (Hurd 2021, 187). Typically, the body gains centre stage attention, culminating into what has been termed a 'biographical disruption', the recognition that the worlds of pain, suffering or perhaps death are not distant possibilities or a plight that affects only others and not oneself (Bury qtd. in Hurd 2021, 187). Central to this literature is the focus on the way that the onset of health issues such as pain, functional losses, or life expectancy associated with chronic illnesses, as well as the social consequences of being ill 'threaten, if not displace, previously held assumptions about one's body, self-concept, future plans and possibilities, and relationships with others' (Bury qtd. in Hurd 2021, 187–8).

The limitations of the successful ageing model with its focus on the possibilities of getting closer to high levels of physical function are further unveiled when age and dementia intersect, since the possibilities of getting dementia increase with ageing, and as a result, people may be doubly stigmatized in dementia: 'people with dementia are likely to experience the stigma that is specifically associated with the disease as well as the broader stigma of ageism' (Evans 2018, 264). For one thing, the weak evidence for the effectiveness of treatments that may ameliorate the symptoms, together with a growing awareness of dementia and its effects – such as ailing memory – has resulted in growing fears about getting dementia (Evans 2018, 264). For another, the physical transformations constitute a central signifier of loss of bodily functions. From this perspective, it may be difficult to find any positive attributes commonly associated with dementia (Evans 2018, 272) which in turn clearly eliminates the possibility of a successful ageing narrative, but also makes it difficult to challenge the naturalization of age-based decline at the heart of ageism.

2. Intersectional exploration of gender privilege, age and disease: Jonathan Franzen's *The Corrections* and 'My Father's Brain'

Jonathan Franzen has narrated his experience with his father's dementia in the essay 'My Father's Brain' and the novel *The Corrections*. While the essay constitutes Franzen's own coming to terms with his father's illness, the novel features at its centre a white, middle-class ageing man with PD as one of its main characters, Albert Lambert.[3]

The Corrections is set in the fictional Midwestern town of St. Jude and pictures Alfred and Enid Lambert, who live on their own in their old age in the house they have shared with their children. The Lamberts are a white, middle-class family whose mother, Enid Lambert, has one central design that is announced early on: to celebrate one last Christmas family reunion in their hometown of St. Jude. As the narration unfolds, there is an impending sense of urgency in Enid's wish, based on her fears about Alfred's PD. The story will thus provide an insight into the personal strain that each member of the family undergoes until at the end, they do actually reunite. As the opening description of the setting suggests – 'trees restless, temperatures falling, the whole northern religion of things coming to an end' (*The Corrections* 3) – the signs of seasonal transformation constitute a symbolic rendering of the effects Alfred Lambert's developing PD have on himself and the family.

The fact that the novel takes place in the Midwest adds a local and conservative background to the action in the novel. As Poole has argued in his

---

[3] As Rutter and Hermeston contend, Alfred 'is referred to throughout the novel as having Parkinson's Disease (p. 64, p. 122, p. 428) and there is also some reference to "depression" or "clinical depression" by family members (p. 179). There are also some implications he may have early Alzheimer's Disease (p. 465). Late in the novel (p. 564) Alfred receives a confirmed medical diagnosis of parkinsonism, dementia, depression and neuropathy of the legs and urinary tract and subsequently dies' 2019, (3).

approach to what he deems Franzen's Midwestern poetics, 'there steadfastly remains a common, nationwide understanding that this is a homogeneous, coherent region: the American heartland' as a signifier for the United States as a nation (2008, 265). Furthermore, the Midwest is the place where what Poole considers 'two ancient American myths' co-exist. Namely, the ideal of the farmer and agrarianism on the one hand, and the old-fashioned and reactionary quality of the region on the other (2008, 269). It is this latter quality which will be central to the construction of privileged identity based on patriarchal gender roles. In particular, Enid constitutes the novel's determined spokesperson for the values of the Midwest, as 'she founds her insistence for remaining in the Midwestern suburbia on the predictability of things, on the reliance of daily routine' (Poole 2008, 277), which contrasts with her son Gary's opinion, who hates the region for its sadness (*The Corrections* 203).

The opening chapter pictures Alfred and Enid's domestic life, he is now a retired man and both of them seem to be haunted by a fretfulness that is difficult to dispel: 'ringing throughout the house was an alarm bell that no one but Alfred and Enid could hear directly. It was the alarm bell of anxiety' (*The Corrections* 3). Such ever-present anxiety translates into Enid's frantically clipping of coupons and her bundling them in a rubber band while stacking them in an all-purpose drawer that keeps them there beyond their expiry date, until the dates become 'historical' (*The Corrections* 4). It also makes her hide a letter from Alfred's former company, the Axon Corporation, because there are aspects about a patent he developed that she and her children are managing and she does not want Alfred to know about. Another reason for Enid's unease is her attempts at decoding Alfred's behaviour, which she reads as essentially erratic. Thus, Alfred sleeps for a long time during the day; he spends long hours painting their love seat but after a month Enid realizes he has only finished painting the legs (*The Corrections* 5). There also appears to be a smell of urine in his workshop – 'perhaps it was only the smell of gasoline and of the dampness of the workshop that smelled like urine (but could not possibly be urine)' (*The Corrections* 6); Alfred also struggles with words – 'every sentence became an adventure in the woods' (*The Corrections* 12) – and is diagnosed with mild hearing impairment by a specialist (*The Corrections* 13). All these symptoms point at the invisibility of the early stages of PD, an aspect that Franzen explores in his essay and that he specifically relates to his own refusal to see: 'I think I was inclined to interpolate across my father's silences and mental absences and to persist in seeing him as the same old wholly whole Earl Franzen' ('My Father's Brain' 15). The changes Alfred is experiencing begin to modify the position he has enjoyed in his life up to then; he is increasingly becoming the recipient of care as a result of his vulnerability instead of being the economic provider of the family.

This opening chapter also provides an interesting rewriting of the process of gender naturalization of male privilege that has operated in the Lambert's home up to then. If we take the process of naturalization to mean 'the framing of problems that result from social processes as merely "the way things are"' (Calasanti and King 2020, 2), we can argue that the gender dynamics exemplified by Enid and Alfred in their marriage reproduce a traditional Midwestern white middle-class patriarchal structure in which Alfred has played the role of the breadwinner while Enid has been a housewife and mother. Part of her role as a mother has been to maintain a tight control of what she perceives as her children's needs and to offer unilateral solutions. In the case of her daughter, Enid focuses on the possibility of finding a suitable husband who will embody the traditional masculine role of breadwinner with very specific features:

> a young man with a neat haircut of the kind you saw in ads for menswear, a really super young fellow who had an upbeat attitude and was polite to older people and didn't believe in premarital sex, and who had a job that contributed to society (. . .) and who came from a loving, stable, traditional family and wanted to start a loving, stable, traditional family of his own. Unless Enid was very much deceived by appearances, young men of this caliber continued, even as the twentieth century drew to a close, to be *the norm* in suburban St. Jude.
>
> *The Corrections* 135, emphasis mine

Enid's role as wife will transform as the novel progresses, moving out from a family fiction of harmony she has constructed for herself to the eventual possibilities for personal realization that materialize after Alfred's death in the last passages of the text. This aspect is also noted in 'My Father's Brain', in which Franzen explores how the effects of living with dementia affect the gender roles between his parents:

He, who had always insisted on being the boss in the marriage, the maker of decisions, the adult protector of the childlike wife, now couldn't help behaving like the child. Now the unseemly outbursts were his, not my mother's. Now she ferried him around town the way she'd once ferried me and my brothers. Task by task, she took charge of their life. And so, although my father's 'long illness' was a crushing strain and disappointment to her, it was also an opportunity to grow slowly into an autonomy she'd never been allowed to: to settle some old scores.

'My Father's' Brain 25

In the novel, Enid's tension between the performance of a submissive wife and the resistance to such a role surfaces early on and finds its culmination at the end of the novel, after Alfred's death. While we learn that 'Enid's world was like a lawn in which the bluegrass grew so thick that evil was simply choked out: a miracle of niceness' (*The Corrections* 135), her thoughts will be revealed to be oppositional and full of anger from the first chapter, resisting to conform to the demands Alfred has put on her in their life as a married couple. Thus, Enid is now 'a guerrilla' who lives 'a refugee existence' against Alfred, her 'ostensible foe' (*The Corrections* 6–7). Her sense of victory over Alfred's dominance will surface in the last chapter in a win-or-lose logic – 'she had to tell him, while she still had time, how wrong he'd been and how right she'd been' (*The Corrections* 653). It is such realization at the end of the story that endows her with a renewed hope for the near future: 'she felt that nothing could kill her hope now, nothing. She was seventy-five and she was going to make some changes in her life' (*The Corrections* 653).

For Alfred, the fact that his identity in the present is framed around ageing and PD with a related severe transformation of his bodily functions forces a redefinition of the gendered and able-bodied privilege that has operated in his life up to then. Thus, as the derived effects of PD in his life post-retirement slowly become more visible, the increasing change in Alfred's bodily functions reveal a vulnerability that triggers a redefinition of gender assumptions. Specifically, this operates in relation to his past masculine identity based on physical violence, emotional detachment, and authority, aspects that have placed him in a position of dominance over his wife and his three children. Hence, his role as the Lambert patriarch is shown to be no longer sustainable, he is the diminishing 'governing force' that witnesses his ascendancy being shrunk: 'unfortunately, Enid lacked the temperament to manage such a house, and Alfred lacked the neurological wherewithal. Alfred's cries of rage on discovering evidence of guerrilla actions (...) were the cries of a government that could no longer govern' (*The Corrections* 7). Such realization results in a struggle to reproduce his male privilege in the face of lessened power. A fundamental signifier in this development are the alterations in Alfred's body.

Alfred's body is one of the clearest sites on which this struggle to maintain his unearned past privilege is enacted, as the tension that arises among the different intersections of privileged and non-privileged sites becomes more visible as the narration unfolds. Alfred's struggle with what he terms 'the betrayals' of his body becomes more and more visible, the tremors in his hands or his difficulty in swallowing. The meaning these transformations have for Alfred is intertwined with his internalized ageism – he reads them as 'childish' – and a loss of male privilege that includes giving orders, possessing or enforcing discipline and obedience:

> His affliction offended his sense of ownership. These shaking hands belonged to nobody but him, and yet they refused to obey him. They were like bad children. Unreasoning two-year-olds in a tantrum of selfish misery. The more sternly he gave orders, the less they listened and the more miserable and out of control they got. He'd always been vulnerable to a child's recalcitrance and refusal to behave like an adult. Irresponsibility and undiscipline were the bane of his existence, and it was another instance of that Devil's logic that his own untimely affliction should consist of his body's refusal to obey him.
>
> *The Corrections* 77

As this passage shows, Alfred's loss of entitlement plays out in both his lack of control over his body, in his age, and in the qualities he feels he has lost as a man, combining thus to form an intersecting position of vulnerability. Alfred's interpretation of his loss of control over his body as a childish aspect, as representing the refusal to obey and submit to discipline, reveals Alfred's perspective on the ways that social relations are structured. The above-quoted passage stands in opposition to Alfred's openly racist comments at several points in the early part of the novel as when he expresses his racist views about African Americans – '"the blacks" would be the ruination of this country,' "the blacks" were incapable of coexisting with whites, they expected the government to take care of them, they didn't know the meaning of hard work, what they lacked above all was *discipline*' (26, emphasis mine). Interestingly, his white privilege is also established upon the notion of discipline he has identified before as being an integral part of his character and thus becoming one of the foundations for his position of dominance.

Alfred's struggle to retain control and self-control over his body will progressively give way to a gradual realization of the increasing vulnerability he feels. This aspect reaches its peak in the chapter entitled 'At Sea', Franzen's brilliant send-up of a sea cruise. In it, Alfred and Enid embark on the *Gunnar Myrdal* in a much-anticipated cruise around Nova Scotia. While at sea, the miseries of their married years together become evident. Ironically, their past sexual routine reveals the extent to which Alfred's dominant masculinity has been dependent on Enid's conscious performance of her expected gendered sexual role as a passive woman:

> To exert attraction, Enid had to be a still, unbloody carcass. Her stillness and self-containment, the slow sips of air she took, her purely vulnerable objecthood, made him pounce. And feeling his padded paw on her ribs and his meat-seeking breath on her neck she went limp, as if with prey's instinctive resignation ('Let's get this dying over with'), although in truth her passivity was calculated, because she knew passivity inflamed him.
>
> *The Corrections* 279

It is also in this chapter that we learn what it means for Alfred to feel 'like a man' (*The Corrections* 283). When the narrator accounts for Alfred's past as a railroad engineer, we discover his ethics of work, essentially structured around long working hours in opposition to 'a new effeminate generation for whom "easygoing" was a compliment' (*The Corrections* 281). Alfred is thus featured as a tough professional, the persistent breadwinner who works long hours in order to provide for his family: 'no man worked harder than he, no man made a quieter motel neighbor, no man was more of a man' (*The Corrections* 283). Alfred's work ethics remain in the past because his present is, once more, guided by transformation; he struggles with incontinence, and the chapter ends with Alfred falling into water and Enid coming to realize 'the falling object as your husband of forty-seven years' (*The Corrections* 289), the utmost emblem of Alfred's inability to control his body.

Imminent change in Alfred's life is plainly perceived by one of his sons, Chip, whose own identity is initially structured around the figures of his parents, whom he defines as 'killers' when they visit him in New York in their endeavour to exert an obvious control over their son (*The Corrections* 17). Chip's life, clothes, and 'tall, gym-built' body are filtered through his parents' 'disappointed eyes' (*The Corrections* 18). Although they cast accusing glances, Chip is also aware that despite Alfred's PD and age, his father's violent and domineering behaviour lingers long:

> Though stooped in the neck now, Alfred was still an imposing figure. His hair was white and thick and sleek, like a polar bear's, and the powerful long muscles of his shoulders, which Chip remembered laboring in the spanking of a child, usually Chip himself, still filled the gray tweed shoulders of his sport coat. (...) For a moment it seemed to Chip that his father had become a likable old stranger; but he knew Alfred, underneath, to be a shouter and a punisher.
>
> *The Corrections* 19, 25

Equally for Gary, the problems he experiences in his marriage to Caroline reproduce the power and gender dynamics he witnessed in his parents, realizing the verbal abuse his father had exerted on his mother; he had been 'a shouter' (*The Corrections* 184). Gary recalls his immobility, his failure to intercede on her mother's behalf while his own sons now play a very different role, they are Catherine's 'allies' in the house (*The Corrections* 184).

Alfred's coming to terms with his condition reaches a climax in the chapter 'One Last Christmas'. In it, Alfred is in the basement with prescription drugs, an enema kit, and a shotgun on the table (*The Corrections* 531). By comparing what he perceives as his now obsolete body with the string of Christmas lights he tries unsuccessfully to light, he reaches the conclusion that 'it was hell to get old' (*The Corrections* 534) and seriously considers suicide as an option. However, Alfred will face up to his condition; he reconsiders what he terms 'the wisdom of surviving' after his ship incident and being hauled out of the water, dried off and wrapped up, 'like a child' (*The Corrections* 534). He also considers suicide, an action he dismisses because he cannot bear to think to be found as a 'finite carcass in a sea of blood and bone chips and gray matter' (*The Corrections* 537). Alfred's awareness of his near death is thus hardened by his realizing that he has to be taken care of.

In contrast, and true to her ever-present capacity for transforming reality, Enid chooses not to publicly accept Alfred's near death and feels shame upon the incidents on the ship 'her shame was crippling and atrocious. It mattered to her now, as it hadn't a week earlier, that a thousand happy travelers on the *Gunnar Myrdal* had witnessed how peculiar she and Alfred were' (*The Corrections* 538). Thus, she decides to start personally handwriting her hundred Christmas cards, in which she includes a short note which reads: 'Loved our cruise to see the autumn color in New England and maritime Canada. Al took an unexpected "swim" in the Gulf of St. Lawrence but is feeling "ship-shape" again!' (*The Corrections* 542). Her attitude contrasts sharply with Chip's, whose life is meant to be a fundamental correction of his father's. Chip's final correction constitutes a negotiation of his identity in the same way that Alfred's is also the end result of a process of transformation we have witnessed in the course of the novel. Thus, refusing to see himself through his father's eyes, he manages to commit himself to Alfred in the final stages of his disease. As Hawkins argues, 'by loving his father, Chip proves that he need not be mired in his father's utilitarianism or in the expressive individualism to which Chip has adhered for much of his life' (2010, 82). Chip understands the pain behind his father's suffering and chooses to stand by him, revealing his capacity for empathy. Despite the hostility that has permeated his relationship with his parents, Chip's masculinity is structured compassion for his father as well as the rejection of the features he has learned to read in his father's life.

3. Conclusion

An analysis of the operation of male privilege in *The Corrections* reveals the ways in which it is qualified and modified by the intersecting parameters of age and disease. As I have argued, Alfred's sense of entitlement derived from the benefits he has gained from the patriarchal dividend during his life, undergoes a process of reconfiguration that has at its foundation the processes of ageing and disease. As a result, the normative masculinity he has performed during his life based on violence, aggressiveness or his sense of entitlement becomes qualified in the later stages of his life by the intersectional positions derived from age and disease. Such reconsideration is concomitant with Alfred's sense of loss at the transformation – a correction – that is made especially visible through the changes that occur in his body. His dismay at the inability to control his bodily functions is symbolic of the parallel loss of authority and exertion of discipline over his family, aspects he has felt all his life he was entitled to. Ultimately, a coming to terms with his vulnerability is forced upon Alfred and thus, *The Corrections* offer in the character of Alfred a complex representation of different identity positions that intersect in old age.

Bibliography

Bartholomaeus, Clare, and Anna Tarrant. 'Masculinities at the Margins of "Middle Adulthood:" What a Consideration of Young Age and Old Age Offers Masculinities Theorizing.' *Men and Masculinities* 19.4 (2016): 351–69.

Calasanti, Toni, Kathleen Slevein, and Neal King. 'Ageism and Feminism: From "Et Cetera" To Center.' *NWSA Journal* 18.1 (2006): 13–30.

Calasanti, Toni, and Neal King. 'Intersectionality and Age.' *Routledge Handbook of Cultural Gerontology.* Eds. Julian Twigg and Wendy Martin. London: Routledge, 2015. 193–200.

Calasanti, Toni, and Neal King. 'Beyond Successful Aging 2.0: Inequalities, Ageism, and the Case for Normalizing Old Ages.' *Journal of Gerontology B Psychological Sciences Social Sciences* Vol. XX: XX (2020): 1–11.

Connell, Raewyn W. *Gender and Power.* Cambridge: Cambridge UP, 1986.

Connell, Raewyn W. *Masculinities.* Cambridge: Polity Press, 1995.

Connell, Raewyn W. *Gender in World Perspective.* Malden, MA: Polity, 2009.

Connell, Raewyn W., and James W. Messerschmidt. 'Hegemonic Masculinity: Rethinking the Concept.' *Gender and Society* 19 (2005): 829–59.

Evans, Simon Chester. 'Ageism and Dementia.' *Contemporary Perspectives on Ageism.* Eds. Liat Ayalon and Clemens Tesch-Römer. New York: Springer Open, 2018. 263–75.

Featherstone, Mike, and Andrew Wernick. 'Introduction.' *Images of Aging: Cultural Representations of Later Life.* Eds. Mike Featherstone and Andrew Wernick. London: Routledge, 1995. 1–16.

Franzen, Jonathan. *The Corrections.* London: Fourth State, 2001.

Franzen, Jonathan. 'My Father's Brain.' *How to Be Alone.* London: Harper, 2004. 7–38.

Gilleard, Chris. 'Cultural Approaches to the Ageing Body.' *The Cambridge Handbook of Age and Ageing.* Ed. Malcom L. Johnson. Cambridge: Cambridge UP, 2005. 156–64.

Gullette, Margaret Morganroth. 'Against "Aging": How to Talk about Growing Older.' *Theory, Culture and Society*. https://www.theoryculturesociety.org/blog/margaret-morganroth-gullette-aging-talk-growing-older [21 December 2017].

Hawkins, Tim. 'Assessing the Promise of Jonathan Franzen's First Three Novels: A Rejection of "Refuge."' *College Literature* 37.4 (Fall, 2010): 61–87.

Hearn, Jeff. 'So, What Has Been, Is, and Might Be Going on in Studying Men and Masculinities? Some Continuities and Discontinuities.' *Men and Masculinities* 22.I (2019): 53–63.

Hearn, Jeff, and Sharon Wray. 'Gender: Implications of a Contested Area.' *Routledge Handbook of Cultural Gerontology*. Eds. Julian Twigg and Wendy Martin. London: Routledge, 2015. 201–9.

Hulko, Wendy. 'From "not a big deal" to "hellish": Experiences of Older People with Dementia.' *Journal of Aging Studies* 23.3 (2009): 131–44.

Hurd, Laura. 'Aging, Gender and the Body.' *The Oxford Handbook of the Sociology of Body and Embodiment*. Eds. Nathalie Boero, and Kathrine Mason. New York, Oxford UP, 2021. 183–9.

Kontos, Pia. 'Dementia and Embodiment.' *Routledge Handbook of Cultural Gerontology*. Eds. Julia Twigg and Wendy Martin. London: Routledge, 2015. 173–80.

McIntosh, Peggy. 'White Privilege: Unpacking the Invisible Knapsack.' *Peace and Freedom Magazine*, July/August (1989): 10–12.

Pease, Bob. *Undoing Privilege: Unearned Advantage in a Divided World*. London: Zed Books, 2010.

Poole, Ralph J. 'Serving the Fruitcake, or Jonathan Franzen's Midwestern Poetics'. *The Midwest Quarterly: A Journal of Contemporary Thought* xlix.3 (Spring 2008): 263–97.

Rutter, Ben, and Hermeston, Rodney. 'The Space Between Words: on the Description of Parkinson's Disease in Jonathan Franzen's *The Corrections*.' *Medical Humanities* 2019. https://dx.doi.org/10.1136/medhum-2018-011536 [6 March 2019].

Sandberg, L. J. 'Dementia and the Gender Trouble?: Theorising Dementia, Gendered Subjectivity and Embodiment.' *Journal of Aging Studies* 45 (2018): 25–31.

Spector-Mersel, Gabriela. 'Never-Aging Stories: Western Hegemonic Masculinity Scripts.' *Journal of Gender Studies* 15.1 (2006): 67–82.

Wehrle, Maren. 'Becoming Old: The Gendered Body and the Experience of Aging.' *Aging and Human Nature: International Perspectives on Aging*. Eds. Mark Schweda et al., 25, 2020. https://doi.org/10.1007/978-3-030-25097-3_6 [30 Sept 2020].

10

Illness memoirs, ageing masculinities and care: The 'son's book of the father'

Heike Hartung

1. Introduction

In the twenty-first century, illness memoirs of dementia have emerged as a new subgenre of life-writing. Whereas a few dementia autobiographies *do* exist, written mainly by people suffering from early-onset Alzheimer's disease (McGowin 1993; DeBaggio 2002, 2007), the overwhelming majority of dementia memoirs are understandably biographies written by relatives. Yet in writing about another person who is no longer able to consent to or reject the representation of him- or herself, the narrators of these memoirs encounter what G. Thomas Couser described as 'vulnerable subjects' (2004a). This specific vulnerability of the person with dementia is added to the trope of biography as a kind of 'taking' of another's life, a fear voiced by the American historian Henry Adams in a letter to novelist Henry James, in which he likened biography to 'literary homicide' and explained his own venture into autobiography as 'a preemptive taking of his own life' (qtd. in Couser 2004b: 198). The distinction between autobiography and biography is blurred in the case of dementia memoirs. Narratives by relatives frequently concern themselves also with death and dying, with the loss of the parent or partner and its impact on the narrator's life.

The popularity of the memoir of the death of a parent was noted in the 1990s by feminist critics as an interest in the cultural consequences of loss

(Claire Kahane 1997, 49).¹ One of the best-known literary examples for this trend is the American writer Philip Roth's book *Patrimony: A True Story* (1991) concerned with his father Herman Roth's dying of a brain tumour. A more recent instance of this genre, which draws in many ways on Roth's earlier text, is the German journalist Tilman Jens's highly controversial book on his father Walter Jens's dementia, *Demenz. Abschied von meinem Vater* (2009; 'Dementia. Farewell to My Father'). This chapter will focus on the intertextual relationship between Tilman Jens's illness memoir and Roth's earlier text in order to analyse how representations of the father's last illness by the son reflect different aspects of ageing masculinities.

From the perspective of age studies, dementia life-writing has been analysed with reference to the social identity and subjectivity of the person with dementia (Ryan et al. 2009), and in terms of the gendered perspectives of relatives as well as the autobiographical perspectives of the patients themselves (Basting 2005; Hartung 2005; Couser 2009; Zimmermann 2017). In his essay on filial narratives of paternal dementia, Couser has noted that, contrary to demographic data of dementia, which show that women are even more frequently affected than men (Dementia Statistics Hub 2018), the majority of (American) memoirs on the illness focus on men. When these are written from a daughter's perspective, the daughter is frequently the main caregiver (Couser 2009, 225–6), while the sons' writing about their father's or mother's illness do this more often from 'a "care-free" distance' (on the repercussions of this term, see Martina Zimmermann's chapter in this volume).

In this chapter I will show how the ethical and representational problematics of writing about others in the context of illness and old age intersect with contemporary notions of care, drawing on two sons' narratives about their ailing fathers in particular. The emphasis on care in the context of illness narratives will also serve as my point of entry for bringing together insights from age studies with those of masculinity studies.

---

¹ As Kahane explains about the historical background and formal aspects of this tendency to narrate a parent's death: 'Provoked in part by our millennial consciousness and the inevitable impulse to look backward, [...] this broad-based retrospection has spawned a dramatic proliferation of memoirs, the genre most overtly motivated by the desire to recapture, or reconstitute, the lost past in language. [...] [T]he contemporary memoir is typically a fragment, a memory-event often traumatic, elaborated after the fact as a meditation that itself engages the issue of memory and loss' (1997, 49). On the cultural function of the illness memoir of Alzheimer's disease, see also Ribbat (2006).

Whereas care has historically been encoded as feminine, feminist care ethics have foregrounded the importance of relationships and responsibility rather than rights and rules in conceptions of care, for instance, in work by Carol Gilligan (1982/2003, 19). She has also drawn attention to different notions of the self: the self as related and connected and the self as separate and objective, identified as different voices upon which both men and women can draw. Arguing against the model of gender difference in Gilligan's work, Joan Tronto has extended her critique to a social and political theory that is 'compatible with the broadest level of care' (1987, 661). With reference to male care, Tronto has analysed two forms of social care as the traditional domain of men: those of 'protection' and 'productive economic activity' (2013, 91) – aspects of care that come into play in public life such as protecting society (covering institutions such as the police and warfare) and providing for the family. These engagements, which have traditionally granted men 'a pass from caring', however, are no longer adequate in their foregrounding of 'the languages of economics, interests, and rights'. As Tronto points out, '[m]en do care, and the changing meanings of care in men's lives currently produce a remarkable amount of anxiety in American life. There is a need, then, for a thorough rethinking of how care responsibilities do and do not align with gender roles' (2013, 93).

Questioning this focus on the public realm within which care has been defined as a feature of hegemonic masculinities, the sociological concept of 'caring masculinities' has shifted its emphasis instead on familial care, promoting fatherhood as a realm for male care beyond the paradigm of protection and productivity. As Toni Tholen has argued with reference to Foucault's double perspective on care, – care of the 'Self' and care of the 'Other' – the conflicts that come to bear on the relationship between masculinities and care have to be considered from a historical and transdisciplinary perspective in order to make the contradictions between (male) subjectivity and forms of subjection visible (2018, 399). In this way, alternative forms of male care, – those which were traditionally conceived of as feminine and were characterized as relational, dependent and re-productive rather than productive – could be analysed in their political, social and cultural framework without reproducing a logic of subjection (Tholen 2019, 215).

The notion of relational subjectivity with its focus on social dependency rather than autonomy and dominance links feminist care ethics to current conceptualizations of masculinities as 'plural and changing over time', as 'not a given but performance, a task that has to be achieved, and a set of norms, differing according to regional, social, and historical contexts, that has to be fulfilled and embodied' (Erhart and Horlacher 2018, 314). Relational subjectivity is also important for my analysis of illness narratives: with Mieke Bal's concept of 'second personhood', a complex, dialogic form of intersubjective communication has been introduced into narrative theory, which links relational subjectivity with the reversibility of subject positions (in narrative) and the attempt (and willingness) to come close to the other person (1996, 182). In the general context of autobiography, Paul John Eakin contrasts the 'supposedly self-determining model of identity that autonomy predicates' with a 'relational concept of selfhood' that focuses on 'relations with others' (1999, 161). Specifically, in the context of illness narratives, Couser argues for an ethical code for narrating and representing 'vulnerable subjects' modelled on the unequal relationship between patient and physician based on trust (2004, 19). Lastly, Anne Davis Basting has introduced an approach to narrative as storytelling into the relationship between dementia and care that is based on improvisation and association rather than on linearity, one that relies on a performative notion of the self (2005).

2. Tilman Jens: *Demenz* (2009) – Between mourning the loss of the father and patricide

With reference to these conceptualizations of relationality that are important also for the context of (male) care and subjectivity, I will now turn to the German journalist Tilman Jens's highly controversial text *Demenz. Abschied von meinem Vater*[2] (2009; 'Dementia. Farewell to My Father') in order to explore how representations of the disease (re-)configure notions of masculinity and how they affect the specific relationship of male kinship and care, of the son's perspective on the father as he is changed by dementia. Comparing this example of a dementia narrative in the German cultural context with Philip Roth's *Patrimony*, I will argue for the importance of a relational approach to the representation of a father's vulnerability.

---

[2] Quotations from this text follow in brackets; translations from the German text are my own.

The public reactions to Jens's text have been compared to some of the more critical responses to John Bayley's memoirs of his wife Iris Murdoch's dementia, although the critique has been much more severe in Jens's case. In the 'case' of Iris Murdoch's illness, public responses focused on the disintegration of mental beauty, which made her suffering from Alzheimer's disease into a most frightful loss. Whereas Bayley was criticized for writing about his wife as a 'vulnerable subject' while she was still alive but unable to respond to his publications about her (Himmelfarb 1997), reviews of Tilman Jens's book about his father charged him with a form of patricide. In particular, literary critic Iris Radisch (in the weekly journal *Die Zeit*, 19 February 2009) dismissed his book as denouncing his defenceless father and ruthlessly turning his illness into a political metaphor. The latter point refers to Tilman Jens's linking his father's emerging dementia with the moment in 2003 when it became public for the first time that Walter Jens, at the age of nineteen, had briefly joined the Nazi party in 1942 and had failed to confront his own past.

Walter Jens, who was diagnosed with dementia in 2004 and died in 2013, like Iris Murdoch was a public intellectual who was identified, and identified himself, with his mind. He was professor of rhetoric, a translator, literary critic, and novelist, who embodied in the post-war period the principles of the *Gruppe 47* that re-established a literary community in Germany after the Second World War based on its commitment to an open society and a literature that reflected that openness. His status as a critical public intellectual, well-known for his extraordinary memory and his critical public voice, made Walter Jens's evasive reaction to news of his brief membership in the Nazi party into a much-discussed public scandal in Germany, even before Tilman Jens's book publication.

The particular scandal of the son's depiction of his famous father in his reduced state – Radisch even talks about 'Denkmalsturz' (the downfall or overthrow of a monument) – seems to be related, like in Iris Murdoch's case, to the heights from which the downfall happened. In addition to this, however, the critical response to Tilman Jens's book frequently took the form of a psychoanalytic reading of his book as an Oedipal fantasy of revenge and retribution to which he has responded in a second book, *Vatermord. Wider einen Generalverdacht* (2010; 'Patricide: Against a General Suspicion').

The reference to Oedipal conflict and patricide in reviews of Jens's books brings up Freud's pronouncement of the death of the father as 'the most important event, the most poignant loss, of a man's life' (qtd. in Kahane 1997, 50). In his construction of the Oedipus complex, Freud situated the death of the father as the pivotal desire of the male subject. Fathers loom large in a German genre that has even been called 'Väterliteratur' ('literature of the father' or 'fatherlit') to designate writings in the post-68 tradition, literary texts by sons and daughters, which are concerned with their fathers' Nazi past (Donahue 2014, n.p.). From this genre, regarded of some literary value, however, Iris Radisch dismisses Tilman Jens's book, which she regards as an expression of a disappointed and misdirected filial love.

The reception of Tilman Jens's book illustrates that the relationship between father and son is perceived as modelled primarily on conflict. It thus remains within the traditional public sphere of male care described by Joan Tronto as encompassing also 'intimate violence' as one of the 'puzzling features of protection as a form of care' (2013, 76). While this external view contrasts with the contents of Tilman Jens's depiction of the 'enlightened' family life of the Jens's, and with Walter Jens's acknowledged pacifism which suggests alternative modes of masculinity, it is Tilman Jens's employment of his father's own words against his embodied self in dementia in the structure of his book that engenders conflict, even 'intimate violence'.

The analogy Tilman Jens draws between his father's onset of dementia and his unacknowledged membership in the Nazi party in his youth has been criticized. It seems to me a misguided form of the kind of metaphorical blame put on the ill person, which Susan Sontag has analysed in *Illness as Metaphor* (1977). In addition, a second theme emerges in Tilman Jens's book: Walter Jens's provocative attitude towards euthanasia in his advocacy of autonomous and humane dying.[3] This second theme is introduced with an initial quotation from Walter Jens's book *Menschenwürdig sterben. Ein Plädoyer für Selbstverantwortung* ('Humane Dying: Advocating Personal Responsibility'). This publication consists of a dialogue with Walter Jens's friend, the theologian

---

[3] The debate on assisted dying is too complex in its repercussions to be treated adequately in the context of this chapter. For a reading of Tilman Jens's book in the context of German debates on assisted dying, which takes issue with his attribution of the 'creatural' to his father and reads it as an objectionable ascription of 'authenticity' to the person with dementia, see Matthias Kamann 2009, 16–27. Disturbingly, at the time of my writing this chapter, Tilman Jens has taken his own life (on 29 July 2020) in response to a devastating physical illness, thus putting into practice the attitude towards autonomous individuality expressed in his book on his father's dementia. He asked his friend, the journalist Heribert Schwan, to make this act of self-determined dying public (Schwan 2020: n.p.).

Hans Küng, on the topic of dignified death. In an essay on this theme, Walter Jens analyses texts ranging from the Bible to modern literature in order to argue for his conviction that modern medicine and the law should make dying less painful and more dignified. The quotation from this book, which Tilman Jens chooses to precede his own book on his father's dementia as a motto for the father's attitude towards a self-determined life and death, is excruciating in its dismissal of the humanity of Walter Jens in his later years of illness, and it is rendered in his own words:

> After a self-determined life, [...] may I not be allowed to have a self-determined death rather than (to) die as a ridiculous thing that has only a passing resemblance with myself? And this last image will remain and outlast the impressions of earlier days, when I used to be an 'I' and not an 'it', when I used to be a thinking being and not a quivering body, a being whose pride may have been its shortcoming – but a rational and acknowledged shortcoming.
>
> T. Jens 2010, n.p.; W. Jens 1995, 196

Tilman Jens begins his book by elaborating on his father's position on assisted suicide, which Walter Jens adapts, in conversation with his son, to the specific case of his being diagnosed with dementia. Walter Jens insists that he wants to be able to kill himself, with the help of his physician, when he is no longer an autonomous human being: 'Ich will sterben – nicht gestorben werden' ('I want to die, not be ushered into death' T. Jens 2009, 10–11).

Tilman Jens gives a clear picture of his father's identification with a life that is determined by language, books, conversation, dialogue, and writing to which he adds Walter Jens's own words on assisted dying. This is contrasted with an image of his father at the age of eighty-five with advanced dementia, whose main pleasure is eating cake when he wakes up in the night and who is looked after by Margit, a farmer and the former cook of the Jens family who has become his devoted carer. Tilman Jens acknowledges Margit Hespeler as his father's main caregiver, and who also becomes his father's main figure of attachment. He thus evokes in some detail what Kathleen Woodward has termed 'the scene of care' in her argument for the necessity to account for new forms of kinship within global care settings by witnessing the experience of the carers who have been neglected in illness writing so far (2012, 35, 41). The description of this care situation with the female carer at its centre reinforces empirical observations that women are still most frequently the main carers, even though care ethics is in the process of reconceptualizing this imbalance (Tholen 2018, 388).

At the end of his book Tilman Jens foregrounds the exceptional status and extraordinary luck of Walter Jens in having his own personal carer, focusing on his emotional, or – as he terms it – 'creatural' existence. However, the contrast between the 'rational', self-determined Walter Jens and his 'emotional' embodiment as a person with dementia remains visible throughout the book and has a harsh and disconcerting effect. It is the formal gesture of intertextuality, in which the son uses the father's own words against his present state of illness, I argue, that produces the negative effect of this memoir, which brings up the question of its ethicality.

3. Intertextual responses to Philip Roth's *Patrimony* (1991): Relational (auto-)biography as the 'Son's Book of the Father'

In addition to using the words of his father, Tilman Jens models his book in its structure on Philip Roth's *Patrimony*. Interestingly, the German translation of Roth's book rendered its title as 'My Life as a Son' (*Mein Leben als Sohn* 1992). Roth's text consists of six chapters with titles referring to his father Herman's emotional expressions, for instance, chapter three: 'Will I be a Zombie?', in which Herman asks Philip Roth this question, when his son tells him about his tumour. Tilman Jens also divides his book into six chapters with titles frequently quoting familiar and familial expressions by Walter Jens, for instance, the first chapter, 'Ich geh dann mal nach oben' ['I am going upstairs'], which refers to Walter Jens's library at the top of the house in Tübingen that used to be his retreat and remains so through the early phase of his illness.

The use of dialogue sequences is a stylistic device used in other books about parental dementia, for instance in Elinor Fuchs's memoir about her mother's dementia, *Making an Exit* (2005), or in Arno Geiger's book about his father, *Der alte König in seinem Exil* (2011; 'The Old King in His Exile' 2017). In both these texts, however, the performative dimension of the use of the person with dementia's speech is more intensely emotional as well as more affirmative. (For a reading of Geiger's book that reveals the complexities of personhood in a son's writing about a father with dementia, see Michaela Schrage-Früh's chapter in this volume.)

Apart from the structural similarities between *Patrimony* and *Demenz*, Tilman Jens quotes directly from Roth's text, a quotation that focuses on the helplessness of the father and the difficulties of witnessing this as a son. The quote introduces the second chapter of Tilman Jens's book, which deals with the public scandal about Walter Jens's early membership in the Nazi party and his silence about this. The chapter further focuses on the father's depression and the onset of his dementia, which occur at the time of this public controversy. Tilman Jens contrasts this incident of depression with his father's major depressive disorder in the 1980s: Walter Jens's reaction then was to make his illness public. After his recovery, he talked about his illness in characteristic fashion in order to make the stigmatized, frequently tabooed and concealed, mental illness publicly visible. In 2003, at the age of eighty, Walter Jens's reaction is a different one. No longer able to work, he regards his life's work as completed, which is no occasion for joy to him. Again, Tilman Jens contrasts his father's present stage of early dementia with his earlier intellectual positions: 'It is at this point that the internalized writer's identification of writing with breathing, and the corresponding identification of no-longer-writing with being dead, bounces back on him with a vengeance' (2010, 36).

Tilman Jens's repeated strategy of contrasting his father's present stage of dementia with his former words makes this intertextual device into a form of judgement that leaves little room for Walter Jens's subjectivity as an ill person. This strategy apparently resembles that of his father's, as Neil Donahue points out in his contextualization of the son's book: 'Tilman does, as son and journalist, what his father had taught him to do and follows his example by examining the contexts and putting to question the possibilities of explanation' (2009, online). Significantly, Donahue's justification of Tilman Jens's book publication remains within the traditional scheme of male kinship, contrasting the 'bad son' (within the scheme of Oedipal revenge and even patricide) with that of the 'good son' (following the father's rational example).

One of the reasons I have pointed out for the disturbing effect of the memoir is the son's use of intertextuality, of the father's own words against the 'vulnerable subject' that he has become. The contrast that the book builds up in pursuing this formal device leads to an almost exclusive foregrounding of the losses, whereas the depiction of Walter Jens's embodied existence in his dementia links him frequently, in an ageist stereotype, with childhood, thus reinforcing the distance between his formerly autonomous existence and his dependant presence. In this way, the narrative technique of intertextuality turns into a punitive form of what I call 'intimate textual violence'.

Investigations into the ethicality of autobiographical writing within the framework of the male kinship relationship, in what Richard Freadman terms 'the Son's Book of the Father' (2004, 122), bring up the question of loyalty *versus* disloyalty, protective silence *versus* public exposure: '[H]owever well intended, books about family are bound to involve some degree of compromise of the sensibilities of others, some measure of indecency. Self-revelation just does entail revelations about others. The moral issue is where to draw the line' (2004, 128). As Freadman further points out, sons' memoirs of the father fuse autobiography with biography, which he characterizes as 'relational (auto) biography' (2004, 128). He sets breaches of confidentiality against 'the notion of a wider public good or common interest' (2004, 125).

The relationality in Tilman Jens's book consists in a dialogue with his absent father that revolves around the two main topics of Walter Jens's position on humane dying and his silence about his early membership in the Nazi party. The focus, furthermore, is on the farewell from the father, as the subtitle announces. The public persona Walter Jens is set against the demented person of his later years, while the book is reticent about the emotional aspects of the relationship between father and son. The breaches of confidentiality, it could be argued, are justified by the 'common interest' in Walter Jens as a public intellectual and by the journalistic ethos of being explicit about an illness that is still stigmatized. The intertextual and intellectual engagement with Walter Jens's own writings could also be seen as part of this moral justification. Why, then, does this book seem to many readers 'highly unethical' (Zimmermann 2017, 55)? In order to reflect on this question, I will turn to Philip Roth's *Patrimony* as an intertext of the 'Jens controversy' and as a different representation of a father–son relationship in relation to illness and dying.

4. Philip Roth's *Patrimony*: Performing masculinity as 'female' care for the father

In his own essay on 'humane dying', Walter Jens used Roth's book as an example of a concrete depiction of death and dying, focusing on a passage in which Philip Roth ponders the meanings of his father's brain after having received the MRI pictures of his father's tumour. This is the passage which Walter Jens quotes:

> Alone, when I felt like crying I cried, and I never felt more like it than when I removed from the envelope the series of pictures from his brain – and not because I could readily identify the tumor invading the brain but simply because it *was* his brain, my father's brain, what prompted him to think the blunt way he thought, speak the emphatic way he spoke, reason the emotional way he reasoned, decide the impulsive way he decided. This was the tissue that [...] had ruled our fate back when he was all-powerful [...], and now it was being compressed and displaced and destroyed because of 'a large mass predominantly located within the region of the right cerebellopontine angles and prepontine cisterns. [...]' I didn't know where to find the cerebellopontine angles or prepontine cisterns, but reading in the radiologist's report that the carotid artery was encased in the tumor was, for me, as good as reading his death sentence. [...] Maybe the impact wasn't quite what it would have been had I been holding that brain in the palms of my hands, but it was along those lines. God's will erupted out of a burning bush and, no less miraculously, Herman Roth's had issued forth all these years from this bulbous organ. I had seen my father's brain [...]. A mystery short of divine [...]
>
> Roth 2016, 6–7

In keeping with Walter Jens's identification with a rational and intellectual self-identity, he picked out this passage on the father's brain, which he uses as an illustration of the precision, visuality, and scientific accuracy literary representations of death and dying have gained in modernity (W. Jens 1995, 109). By contrast, Tilman Jens quotes a passage from Roth's book that is concerned with the weakness of the father who used to be a strong man, thus focusing, once more, primarily on loss.

The passage from Roth's memoir illustrates some of the characteristics of this literary text, above all the strong emotional link between son and father that is apparent even in this scene's focus on the materiality of the diseased brain, the MRI pictures. Roth frames this viewing of the brain scan, first, in his own emotional affect. Crying, alone in his hotel room, Roth expresses his emotional connection to his father, while making explicit the meaning of the brain scan for him as the death sentence for his father. Second, Philip Roth contextualizes the material image of the (diseased) brain in the father's individuality, in his characteristics, his emotional and impulsive being. Thus, he acknowledges him as a subject and places him in relation to his family and to himself.

The quoted passage also indicates the emotional tone of the memoir, which has been described as 'a deeply moving account' of the relationship between father and son (Berman 2012, 75). In spite of its explicitness, Roth's book has been regarded largely as benign in its representation of the father. This is astonishing in view of a central scene in the book, which is related to the meaning Roth attaches to 'patrimony' and which, according to Eakin 'poses so starkly the ethical dilemmas of life-writing' (185; qtd. in Gooblar 2008, 37). In this scene, Herman Roth, who convalesces in his son Philip's house after a hospital visit that has left him weakened, has, as he calls it, 'beshat myself' (2016, 120, 121). In a detailed description that borders on 'representational excess' (Kahane 1997, 50), Philip Roth narrates his father's shame about his incontinence while detailing his cleaning up of his father's shit. At the end of this extended scene, Roth describes his feelings of acknowledgement of his father, and that he even emphatically embraces the situation because he comes to understand it as his patrimony: 'So that was the patrimony. And not because cleaning it up was symbolic of something else but because it wasn't, because it was nothing less or more than the lived reality of what it was. There was my patrimony: not the money, not the tefillin, not the shaving mug, but the shit' (2016, 123–4).

In this scene, Roth deconstructs the notion of patrimony by identifying it with excrement as a universal object of devaluation. While reducing his father in this scene to abject matter, Philip Roth, in Kahane's reading, 'identifies with his father's humiliation, and with the corporeal vulnerability that he and his father share, conveying this mutuality through an "anal humour" that gives bodily functions more than their due' (1997, 50). By grounding his writing about his father in the material aspects of his existence, or – as Nancy K. Miller has argued – 'in the spectacular but nonetheless ordinary mess of human life' (1992, 20), Roth evokes – both in the epiphanic 'shit scene' and in the 'brain scan scene' – a sense of his father's characteristic and ordinary subjectivity. This form of 'productive' male care seems different from the traditional forms Tronto describes for the public realm. In a specifically writerly form of public care, patrimony can be read as a caring rather than destructive or violent form of textual inheritance, in which 'the memoir almost becomes a kind of posthumous grandchild' (Miller 1992, 32).

A contrast between Tilman Jens's book on his father and Roth's *Patrimony* emerges that is not primarily related to the question of writing ethically about a 'vulnerable subject'. At the end of his book, Tilman Jens concludes that the life of his father in his dementia is still valuable and that this is mainly due to his privilege of having his own carer Margit, who caters to the physical needs that have become predominant for him. He describes the 'new' father that he perceives after the public intellectual Walter Jens has gone: 'The father I knew has disappeared long ago. [. . .] But now, after he has gone I have discovered a completely different father, a creatural father – a father who simply laughs when he sees me, who cries a lot, and then again, a few minutes later, is pleased with some cake or a glass of cherry juice' (2010, 152). This final image of a 'creatural father' does not counteract the structural effect of 'intimate (inter) textual violence', with which the book juxtaposes the words of the 'rational' Walter Jens, in particular his position on euthanasia, with his 'emotional' self in dementia. With its insistent focus primarily on what is lost in dementia, Tilman Jens's writing about his father remains within the traditional public realm of male care.

By contrast, Philip Roth's approach to his father's dying is more emotional, relational and embodied. Even though Roth apparently betrays his father's trust by making his humiliation into the central epiphany of his book, his 'care' for his father, by transgressing boundaries of representation, also creates something new in terms of 'textual intimacy'.

Towards the end of the book, Roth also thinks about the meanings his father and his father's dying have for him. Acknowledging that his love for his father in his vulnerability borders on idealization (Berman 2012, 93), Roth links his emotional engagement with his father to an idea of fatherhood that repeats the intensification of the external or material of the earlier quotation: 'He wasn't just any father, he was *the* father, with everything there is to hate in a father and everything there is to love' (2016, 127). Immediately following this statement, Roth overhears his father telling his partner that 'Philip is like a mother to me'. Roth, surprised by this statement, would have expected him to compare his care for him to that of a father, but concedes that his father's description was 'more discriminating than my commonplace expectations while at the same time much more flagrant, unblinking, and enviably, unself-consciously blunt' (2016, 127).

Without wishing to essentialize the focus on relationality and emotional connection with female care, I argue that Roth's text readjusts the relation between masculinity and care by accepting a kind of 'motherliness' towards his dying father. In thus departing from the more frequent 'care-free' perspective of the son, Roth embraces the private and familial form of 'caring masculinity' while making it, as a writer, public.[4] With reference to the relation between masculinity and care, then, Philip Roth's book performs a shift from a conflicted to a caring, even 'maternal', relationship between son and father, whereas Tilman Jens's book remains within 'the long tradition of depicting relationships especially between sons and fathers as an unsolvable conflict' (Tholen 2018, 401).

5. Conclusion

In spite of the differences in form between a literary and a journalistic memoir, and in the contents of the texts between a father dying from a brain tumour and one dying from dementia, the comparison between Philip Roth's and Tilman Jens's books about their fathers illustrates the difficulties of determining where to draw the line in writing about 'vulnerable subjects'. Whereas Tilman Jens may continue what his father has done throughout his conscious life, when he intertextually engages with the father's writings, the difference is that

---

[4] Roth's embracing of an alternative form of 'caring masculinity' is particularly astonishing in its contrast with the hypermasculine persona in many of Roth's novels. With reference to *Patrimony*, this shift has been interpreted as a contrast between the 'bad son' as the 'transgressive son who rails against his castrating mother and ineffectual and submissive father' in many of the novels and the 'good son' in the autobiographical books 'who honors his parents and defends them from attack by others' (Berman 2012, 102).

it *is* no longer Walter Jens who is speaking, but that his earlier words are turned relentlessly against his embodied self, however changed. There is a difference, particularly in the case of writing about mental illness, in *who* is the speaker of the utterance.

If one of the fundamental paradoxes of biography is its attack on private life, it is surprising that it is Philip Roth's book with its apparent transgression of intimacy, which successfully evokes the father not primarily as a 'vulnerable' but a complete subject, whereas Tilman Jens by following his father's example and writing what the father had taught him to do leaves little room for the 'no longer rational' subject. Whereas Tilman Jens's book on his father remains within the traditional framework of rational masculinity, Philip Roth's text in its performative and transforming aspects opens up alternative forms of the relation between masculinity and care.

Relational subjectivity also comes to bear on these different representations of son–father relationships. Whereas in Tilman Jens's book the structural emphasis on the topics of guilt and memory loss, humane dying and individual autonomy matches the predominant images of crisis and decline, Philip Roth's *Patrimony* with its invocation of remembrance – 'You must not forget anything' (170) is the book's last line – and its evocation of the materiality and specificity of human subjectivity succeeds in fostering an engaging image of his father as well as providing an unconventional perspective in an imaginative and empathetic 'son's book of the father'.

Bibliography

Alzheimer's Research UK. 'Dementia Statistics Hub: Prevalence by Gender in the UK.' https://www.dementiastatistics.org/statistics/prevalence-by-gender-in-the-uk/ [1 November 2020].

Bal, Mieke. 'First Person, Second Person, Same Person.' *Double Exposures: The Subject of Cultural Analysis.* New York: Routledge, 1996. 165–94.

Basting, Anne Davis. 'Dementia & the Performance of Self.' *Bodies in Commotion: Disability and Performance.* Eds. Carrie Sandahl and Philip Auslander. Ann Arbor: U of Michigan P, 2005. 202–13.

Berman, Jeffrey. *Dying in Character: Memoirs of the End of Life.* Amherst, MA: U of Massachusetts P, 2012.

Couser, G. Thomas. *Vulnerable Subjects: Ethics and Life Writing*. Ithaca, NY: Cornell UP, 2004a.

Couser, G. Thomas. 'When Life Writing Becomes Death Writing: Disability and the Ethics of Parental Euthanography.' *The Ethics of Life Writing*. Ed. Paul John Eakin. Ithaca: Cornell UP, 2004b. 195–215.

Couser, G. Thomas. 'Memoir and (Lack of) Memory: Filial Narratives of Paternal Dementia.' *New Essays on Life Writing and the Body*. Eds. Christopher Stuart, Stephanie Todd and Timothy Dow Adams. Newcastle upon Tyne: Cambridge Scholars, 2009. 223–40.

DeBaggio, Thomas. *Losing my Mind. An Intimate Look at Life with Alzheimer's*. New York: Free P, 2002.

DeBaggio, Thomas. *When It Gets Dark. An Enlightened Reflection on Life with Alzheimer's*. New York: Free P, 2007.

Donahue, Neil H. 'The Political Pathology of Amnesia in Postwar Germany: Tilman Jens' Demenz: Abschied von meinem Vater (2009).' *Glossen: German Literature and Culture After 1945*, 39 (2014). https://www.blogs.dickinson.edu/glossen/archive/most-recent-issue-glossen-392014/neil-h-donahue/ [17 December 2020].

Eakin, Paul John. *How Our Lives Become Stories: Making Selves*. Ithaca: Cornell UP, 1999.

Erhart, Walter, and Stefan Horlacher. 'Editorial: Themenschwerpunkt: Comparative Masculinity Studies and the Question of Narrative.' *Internationales Archiv für Sozialgeschichte der deutschen Literatur* (IASL) 43.2 (2018): 312–26.

Freadman, Richard. 'Decent and Indecent: Writing my Father's Life.' *The Ethics of Life Writing*. Ed. Paul John Eakin. Ithaca: Cornell UP, 2004. 121–46.

Gilligan, Carol. *In a Different Voice: Philosophical Theory and Women's Development*. Cambridge, MA: Harvard UP, 2003.

Gooblar, David. 'The Truth Hurts: The Ethics of Philip Roth's "Autobiographical" Books.' *Journal of Modern Literature* 32.1 (2008): 33–53.

Hartung, Heike. 'Small World? Narrative Annäherungen an Alzheimer.' *Siegener Periodicum zur Internationalen Empirischen Literaturwissenschaft* 24 (2005): 163–78.

Himmelfarb, Gertrude. 'A Man's Own Household His Enemies.' *Commentary* 108.1 (July–August 1997): 34–8.

Jens, Tilman. *Demenz. Abschied von meinem Vater*. München: Goldman, 2010.

Jens, Tilman. *Vatermord. Gegen einen Generalverdacht*. Gütersloh: Gütersloher Verlagshaus, 2010.

Jens, Walter. 'Si vis vitam para mortem. Die Literatur über Würde und Würdelosigkeit des Sterbens.' Walter Jens und Hans Küng. *Menschenwürdig Sterben. Ein Plädoyer für Selbstverantwortung*. München: Piper, 1995.

Kahane, Claire. 'Gender and Patrimony: Mourning the Dead Father.' *differences: A Journal of Feminist Cultural Studies* 9.1 (Spring 1997): 49–56.

Kamann, Matthias. *Todeskämpfe. Die Politik des Jenseits und der Streit um Sterbehilfe.* Bielefeld: Transcript Verlag, 2009.

McGowin, Diana Friel. *Living in the Labyrinth: A Personal Journey Through the Maze of Alzheimer's.* San Francisco: Elder Books, 1993.

Miller, Nancy K. 'Autobiographical Deaths.' *The Massachusetts Review* 33.1 (Spring 1992): 19–47.

Radisch, Iris. 'Der Mann seines Lebens: Tilman Jens verklärt und denunziert seinen an Demenz erkrankten wehrlosen Vater Walter Jens.' *Die Zeit* 9 (19 February 2009).

Ribbat, Christoph. 'Authorship, Alzheimer's, and the Illness Memoir.' *Colloquium Helveticum* 37 (2006): 179–97.

Roth, Philip. *Patrimony: A True Story.* [1991] London: Vintage, 2016.

Ryan, E.B., K.A. Bannister, and A.P. Anas. 'The Dementia Narrative: Writing to Reclaim Social Identity.' *Journal of Aging Studies* 23 (2009): 145–57.

Sontag, Susan. *Illness as Metaphor.* New York: Farrar, Straus and Giroux, 1977.

Schwan, Heribert. 'Tilman Jens ist tot.' https://www.heribert-schwan.de/tilman-jens-ist-tot [17 December 2020].

Tholen, Toni. 'Narrating the Modern Relation between Masculinity and Care. Perspectives on a Transdisciplinary Problem.' *Internationales Archiv für Sozialgeschichte der deutschen Literatur* (IASL) 43.2 (2018): 38–402.

Tholen, Toni. 'Caring Masculinities? Probleme und Potenziale.' *Caring Masculinities? Männlichkeiten in der Transformation kapitalistischer Wachstumsgesellschaften.* Eds. Sylka Scholz and Andreas Heilmann. Munich: Oekom, 2019. 213–24.

Tronto, Joan C. 'Beyond Gender Difference to a Theory of Care.' *Signs: Journal of Women in Culture and Society* 12.4 (1987): 644–63.

Tronto, Joan C. *Caring Democracy. Markets, Equality, and Justice.* New York, London: New York UP, 2013.

Woodward, Kathleen. 'A Public Secret: Assisted Living, Caregivers, Globalization.' *International Journal of Ageing and Later Life* 7.2 (2012): 17–51.

Zimmermann, Martina. *The Poetics and Politics of Alzheimer's Disease Life-Writing.* Cham: Palgrave Macmillan, 2017.

Index

Aber, Rita A. 84
Adams, Henry 179
After a Diagnosis of Dementia: What to Expect from Health and Care Services (UK Department of Health and Social Care pamphlet) 22
Ahmed, Sara 54, 58–60
Alte König in seinem Exil, Der [The Old King in his Exile] (memoir by Arno Geiger) 78, 81 n.12, 93, 145–54, 186
Althusser, Louis 13 n.4
Alzheimer, Alois 80
Alzheimer's disease (AD) 1–13, 105 n.1
   Achilles's helmet as a metaphor for 94
   autobiographies 53, 179, 182, 188
   checking ledgers and 111
   crime narratives and 113, 125–40
   drugs and 42, 45–7
   exile and 146, 149, 149 n.2, 152–7, 159
   journal writing and 132–5, 137, 140
   life-writing and 22, 26, 27, 33, 132–3, 179, 180, 190
   list making and 95
   memorabilia and 31
   memory vs. experience and 148
   note taking and 95
   painting and 4, 6
   poetry about 73–88, 91–100
   poetry and 4, 6, 13, 131, 131 n.4, 133, 134, 137
   sexuality and 38, 44, 98 n.9, 99 n.10, 105–22
   storytelling and 53
   voice memos and 132–5, 139, 140
Alzheimer Fest 22, 22 n.5, 33
Alzheimer na Periferia (documentary film by Albert Klinke) 40
Alzheimer's Poetry Project 13, 74 n.3
And When Did You Last See Your Father? (memoir by Blake Morrison) 27, 31 n.7, 33

Andrei Rublev (film by Andrei Tarkovsky) 82–3, 87
aphasia 4, 74
Arber, Sara 32
Armengol, Josep P. 120
Armour, Ellen T. 6
assisted dying, 184 n.3, 18
   see also euthanasia
'Auguste D.' 80–1
Austria 146, 150, 159

Baker, Kevin 41
Bal, Mieke 182
Balibar, Etienne 13 n.4
Banerjee, Mita 8
Barry, Elizabeth 148
Bartholomaeus, Clare 166–7
Bastide, Roger 38
Basting, Anne Davis 5, 180, 182
Bauman, Zygmunt 33
Bayley, John 78, 183
Beam, Christopher R. 10
Bear Came Over the Mountain, The (short story by Alice Monro) 77
Beckett, Samuel 4, 8, 12
Behuniak, Susan 145
Being Mortal: Medicine and What Happens in the End (book by Atul Gawande) 23, 29, 31
Benjamin, Walter 57
Berman, Jeffrey 190, 191, 192 n.4
Bernstein, Charles 97
biography 73, 98 n.8, 179, 182, 188, 193
Bitenc, Rebecca A. 3, 6 n.2, 32
Bolaki, Stella 20
Bolsanaro, Jair 49–50
Boniol, Mathieu 32
Boratav, Hale B. 49
Bourdieu, Pierre 67, 131 n.3
Bowen, Mary E. 40
Boyle, Geraldine 150

Brandt, Timo 74–5
Brannon, Robert 109–10
Brazil 37–50
Brigeiro, Mauro 39
Britton, Anthony 22
Buck, Matthew 108
Burke, Lucy 27, 31
Bury, Michael 168

Calasanti, Toni 40, 163, 164, 167, 168, 171
Calitri, Raff 56
Capgras syndrome 25–8, 34
Care Manifesto: The Politics of Interdependence, The (book by The Care Collective) 11
caregivers/carers
　family 7–8, 19 n.1, 33, 41–50, 83, 147, 149, 154, 154 n.4, 159, 172, 180
　female 7–8, 19 n.1, 32, 33, 37, 39, 41, 83, 139 n.5, 151, 154 n.4, 172, 180, 181, 185–6, 191, 192
　male 3, 19, 19 n.1, 32, 33, 39, 41, 181
　non-professional 7–8, 23, 39, 151–2, 154 n.4, 185, 191
　professional 22, 39, 152
　violence towards 151
Carrijo, Elisângela 38, 45
Carson, Anne 91–100
Cavigioli, Rita C. 20
Chakrabarti, Subho 19, 20
Choi, Chungmoo 128
Choi, Jinhee 126
Christianity 40
Clarens, Carlos 126
Coelho, Juliana S. 38
Cohen, Lawrence 5 n.1
Cohen-Shalev, Amir 126
Comas-d'Argemir, Dolors 21
comedy films *see* films on AD/dementia, comedy
Connell, Raewyn 109, 165, 166
control, maintaining as a child of a parent/parents with dementia 22, 25, 33–4
Corrections, The (novel by Jonathan Franzen) 77, 163, 169–77
Coston, Bethany 109–10, 119

Couser, G. Thomas 22, 27, 179, 180, 182
Covid-19 50
cuidadora 39
　see also caregiver, female; and caregiver, professional

da Silva, Luiz Inácio Lula 49
da Silva Cabral, Cristiane 38
David, Deborah S. 109–10
de Oliveira, Amanda M. 39
de Souza, Márcio Ferreira 40
DeBaggio, Thomas 179
Debert, Guita G. 39
Decker, Christof 108 n.5
DeFalco, Amelia 145
Dementia Statistics Hub 180
dementia ventriloquism 7–10
Demenz. Abschied von meinem Vater [Dementia. Farewell to My Father] (memoir by Tilman Jens) 78, 180, 182–6, 187
Diagnostic and Statistical Manual (DSM) of the American Psychiatric Association 1
Differences Between Women and Men in Incidence Rates of Dementia and Alzheimer's Disease (study) 10
dignified dying *see* euthanasia
divorce 43, 86 n.16
Doka, Kenneth J. 84
Donahue, Neil 184, 187
Draaisma, Douwe 25, 26
Drummond, Neil 25
Dummer August 80–1

Eakin, Paul John 182, 189
Egloff, Boris 33
Eighteenth Brumaire of Louis Napoléon, The (essay by Karl Marx) 7 n.3
Eklöf, Gunnar 82 n.14
Elegy for Iris (memoir by John Bayley) 78
Elfving-Hwang, Joanna 128
Eliot, T.S. 82 n.14
empregada 39
　see also caregiver, non-professional; and caregiver, female
Endemann, Till 108
　see also Vater Morgana

Engel, Cíntia 38, 45, 47
Engel, Thomas 108
England 20, 22
    see also United Kingdom
England, Suzanne E. 6 n.2
Epistemology of the Closet (book by Eve Kolofsky Sedgewick) 13 n.4
Erhart, Walter 182
Ernst, Christoph 64 n.5, 68
Eurydice *see Orpheus and Eurydice*
euthanasia 184–5, 191
Evans, Simon Chester 168, 169
experience 58

Falcus, Sarah 3, 159
Farina, Michele 20–8, 29, 33–4
Featherstone, Mike 166
Fenech, Freddy 82
films on AD/dementia 5
    comedy 105–22
    crime 127–40
    documentary 40
Finale, La (film) 108, 110–12, 118–21
Firmo, Josélia O.A. 38
Fisek, Güler O. 49
Fleming, Joan 91 n.1
Forceville, Charles J. 67
Foucault, Michel 54, 55, 57, 59, 62, 181
Fox, Ragan 84
France 110–12
Franzen, Earl 8, 171
Franzen, Jonathan 8, 77, 84, 163, 169–77
Freadman, Richard 188
Freire, Paulo 38
Freud, Sigmund 86 n.15, 86 n.16, 92 n.3, 98, 98 n.9, 99 n.10, 183–4
Fuchs, Elinor 4, 186
Fürholzer, Katharina 82 n.15
Furlini, Linda 84

Garrie, Alaina J. 74 n.3
Gawande, Atul 22, 29, 31
Geiger, Arno 78, 81 n.12, 93, 145–54, 158–9, 186
Geiger, August 78, 147–54
Gelman, Caroline Rosenthal 26
gender equality, 38
generation Nutella 23

Genova, Lisa 77
Germany 107, 108 n.5, 112–16, 182–4, 188
Giacomin, Karla C. 38
Gilbert, Nigel 32
Gilleard, Christopher 2, 29, 30, 167
Gilligan, Carol 10–11, 181
Gleeson, Sinéad 66, 145, 148
Global North 5, 11, 21
Goldstein, Gary 108
Gooblar, David 189
Goyer, Amy 7
'Greatest Gifts of All, The' (blog post) 7
Greer, Christine 26
Grossberg, Lawrence 6
Grover, Sandeep 19, 20
'Gruppe 47' 183
Gu Miyoung 128–9
guilt and atonement, children's 33
Gullette, Margaret Morgenroth 2, 165–6

Happy Tears (film) 106
Hardt, Michael 6
Hartung, Heike 3, 54, 81 n.11, 145, 149, 180
Hawkins, Anne Hunsaker 31
Hawkins, Tim 176
Head Full of Honey (film) 107–9, 113–17, 119–21
Hearn, Jeff 33, 163 n.2, 164
Heilborn, Maria L. 38
Hejinian, Lyn 94 n.5
Henning, Michele 58
Heo MinSook 130
Hermeston, Rodney 169 n.3
Hespeler, Margit (carer for Walter Jens) 185, 191
Higgs, Paul 2, 29, 30
Himmelfarb, Gertrude 183
Hirsch, Edward 76 n.6
Hirst, Michael 32
Honig im Kopf (film) 107–9, 113–17, 119–21
Hope, Donna P. 105
Horlacher, Stefan 106 n.3, 107, 120 n.10, 182
Hulko, Wendy 167
Hurd Clarke, Laura 165, 168

Illness as Metaphor (essay by Susan Sontag) 184
IMF crisis (1997) 126–8
insidekino.com 107
Ireland 155–7, 159
Iris (film) 106, 106 n.2
Iron Lady, The (film) 106 n.2
Italy 20–5

James, Henry 179
James, William 94 n.5
Jang, Jung Yun 10
Janson, C.G. 74 n.3
Jeffers, Jennifer M. 12
Jens, Tilman 78, 180, 182–6, 187–8, 189, 191, 192, 193
Jens, Walter 78, 180, 183–6, 187–8, 189, 193
Johar, Omesh, 60
John Joe (grandfather of Ian Maleney) 154–8
Johnson, Marc 56, 57, 58, 63, 64 n.5, 67
Johnson, Vida T. 82
Jutel, Annemarie 27
Jutel, Thierry 27

Kafka, Franz 149 n.2
Kahane, Claire 179, 180 n.1, 189
Kahn, Robert 167
Kamann, Matthias 184 n.3
Kamm, Jürgen 107
Katz, Stephen 38
Keady, John 25
Kessler, Lilian 4
Kim, Kyung Hyun 127
Kim, Y.M. 129
Kimmel, Michael 109–10, 119
King, Nicola 27, 163, 164, 168, 171
Kittay, Eva Feder 11
Klinke, Albert 40
Kontos, Pia C. 54, 67–9, 131 n.3
Korean War 127
Korotchenko, Alex 165
Kriebernegg, Ulla 93
Krizan, Zlatan 60
Krüger-Fürhoff, Irmela Marei 25
Krutnik, Frank 126
Küng, Hans 185
Kunow, Rüdiger 3, 86 *n*15
Kyung Hyun Kim 127

Laing, Olivia 28
Lakoff, George 56, 57, 58, 63, 64 n.5, 67
Lee Chang-dong 131 n.4
Lee, Nikki J.Y. 126
Leibing, Annette 3, 38, 45, 47
Leitch, Thomas 126
Li, Aijun 63
Lipkov, Aleksandr 82
Lovitt, Carl 132
Luira, Alexander 98 n.8

MacDonald, Tanis 92 n.2
McDonell, Eilis 32
McGowin, Diana Friel 179
machista 37, 41, 42, 44, 49
McIntosh, Peggy 165
McTaggert, J. Ellis 136
Maginess, Tess 3
Making an Exit (memoir by Elinor Fuchs) 4, 186
Malabou, Catherine, 92, 92 n.3, 98 n.8, 98 n.9, 98–9, 99 n.10
Maleney, Ian 145–7, 154–9
Marcus, Esther 126
maricas 50
Marshall, Barbara 38
Martin, Wendy 131 n.3
Marx, Karl 7 n.3
Matthews, Eric 131 n.3
Medeiros, Paulo Adão 38
Medina, Raquel 3, 107, 126
Meet Me at MoMA (project) 8, 13
Memoir of a Murderer (film by Won Shin-yun, based on the novel by Kim Young Ha) 125, 127, 129–40
Menschenwürdig sterben. Ein Plädoyer für Selbstverantwortung (book by Walter Jens) 184
Merleau-Ponty, Maurice 67
Mescher, Kris 56, 57
Messerschmidt, James W. 166
Meteyard, Lotte 3
Mexico 29, 32
Meyer, Steven 94 n.5
Miller, Nancy K. 190–1
Minor Monuments (essay collection by Ian Maleney) 145–7, 154–9
Mitterer, Felix 77

MoMA (Musem of Modern Art, New
    York) 8, 13
Morrison, Blake 27, 31 n.7, 33
Mouzon, Dawne 20
Mr Holmes (film) 106
Munro, Alice 77
Murdoch, Iris 78, 183
Murphy, Fiona 158
*My Father's Brain: What Alzheimer's Takes
    Away* (essay by Jonathan Franzen)
    8, 84, 169, 171–2

Necessary End, A (memoir by Nick Taylor)
    20, 28–32
Neumann, Birgit 107
Nietzsche, Friedrich Wilhelm 131,
    137, 140
Norén, Lars 82 n.14
Notebook, The (film) 96

O'Callaghan, Ruth 74
O du lieber Augustin (Austrian folksong)
    79 n.10, 79–81
Ohio Impromptu (play by Samuel Beckett)
    9–10
Old King in His Exile, The see *Alte König in
    seinem Exil, Der*
Ong, Aihwa 5
Orpheus and Eurydice (myth) 84–6
othering/otherness 60–1
Oyebode, Femi 148
Oyebode, Jan 148

Panther, Der (play by Felix Mitterer) 77
Park Chung-hee 128
Parkinson's disease (PD) 22–32, 34, 163,
    169 n.3, 169–77
pater familias 88, 118
Patrimony: A True Story (memoir by
    Philip Roth) 24, 31, 33, 180, 186–93
Patterson, Karalyn 3
Pease, Bob 164, 165
Peberdy, Donna 127
percept cycles 54, 63–9
Pereira, Erik G.B. 38
Petrie, Graham 82
pharma-literacy 38
poetry
    about dementia 91–100
    and murder 131, 134
    as therapy 13, 131 n.4, 133
Poole, Ralph J. 169–70
Price, Elizabeth 120
privilege, male 163, 165, 167, 173–4, 176
pyjamas (male homebodies) 39

*Quando andiamo a casa? Mia madre e il
    mio viaggio per comprendere
    l'Alzheimer. Un ricordo alla
    volta* (book by Michele Farina)
    20–5
Quant, James 81

Radisch, Iris 183–4
Rafter, Nicole 126
relationships
    father–daughter 7, 41, 73–88, 92 n.2,
        95, 134
    father–son 19, 25–8, 28–32, 76 n.6, 78,
        93–4, 146–54, 159, 180–93
    grandfather–grandson relationships
        146–7, 154–9
    mother–daughter relationships 4, 42–3,
        45–8
    mother–grandchild relationships
        44
    mother–son relationships 21–5, 28–32,
        45–50
    partner relationships 37, 40–3,
        169–76
Ribbat, Christoph 180 n.1
Ribeiro, Oscar 146, 150
Ricoeur, Paul 136
Rifiotis, Theophilus 39, 41, 49
Rilke, Rainer Maria 82 n.14
Roach, Pamela 25
Rober, Franziska 106 n.3, 120 n.10
Robinson, Carol 41
Rosenberg, Francesca 8
Roth, Herman 186, 189–93
Roth, Philip 24, 31, 33, 180, 186, 189–93
Rousseff, Dilma 49
Rowe, John 167
Rudmann, Laurie A. 56, 57
Russell, Richard 41
Rutter, Ben 169 n.3
Ryan, Assumpta A. 32
Ryan, E.B. 180

Sacks, Oliver 98 n.8
Sako, Katsuro 3, 159
St. Ville, Susan M. 6
Sandberg, Linn J. 106, 110, 120, 149, 150, 167
Santos, Sílvia 39, 41, 49
Scheibling, Casey 49
Schicktanz, Silke 3
Schmukle, Stefan C. 33
Schwan, Heribert 184 n.3
Schweda, Mark 2, 3
Schweiger, Til 107–9, 111, 113–17, 121
Schwickert, Martin 108
Second World War 126, 150, 183, 184, 187–8
Sedgwick, Eve Kosofsky 13 n.4
self-care, male 38–9
Semmel, K.E. 73
Seng, Joachim 73
Shainberg, Lawrence 12
shame, feelings of 54, 58–64, 69, 98, 156, 176, 190
Sharma, Nidhi 19, 20
Simon, Linda 87
Sontag, Susan 184
Soronellas, Monserrat 21
South Korea 125–9, 130 n.2, 138, 139 n.5
Specht, Jule 33
Spector-Mersel, Gabriela 167
Spivak, Gayatri Chakraworty 9
Springer, Kristen W. 20
Staszak, J.F. 55, 57
Steck, Barbara 26
Stein, Gertrude 92, 93, 94–7, 97 n.7, 99–100
Steinberg, Shirley R. 38
Still Alice (film by Richard Glatzer and Wash Westmoreland) 5, 106 n.2
Still Alice (novel by Lisa Genova) 77
storytelling 5, 9, 53, 133, 136, 137, 182
Stott, Andrew 106
Streb, Elizabeth 97–8
Stringer, Julian 126
Swinnen, Aagje 2, 3
Sykes, Robin 108
  see also *Finale, La*
symptomatic reading 13 n.4

Tafdrup, Pia 73–88
Takahashi, Yasunari 9
Take Me Home: Parkinson's, My Father, Myself (memoir by Jonathan Taylor) 20, 25–8
Tarkovsky, Andrei 79, 82 n.13, 87
Tarkovsky's Horses (poetic cycle by Pia Tafdrup) 73–88
Tarrant, Anna 167
Taylor, Clare 28–32
Taylor, Jack 28–32
Taylor, John 25–8
Taylor, Jonathan 20, 25–8, 33–4
Taylor, Nick 20, 28–34
Tholen, Toni 153, 181, 186, 192
Tobler, Stefan 146 n.1
Tolhurst, Edward 119, 150, 151, 155
Trabucchi, Marco 21
Traxler, Patricia 74
Trevitt, Corinne 145, 152, 153
Tronto, Joan C. 10, 181, 184, 191

United Kingdom (UK) 22 n.4, 40
United States of America (USA) 5, 10, 20, 28, 107–9, 115–16, 169–76, 180
Urios-Aparisi, Eduardo 67

van Gogh, Vincent 8
Vater Morgana (film by Til Endemann) 108–9, 112–14, 118–21
'Väterliteratur' 184
Vatermord. Wider einen Generalverdacht (book by Tilman Jens) 182
Vietnam War 128, 129, 138
Viki, G. Tandayi 56
Vilela, Renata 39
violence 54, 57, 61, 65, 68, 82, 87, 130 n.2, 131 n.4, 151, 155, 172, 175, 176, 184, 188, 191
violence in film see *Memoir of a Murderer*
violence, textual 191

Ward, Richard 120
Weicht, Bernhard 119, 150, 151, 155
Werhle, Maren 165
Wernick, Andrew 166
Williams, Angie 109

Won Shin-yun 125–7
    see also *Memoir of a Murderer*
Woodward, Kathleen 22, 185
word salad 94
wordplay 153
World Health Organization (WHO) 105 n.1
Wray, Sharon 164

Zarit, Judy M. 84
Zarit, Steven H. 84
Zeilig, Hanna 74 n.2, 75, 145
Zimmermann, Martina 3, 19, 19 n.1, 22, 30, 32, 33, 133, 139, 147, 148, 180, 188
Ziya, Hande E. 49
Žižek, Slavoj 92, 92 n.3, 99 n.10, 99–100

www.ingramcontent.com/pod-product-compliance
Lightning Source LLC
Chambersburg PA
CBHW062228300426
44115CB00012BA/2259